WHAT´S LOV

GOT TO DO

WITH IT?

Also by David Wagner

*The New Temperance: The American Obsession with Sin and Vice*

*Checkerboard Square:*
*Culture and Resistance in a Homeless Community*

*The Quest for a Radical Profession:*
*Social Service Careers and Political Ideology*

# WHAT'S LOVE GOT TO DO WITH IT?

*A Critical Look at American Charity*

DAVID WAGNER

THE NEW PRESS  NEW YORK

Library of Congress Cataloging-in-Publication Data

Wagner, David.
    What's love got to do with it? : a critical look at American charity /
David Wagner.
        p.   cm.
    Includes bibliographical references and index.
    1. Charities — United States.   2. Nonprofit organizations — United
States.   3. Human services — United States.   4. Public welfare —
United States.   I. Title.
HV91.W24   2000
361.7'0973 — dc21                            99-35845

Published in the United States by The New Press, New York
Distributed by W. W. Norton & Company, Inc., New York

The New Press was established in 1990 as a not-for-profit alternative to the large, commercial publishing
houses currently dominating the book publishing industry. The New Press operates in the public interest rather than for private gain, and is committed to publishing, in innovative ways, works of educational,
cultural, and community value that are often deemed insufficiently profitable.

www.thenewpress.com

Printed in the United States of America

9  8  7  6  5  4  3  2  1

# Contents

# —Acknowledgments

Every piece of written work has its intellectual roots. While any missteps and mistakes contained within are entirely my responsibility, this book would not be possible without the prior work of many others, particularly authors Frances Fox Piven and Richard Cloward. Their critical work beginning with *Regulating the Poor* in 1971 stimulated thousands of students, workers, and intellectuals to move beyond sentimentalism in looking at issues of social welfare (at least for a time anyway). I was extremely lucky to have entered graduate school in the days when *Regulating* was being debated, and when they were working on their forthcoming book, *Poor People's Movements*. I have been privileged to maintain an ongoing relationship with Piven and Cloward over the years for which I am extremely grateful.

A second intellectual debt I owe for all my books is to Marcia B. Cohen, my wife, sometime co-author, and always first editor and intellectual sounding board. Although we have both worked with poor people and some social agencies, she has been far more active than I in these regards of late. Her feedback was critical for this work, since there is always a danger of living in a fantasy world as one writes.

My students at the University of Southern Maine have also had a big influence on me. When I started teaching Social Welfare Policy, questions and discussion led us all to ask "What [does] Love Have to Do with It?" e.g., is altruism the real sum total of what social service work and charity is really about? This is the view that most textbooks and professors seem to offer, but it was greeted with well-founded skepticism by students who are overwhelmingly working class or poor, many of whom have been in "the system" themselves. Students also read parts of this book in developing form. While students at USM are far too nice to offer biting criticism, it is interesting that in recent semesters I have been defending altruism a bit against many students who are sometimes even more skeptical than I that the whole system is not set up only for social control purposes.

A number of readers also have my deep appreciation. Piven and Cloward's comments on this work, positive and critical, have been indispensible. Robert Fisher of the University of Houston and Donileen Loseke of the University of Southern Florida read drafts of the manuscript and offered helpful suggestions; Thomas Knoll of Halmsted University and Ingrid Sahlin of the University of Gothenberg again offered me an invaluable international perspective as they did with my previous work; and two excellent writers, John Buell and Dennis Must, have become increasingly important to me in making sure a nonspecialist can discern what I am trying to say.

This book appears in the aftermath of the disappearance of my editor Joe Wood, whom I got to know only too briefly as we worked on this project. I thank him for his great help and wished we had worked together earlier. My hopes and wishes go to his family, friends, and colleagues. Barbara Chuang, Grace Farrell, and Diane Wachtell of The New Press have all helped on this project, despite the exceptionally trying circumstances, to move things forward. They have my lasting appreciation.

# Preface

I must admit to a certain fear after writing. For as much as the printed page provides the writer a wonderful opportunity to communicate, it also provides a place to be misunderstood. Sometimes I fear that the number of friends I have may decrease with each new book I write.

So in challenging the self-congratulatory American myth of altruism, I hasten to add that this book is not meant to criticize colleagues, friends, students, and former students employed in the human services. In fact, I have worked for most of my adult life in the social services, from feeding and bathing severely mentally retarded patients who were institutionalized, to consoling scared candidates for neurosurgery in a medical center, to finding field internships for social work students, to teaching hundreds of students the history of social welfare and how to work to improve human service organizations. By far the vast majority of people I have worked with have been compassionate, dedicated, sensitive, and, at least initially, driven to the work by idealism.

But the question I ask in this book is, what do these altruistic motives come to? What do professions of "love" and caring amount to in America's increasingly privatized social welfare system? After all, much human activity takes as its discourse "love" or "compassion." Destructive personal relationships rarely advertise themselves as harmful, even when violence is occurring in the home; nonetheless, more often than not "love" is espoused. Wars are rarely declared by politicians with manifestly belligerent justifications, but are usually undertaken to "save" the people of faraway places (from Communism, authoritarianism, or other threats) in order to meet our moral obligations or to protect ourselves from "barbarism" or "slavery." Politicians likewise *always* profess to be compassionate. They tell us they feel the pain of their constituents and claim to "love" them, regardless of their party or ideology.

*What's Love Got to Do with It?* questions why the actions of so many good people don't amount to more. How, in a nation that can't stop talking of volunteering, expressing feeling, and giving to charity, do we have so much poverty and misery, and so few actual material benefits for our people (as we recently demonstrated by "ending welfare as we know it")? Why are we almost the only nation in the industrialized world to murder our citizens by capital punishment? Why do we imprison the highest percentage of our population, often for merely possessing an illegal substance? "Love" seems to have little to do with American economic, social, and political life.

The American love affair with charity reveals a nation that "protests too much," that has a surplus of guilt because of our inability to arrange a better organization of our overall community life. A core of nice people and a rhetoric of kindhearted feeling cannot replace a more intelligent and generous social policy. Indeed, in one way or another, many social workers, students, and former clients of mine know this even if they don't always use the same words to explain it.

Former students who entered the human services often have left; they often say that other work involves less stress and more money. Or they apologetically explain why they no longer work with poor people but now have a private psychotherapy practice. Consumers of social service who become active in human service organizations complain of being unappreciated or "burned out" on activism, and cease attending meetings. The professions of human service often blame these people (their own trainees or clients) for not "sticking with it," but in a way they are blaming the victims. For much of the real problem lies in how quickly sentimental rhetoric and idealistic speeches become transparent to intelligent people over time—and how little social service, volunteering, or charity really achieves.

This book attempts to demystify charity. Perhaps it may disappoint some who work tirelessly fundraising for good causes, but perhaps others might consider their commitment to the limited possibilities of America's social service system.

# WHAT'S LOVE GOT TO DO WITH IT?

# Introduction: Charity as an American "Glorifying Myth"

*Compassion may itself be a substitute for justice . . . compassion always already signifies inequality. The compassionate intend no justice, for justice might disrupt current power relationships.*

Hannah Arendt[1]

*It may be that he who bestows the largest amount of time and money on the needy may be doing the most by his mode of life to produce the misery he strives in vain to relieve. . . . Philanthropy was the only virtue sufficiently appreciated by mankind. Nay, it is greatly overrated.*

Henry David Thoreau[2]

## THE VIRTUOUS AMERICAN

To hear most Americans talk, we are the most virtuous and glorious people, moved by our compassion and commitment to help others. On the one hundredth anniversary of the United Way in 1986, then-President Ronald Reagan proclaimed:

> Since earliest times, we Americans have joined together to help each other and to strengthen our communities. Our deep-rooted spirit of caring, of neighbor helping neighbor, has become an American trademark—and an American way of life. Over the years, our generous and inventive people have created an ingenious network of voluntary organizations to give help where help is needed . . . [3]

Eleven years later, at a nationwide "summit" on voluntarism, President Bill Clinton, flanked by luminaries ranging from Colin Powell to Jimmy Carter and by both conservative and liberal activists, declared altruism the American way. Without a hint of irony, the President, who had recently signed a bill ending "welfare as we know it," praised the American spirit of helping: "Citizen service belongs to no party, no ideology. It is an American idea, which every American should embrace."[4]

Whatever one thinks of Ronald Reagan or Bill Clinton, they are essentially correct. Americans have always glorified their virtues of charity, voluntarism, and compassion, and such glorification has always crossed partisan and mainstream ideological positions. While the much quoted nineteenth-century observer of American life Alexis de Tocqueville commented that "in the United States, hardly anybody talks of the beauty of virtue, but they maintain that virtue is useful and prove it every day," in fact, more typically, as historian Robert Bremner observed:

> . . . celebration of American philanthropy has reached such heights that one can scarcely read a newspaper or magazine without being reminded, in editorials or advertisements, that the United States is the country with a heart, that giving is the great American game, and that philanthropy ranks as one of the leading industries of the age. Americans seem never to tire of saying . . . that they are generous to a fault—the most compassionate, open-handed people the world has ever known.[5]

While, of course, serious differences exist between conservative proponents of charity who believe (in George Bush's words) that "the thousand points of light" can replace public social services, and the more liberal American tradition of supporting at least some public sector "safety net," currently no major political group opposes in principle the nation's widespread lovefest for charity, voluntarism, and social service. Nor does any major political force support expanding the public social welfare system in a way that would even begin to approach European standards. In fact, even groups on the Left have often sought to secure the mantle of charitable virtue. Some feminists have argued, for example, that charity and philanthropy should be appropriated as women's issues: "Women's giving and voluntarism played a central, albeit unheralded role in women's history, providing access to power outside the masculine realms of government and commerce. Through gifts of time and money, women have built institutions, provided charitable services . . ."[6] And some on the Left can wax rhetorical about alternative philanthropy: "The emergence . . . of . . .

alternative funds has all the markings of a new, broad-based social movement . . . It is rooted in fundamental values that are at the heart of our national ethic — self-determination, self-reliance, democratic pluralism, competition, free exchange of ideas, compassion, and justice."[7]

This love affair with charity, as embedded in the American psyche as it is, was hardly shared by all Americans in the past. For a long time, social critics (such as Thoreau, quoted at the chapter's start) and those on the Left were quite critical of both charity as an idea and charity as an institution, for example, private giving by the more affluent. To take one example, Eugene V. Debs, the prominent Socialist Party leader during the first decades of the twentieth century, urged the public to refuse the gifts of philanthropist Andrew Carnegie, replying that workers would build their own libraries rather than accept the "blood money" of capitalism.[8] More recently, Ferdinand Lundberg was typical of 1960s critics when in his muckraking book *The Rich and The Super-Rich* he critiqued charity as legitimizing the very wealthy:

> Wealthy men and women today are almost all freely labeled by the public prints as philanthropists. In such mindless parroting the word has acquired the operationally extended meaning of "wealthy person"; and "wealthy person" means, reciprocally, "philanthropist." . . . Contrary to reasonable supposition and statistical fact the wealthy are not endeavoring to increase their wealth but are feverishly endeavoring to give it away for good works.[9]

Yet, as I write, few institutions in American society are as sacrosanct and vaunted as our charitable and social service sector. At least rhetorically, one of the few things that seems to unite business and labor, liberals and conservatives, Catholics, Protestants, Jews, and Muslims, whites and nonwhites, is the provision of nonprofit charity and social services. Not only is our vast array of voluntary social services a particularly American phenomenon, but the "therapeutic state"[10] (as one author calls it), more and more seems a shared American vision in which a rhetoric and sentiment of "caring" ("I feel your pain") comes to replace structural efforts at income redistribution or eliminating poverty. Like the proverbial symbols of the flag and motherhood, or perhaps more currently the internet and MTV, neither charity nor the claims of social service are to be challenged.

## WHY CRITICIZE AMERICAN ALTRUISM?

Given all this wonderful "virtue talk" and feeling good about ourselves, why am I playing Scrooge at Christmas by casting doubt on American altruism? To challenge the American "glorifying myth" is, after all, to challenge what for most people is a noble tradition.

But is all this "patting on the back" we give ourselves appropriate considering the real American condition? The United States has the sharpest rates of income inequality in the Western world, the sparsest public social welfare system in the industrialized world, among the highest poverty rates in the Western world, and a host of festering social problems that produce more violence and prisons than elsewhere. If Americans have " a deep-rooted spirit of caring" (Reagan), practice the "beauty of virtue" (de Tocqueville), and live in "the country with a heart" (Bremner), how is it that for hundreds of years the poor were punished by being sent to poorhouses and workhouses, that poor children were auctioned off or forced onto "charity trains," and that even the treadmill was brought over from England to punish the "indolent and vicious"?[11] Why do most societies provide their citizens with family allowances to support children, free health care, and other services as a basic right, while the United States does not? As a general rule, Americans are harsher and more punitive towards poor people and others in need than the governments of most other nations.

Further, the major positive changes in the conditions of poor people have come *not* from philanthropy or goodwill, but from social struggles, particularly in the 1930s and the 1960s and 1970s. Labor unrest, civil rights struggles and ghetto riots, even demands of the elderly have been far more central to the creation of an expanded and improved social welfare system than the actions of charity officials, social workers, or religious volunteers. But even with the changes that have occurred, conditions in America's inner cities shock visiting foreign observers. I argue in this book that America's "virtue talk" has a great deal to do with obscuring how little we as Americans *actually do* for people who find themselves in adverse circumstances. More subtly, America's worship of giving, volunteering, and nonprofit human service work as the center of moral acts and heroic achievement allows the two other sectors of American life—the for-profit business sector and the government—to be legitimized. Americans seem to ignore the decline in real wages over the last twenty-five years and the crushing of unions by corporate America, and generally support the war on drugs, the growth of prisons and capital punishment since the 1970s, and the demise of public benefits for the poor. After all, the needy can receive charity, and we give so much.

Secondly, just as we ignore the massive war against the poor today, which places as many as one in four young African-American males in the correctional system,[12] we need to be honest about the roots of the rhetoric of "virtue" and how it was embedded in our past. The rhetoric of virtue has always coexisted with a deep-seated streak of violent repression in America: the physical and cultural genocide against American Indians, the enslavement of Africans, and the conquering of foreign lands. It is not merely that the rhetoric of caring and the roots of philanthropy are inadequate to assist those who need help, but that their very nature is tainted historically with American visions of control over inferiors. The origins of our charitable institutions are integrally connected with a vision of repression over those deemed different, dangerous, or "deviant." As we shall see in chapter 1, from the seventeenth century through most of the twentieth century, American reformers and philanthropists spearheaded efforts to "civilize" the American Indian population. They saw themselves as virtuous and noble because they usually argued against out-and-out extermination of the Indian nations. Yet the "liberal" position of philanthropists and reformers never meant for the Indians to live as they desired, but rather to remove them from their land, take their valuable resources, turn them into Christians, and save these "heathens" from "barbarism" by changing their attire, destroying their language and customs, and reversing communal property relations.

Behind the philanthropist always lurked the soldier and settler. As Indian scholar Vine DeLoria comments, in many ways the missionaries were more dangerous than the soldiers, since they were more confusing to indigenous tribes and proved better able to move the Indians from traditional ways than the soldiers.[13] A similar argument can be made about the success of charity and philanthropy in overcoming resistance to exploitation at the hands of big business among the poor and workers. The symbols of Christian charity and philanthropic virtue have been arguably far more successful in absorbing dissent in America than violent repression has.

While, of course, it would be ludicrous to tar all charity and social welfare workers and volunteers with the misdeeds of the past, the failure of the rhetoric of caring and compassion either to represent adequately the American past *or* the contemporary American scene should give us pause. Are the manifest claims of people to be charitable and well-meaning an assurance that they are indeed *helping people*?

As the quote from Hannah Arendt at this chapter's start suggests, compassion and altruism may not always be as they seem. We need to explore how the structured inequalities of social systems (slavery, feudalism, and capitalism, for example) lead those in power to develop secondary and subsidiary institutions such as charity and social services to mitigate their guilt and attempt, at least symbolically, to display sympathy for the "Other," while at the same time economic and political systems work to maintain poverty and inequality. There may even be a harsher side to altruism: sometimes people say the *opposite* of the truth because their values or ideological systems allow them little choice. The doublespeak predicted by George Orwell need not always be intentional, or part of some plan devised by a totalitarian leader or slick public relations professional (although there is some evidence of this as singer Tracy Chapman asks, "Why are the missiles called Peacemakers?"). It is possible that ideology and cultural commitments often make us grotesquely transform reality to fit our self-concept.

Perhaps one of the earliest examples of such transmogrification was the Massachusetts Commonwealth seal developed by Cotton Mather. Side by side stand a colonialist and "a poor Indian having as a label from his Lips, expressing this Cry, COME OVER AND

HELP US!"[14] This seal conveniently rewrote history only a number of decades after the Pilgrims landed, a revision that portrays the brave colonialists as guests *invited* to the New World by heathens who wished to enjoy conversion and other good deeds of the settlers. But this is not merely propaganda. Just as most contemporary Americans believe we are the most virtuous people in the world, so too the Massachusetts settlers came to believe that they were humanitarian philanthropists, continuing the original Puritan mission of the "city on the hill" by aiding the poor Indians with Christian Bibles, the English language, and civilized schools and clothes. That they were literally destroying millions of lives was evidently beside the point. Social critic John McKnight makes a similar challenge to the language of Christian "caring":

> There is a problem, however, with our dedication to service as the ultimate Christian ideal. After all, the Crusaders thought they were servants of Christ. We doubt it today. The conquistadors thought they were servants of Christ. We doubt it today. The missionaries who went to Africa and Asia thought they were servants of Christ. We doubt it today.[15]

Western religion and the successive developments of the ideology of charity are suspect not only for the use they have been put to, but for the ideology of proselytization itself. That is, an imperial drive to make everyone the same always defines some as nonbelievers and hence nonhuman. Not only did Christian settlers dehumanize the indigenous peoples and others of different races, but the white Christians of the dominant classes defined recipients of charity and social service as objects of moral proselytizing. To the extent the norms and behavior of the poor, the mentally and physically disabled, or those deemed sexually deviant differed from the dominant culture, altruistic gestures were in part a strategic effort at resocializing and taming their "animal" spirit.

## LIFTING THE SENTIMENTAL VEIL: CHARITY OR SOCIAL JUSTICE?

Not only the public, but experts and intellectuals often get lost in a sentimental haze when words like "social welfare," "social ser-

vices," or "charity" are used. Frances Fox Piven and Richard Cloward noted that self-interest makes even experts soft around the
edges on such subjects. Social service workers, administrators, and
academic experts on social welfare, for example, are so "enmeshed
within the system itself" they tend to justify it and "view the system
as shaped by morality—by their good intentions, or by the mis-
taken intentions of others."[16] This self-interest also combines with
the ideological tendency in America—even among groups such as
academics—to view history in an idealistic way, as reflecting
progress by elites who discover (generally altruistically and rationally) the correct path, rather than view social welfare through a
social conflict perspective.[17] Add to these tendencies some real ter-
minological confusion, and intelligent discussion about social welfare sometimes seems impossible.

An examination of the broad topic of American charity needs to
distinguish between *public* aid and *private* assistance, and between
*material social welfare* benefits provided to those in need (some of
which may be redistributive in nature or part of what Europeans
refer to as the "social wage") and *therapeutic social services* aimed
at character amelioration or even punishment or repression. As a
general rule, activists on the Left and social movements of the lower
classes have favored public social welfare as a tool of social justice
that would provide income or other material support to those in
need. The rhetoric of charity, on the other hand, emphasizes moral
uplift and (more recently) professional treatment and services.

Classically, social welfare observers have stressed the differences between public services and those provided by private parties, primarily by nonprofit charities (although increasingly for-
profit businesses are emerging as major "service providers"). I will
explore in this book primarily the "voluntary" not-for-profit sector,
which is associated with those institutions that Americans know as
"charity." I do so despite strong evidence that "public" and "private" have always been intertwined in America, and that from the
early days these sectors were ambiguous and overlapping.[18] A further complexity is that today's nonprofit sector is supported greatly
by government through a combination of direct subsidies and public tax policies. The public sector, in social welfare no less than in

defense or banking regulation, is highly influenced by the needs of private business as well as self-interested bureaucracies that control policies. There is nothing "pure" or inherently "good" about government services, as anyone who has ever been on public assistance can attest.

Yet despite criticisms of government, throughout American history and around the world, social movements of the poor and working class have strongly supported public programs as entitlements of citizenship: for example, Social Security pensions, national health care, and other income supports. "Charity," or the voluntary provision of aid, requires supplication and meekness, while public social welfare, once achieved, becomes a right of citizenship. Public programs may also add to the well-being of citizens by increasing the bargaining power of workers and limiting the freedom of employers to cut wages and lay off workers. Further, if progressive taxation accompanies material benefits for those less affluent, a potential for income redistribution exists. Charity is a poor instrument for social justice on two accounts. Not only is it badly equipped in scope for the task of social justice, it is privately run by boards of directors or trustees who are unelected and not directly accountable to the public (see chapters 4 and 5).

Another distinction must be made between the nature of the programs or services offered to the public. Some programs, such as Social Security or Medicare, clearly provide material aid to help people survive. But most programs labeled *social services* provide assistance that has little relation to material benefits (money, housing, food, medical care, etc.) or other actual resources. Rather, programs aimed at changing character and/or punishing people have grown at a far more rapid rate than any income-providing programs, particularly in the last two decades. "Social services" may refer to anything from night basketball games to juvenile detention programs to substance-abuse services; from private psychotherapy and counseling services to programs that combat domestic violence and sexual abuse, to name just a few possibilities. The prevailing public debate rarely distinguishes among the different dimensions of "social welfare expenditures," hence allowing an obfuscation of what is accomplished (or even intended) by funds spent by private or public parties on the vaguely termed "philan-thropy" or even "social welfare."

Until quite recently, discussion of "social welfare" centered on broad strategies for addressing human need such as providing ad-equate health care, income, housing, and so on. The term "social services" originally represented a small subset of social welfare pro-grams, usually associated with counseling and personal assistance, and staffed by social workers and similar specialists. As I will dis-cuss in later chapters, these terms have begun to be used inter-changeably in the political and professional discourse in the last two decades or so. Somewhat surprisingly, social services have grown in recent years, even at a time when many social welfare pro-grams which distribute material benefits to the poor, have been cut. Popular opinion clearly approves of social service programs — from night basketball games to Big Brother programs to job train-ing programs — which do *not* entail material benefits. But as with the recent "ending welfare as we know it" campaign, tremendous unpopularity surrounds many social benefit programs. I intend, for discussion, to separate recreation, counseling, training, and com-panionship programs from material benefits central to a social jus-tice perspective of the welfare state. By doing so, I do not mean to denigrate the importance of counseling or recreation or services. I suggest, however, that social services are quite a different thing from securing a potentially lifesaving Social Security check or Medicaid card. Services are cheaper, involve no income redistribu-tion, are less risky politically, and are usually less subject to any clear evaluation of benefit. Hence, social services, like the idea of charity, are popular across the political spectrum due both to their very vagueness and to their association with the symbolism of charity.

## THE POWER OF SYMBOLISM, THE TRIUMPH OF THE RELATIONSHIP

Although part of the purpose of this book will be to revive a debate about social justice as opposed to America's love affair with charity and social services, to stop there would be sorely incomplete. The fact is that the sociological dictum "As people perceive things as real, they are real"[19] holds a great deal of truth. The growth and dissemination of the stance of "caring" in our society (simultaneous with cuts in public services) by political, religious, business, and professional leaders deserves greater attention than it has received. This book will explore not only the limitations of charity but the appeal of altruistic claims and therapeutic relations. I will postulate two central features behind the success of the "love" discourse that help constitute the American glorifying myth of charity and service.

First, the discourse of "caring" is magnificent symbolism, which historically emanates from the Christian tradition. In today's more secular society, religious belief has melded with the strategies of business, professionals, and the media to approach issues of concern (not only poverty or traditional social service issues, but race relations or threats to societal consensus of any kind) with a therapeutic response. So often we hear political, business, academic, and social service officials make remarks such as, "I feel your pain," "We hear what you are saying," "Why can't we all just get along?" But a caring discourse is still, after all, only talk. Symbolism and sentiment apparently require no evaluation: they assert a quasi-religious mystique of "doing good." I propose to trace the power of such symbolism by examining the adaptation of the religious symbol of service to business, the professions, and the nonprofit sector in particular.

Second, the power of symbolism has grown largely through the development of personal relationships between "givers"—or those of higher status—and "recipients," or the lower-status people being "served." In the eighteenth, nineteenth, and early twentieth centuries, American missionaries, settlement house workers, and early social workers understood this and proudly proclaimed that one way to solve class antagonism was to personally visit the poor, immigrant workers, Indians and African-Americans, and others. The turn-of-the-century motto of the friendly visitor ("Not alms, but a Friend")[20] has actually succeeded far more than many historians have acknowledged.

Advances in the language of "caring," the professionalization of the helping relationship, and the social movement of self-help have all, of course, modified the paternalism of the old friendly visitors to make the helper more respecting, often a positive contributor to the life of the helped. Yet, at bottom, efforts even today by many volunteers or human service workers to "be with" the sick, the poor, the old, or the hurt are successors to Christian missionary and charity organization workers. Rarely, for example, do volunteers or workers focus on financial or economic aid, much less political mobilization. More often, the mission remains to provide inspiration, care, solace, or support. The wide appeal of this relationship to all parts of American society is evident in the tremendous number of people who enter the helping professions, who volunteer their time, and the number of "recipients" who welcome these visitors into their lives. This appeal needs both analysis and criticism. Clearly the transaction between people of different classes, in different life stages or states of health, is a powerful thing and provides some measure of solace and sometimes critical help. Yet the possibility is also present that in the "one-on-one" dealings between helper and helped, the relationship therapy that has so triumphed in America, we may also have lost some of the forest for the trees.

## ORGANIZATION OF THE BOOK

It is beyond the scope of this book to provide a complete history of social welfare, either of the public or charitable sector. My objective is rather to explore those dimensions of American charity which have been hidden from discussion, in part because of the self-interest of a host of political and professional forces. In exploring these controversial paths, I by no means seek to call into question the well-meaningness of most individuals and groups who provide aid in modern America. Indeed, the book answers its rhetorical question by saying (at least in a vague way) that "love" may have everything to do with it! Yet, in our society at this point, exaltation of the charitable, the volunteer, the therapist, and the helper is everywhere; it does not need this author's praise. I do wish to call into question the sanctity and efficacy of the largest voluntary and not-for-profit enterprise in the world: What are the roots of its sanctity, what does it achieve, and what are its failures? Why is it so sacrosanct considering the vagueness of its accomplishments?

In chapters 1 and 2, I explore how, historically, claims to altruism have often coincided with cruel and even violent repression of those who were different. I call this phenomenon "repressive benevolence," to indicate that the policy of repression was spearheaded by those who believed they were "doing good." In the case of the destruction of America's indigenous peoples (chapter 1), a clear philanthropic objective was to assimilate the Indian into the white, civilized way at whatever cost. The difference between white armies and marauders, and missionaries and charity officials, was not one of objective but of means. In chapter 2, in examining some aspects of how the poor have been treated in America's past, I suggest similar motives of repression (while less extreme) were at work. Citing Biblical morality, for hundreds of years a variety of reformers and visitors went to the slums hoping to socialize and change the "dangerous classes," fearing that social disorder, even communism, would emerge if the bad habits of the poor were not remedied.

The second half of the book moves to an interesting but almost totally unanalyzed element of American history: how is it that even after the passage of government legislation at the federal level that provided major social welfare benefits, the charitable sector has grown so enormously and, in contrast to its reputation with the Left and some of the poor in earlier days, has managed to become a sacrosanct and glorified institution? Government, in contrast, has become almost synonymous with repression or incompetence, or both, simultaneously.

In chapter 3, I briefly present some of the elements of Christian thought which helped elevate the vague notion of charity into a noble act, in part placing this symbolic ritual at a moral level far different from (and above) government aid. Chapter 4 suggests that the wealthy utilized the religious veil of sentimentality to modify their poor reputations, particularly during the Gilded Age, and gradually developed an infrastructure of nonprofit social agencies, foundations, community chests (later united ways), and other institutions to legitimize their existence. In chapter 5, I return to the organization of the nonprofit world in contemporary times, tracing the continued self-interest of the powerful and examining the strange paradox of the nonprofit sector's providing less service to the poor while greatly fragmenting the existing service sector. In chapter 6, in light of these paradoxes, I return to the question of how the charitable sector retains such legitimacy, including with those who are its "clients" and with the remnants of the Left. I argue that the nonprofit world, through its symbiotic relationship with government and corporate America, has served as one element in the general encapsulation of previously dissident elements in our society. In the concluding chapter, I briefly explore the alternatives to charity. How can those interested in social justice rather than symbolism move beyond clichés and the tyranny of conventionality to affirm that there are other avenues of "love"?

# Part One

# AMERICAN ALTRUISM AND REPRESSIVE BENEVOLENCE

# American Altruism and
# Repressive Benevolence

Western culture tends to dichotomize human action. Good or noble acts contrast with evil or sinful acts. If life were quite so simple, we could stop our inquiry now and simply indict Euroamericans as completely "evil" and leave it at that. The record of Euroamericans is one of extermination of the indigenous peoples of the American continent, enslavement of African peoples, and a fair amount of repression against their "own" kind. But it is far too simple merely to condemn the evils of the past; in some ways it is almost as shallow as the "glorifying myths" discussed in the introduction. To shake our heads and "tut-tut" may allow us to feel superior to those who went before us, but it does not help us understand the issues of Western culture any better.

The following two chapters locate "doing good" in American history within a broader context that was less than good. Conceptions of "good" and "proper" treatment are socially bound and cannot be divorced from the sociological, ideological, and moral constructions of the time. People often act with good intentions. But intentions occur within a broader context and social structure. For example, caught up in war, some soldiers can be heroic, some charitable, and some brutal. No one would evaluate the entire war based on the acts of individuals or even units of soldiers. If a war's *purpose* is unjust, then the actions of a few soldiers or citizens can hardly make it just.

The American focus on altruism and charity, like that on war heroism or valiant first aid workers, obscures the forest for the trees by taking individual action out of a social context and glorifying it. I will argue that being "civilized" and "good" throughout most of American history has been defined in such a way that it encompasses the belief in "righteousness" while *simultaneously* bringing punishment and sometimes even countenancing violence on those not "civilized." That is, if the overall purpose of an activity and the broader mission of a society is repressive, then donning the mantle of charity no matter how sincere does not mitigate the broader damage.

*Repressive benevolence* can be used to describe the actions and attitudes of those who claim to do good, but because of cultural and power differentials often harm their intended subjects. Underlying repressive benevolence is the strong American ideological belief that its churchgoing, white, middle-class citizens know what is best for others as well as themselves, and hence are summoned to "do good" by spreading their gospel of living to others. Such spreading of the good life is considered well-meaning and constitutes a strand from the Puritans of old to American soldiers in Vietnam or the Middle East in the twentieth century. When "superior" meets "inferior," acts by the former are almost always repressive since the goodwill of the white churchgoing citizen is conditioned on the behavioral and character change of the subject or client of the mission.

In chapter 1, I explore the tragic history of Euroamerican genocide against American Indians, and in chapter 2 the harsh treatment of citizens of all races and ethnicities who were poor or judged "deviant" during centuries of American history. In both cases, "do-gooders" who were known as "humanitarians" or "reformers" played a large role, and were sometimes successful in implementing repressive measures even more effectively than people who openly suggested violent or harsher measures. To "civilize" people, to make them Christian and "proper," was enshrined as noble and compassionate, yet actions against those who were different often turned ugly. The missionary approached the Indian with a smile and a Bible, but after some time if this strategy didn't work, other measures were needed to civilize the "barbarian." It is true that the missionary and later the humanitarian "Friend of the Indian" may have meant well, but how much is this claim worth to America's indigenous peoples? Poor transients of colonial times may have been offered alms in some New England towns, but if or when they lingered too long, strong punitive action was taken. Not all missionaries approved of the violence done by many settlers, and not all upstanding citizens favored the lash or other punishments for the poor, but neither did they see them as unnatural.

Of course, the following chapters are hardly meant to be a comprehensive treatment of American charity or social welfare, either in terms of specific issues treated or the general character of all Americans' interaction with those in need. There were always exceptions to those whose charity was conditioned on reform and assimilation, and many did indeed use the offices of charity to perform good acts. In general, charity which crossed lines of class and race—such as relief from floods or other natural disasters—and some efforts at helping the physically disabled, the blind, the deaf, and the old, tended to be more altruistic. Nevertheless, it is fair to say that the Anglo-American charitable heritage is largely one of repressive benevolence, and while things have improved considerably for many over time (certainly the rights and conditions of women, children, people of color, and those with disabilities), we are hardly removed from this type of tough love today. Recent actions and rhetoric directed at the poor or others judged "deviant" today—from the "ending of welfare as we know it" to the continuing violent war on drugs with its dramatic devastation of African-American urban life—reflect once again this contradiction between our claims to do good while actually doing bad.

# 1—Charity, Philanthropy, and the Indian: Overlooked Aspects of Genocide

*When civilization and barbarism are brought into such relation that they cannot coexist together, it is right that the superiority of the former should be asserted and the latter compelled to give way. It is, therefore, no matter of regret or reproach that so large a portion of our territory has been wrested from its aboriginal inhabitants and made the happy abode of an enlightened and Christian people.*

Luke Lea, U.S. Indian Commissioner[1]

*A great deal of damage can be carried out under the cloak of benevolence.*

Annette Jaimes, Indian scholar[2]

*It is said of missionaries that when they arrived, they had only the Book and we had the land; now we have the Book and they have the land.*

Vine DeLoria, Indian scholar[3]

Traditionally, most social welfare experts begin the historical treatment of charity and social welfare by focusing on the English Poor Laws, which were transplanted to the American colonies, then discuss the history of early charity societies, hospitals, or orphanages in Eastern seaboard cities. Often absent from this discussion is the fact that America was a settler nation whose character was firmly stamped by its interactions with the inhabitants already present in this continent. For over five hundred years after Columbus led the European invasion of the New World, Western European settlers with their "civilization" confronted "barbarism" (that is, the indigenous peoples and their own set of social institutions). One part of this tragic story of physical and cultural genocide of the indigenous peoples of the Americas is the story of charity and philanthropy.

This chapter has two purposes. One is to highlight that much of this assault was conducted not by armies and rabid Indian-hating settlers but by benevolent armies of religious missionaries, charity officials, and philanthropists. Second, while not at all negating the historic uniqueness of the Indian experience, significant parallels will be drawn between the charitable construction of Indian "savagery" and "barbarism," and the definition of others, including Caucasians, who were also "savage." Religious missionaries pioneered what might be called a moral technology as an alternative to a military option for dealing with the "barbarians." This technology, while often resisted by Indians, was successful on many occasions. Missions to the Indians were a part of America's development of a wide range of benevolent and charitable societies aimed at helping a large number of populations, and it gradually moved from being a religious to a secular feature of late nineteenth- and early twentieth-century America.

To situate the discussion of "altruism" in the Indian removal process, an all too brief introduction is needed to show why the indigenous peoples were seen as barbarians and savages.

## "CIVILIZED" VERSUS "BARBARIAN"

Despite the irony that today many of us would see the roles as reversed, Euroamericans classified indigenous peoples as barbarian while they represented themselves as the superior culture. While discussion of native cultures lumps together as many differences as similarities, still the following generalizations are accurate: at a time when Columbus's Spain and Henry Hudson's England were ruled by monarchs and feudal lords, most Indian nations had consensual, collective decisionmaking processes; at a time when European peasants worked under miserable conditions, the hunting societies of America had more leisure and relative material prosperity than European society; at a time when harsh corporal punishment, mistreatment of women (such as the burning of witches), and incarceration and execution of dissidents was rampant in Europe (the Inquisition, for example), violence was usually absent in Indian nations; and in contrast to the huge pauperization of Europe that accompanied the unraveling of feudalism, the Indians had no paupers as they shared the fruits of their labor in a more egalitarian manner than either feudal or later capitalist systems would ever do. This viewpoint is (as we shall return to) not modern romanticism or one of "political correctness." Thomas Morton, an early Massachusetts settler who led a number of colonialists into a cooperative life with the Indians (the first known white to "go native"), observed in 1632:

> Yet all things are used in common amongst them. A bisket cake given to one; that one breakes it equally into so many parts, as there be persons in his company, and distributes it. Platoes Commonwealth is so much practised by these people . . . they make use of those things they enjoy . . . as common goods, and are therein, so compassionate that rather than one should starve all, thus doe they passe away the time merrily, not regarding our pompe (which they see dayly before their faces) but are bettre content with their owne. . . .[4]

As one other example, Moravian missionary John Heckewelder wrote in 1819 of his experience with an Indian nation:

> Whatever liveth on the land, whatsoever groweth out of the earth, and all that is in the rivers and waters flowing through the same, was given jointly to all, and every one is entitled to his share. From this principle, hospitality flows as from its source. With them it is not a virtue but a strict duty. Hence they are never in search of excuses to avoid giving, but freely supply their neighbor's wants from the stock prepared for their own use. They give and are hospitable to all, without exception, and will always share with each other and often with the stranger, even to the last morsel . . . the stranger has a claim to their hospitality . . . for if the meat . . . was taken from the woods, common to all before the hunter took it; if corn or vegetables, it had grown out of the common ground, yet not by the power of man, but by the Great Spirit. . . .[5]

Yet despite Morton and Heckewelder's recognition of and admiration for the powerful collectivity of Indian culture, these observers did not represent official thinking. To most early explorers, settlers, and missionaries, the Indians were barbarians by two standards. First, of course, they were not Christians, but heathens. Disposition of "infidels" was taken up as early as the Crusades by papal bulls, yet in the sixteenth century the fate of the heathens found in the New World was still being debated in Rome. One set of church philosophers favored enslaving the indigenous people, while others sought conversion. Pope Pius V finally sided with the latter.[6] The religious difference (being heathen) was, to say the least, no small matter in those days, as fresh graves in Europe from the Inquisition proved.

Along with Christian versus heathen came a second distinction between "civil" and "savage." European feudal society was heavily influenced by the uncertainties and dangers that large forests and other "unsettled" areas held in the Middle Ages. Forests were associated with highwaymen, vagrants, vagabonds, and other uncivilized ruffians and criminals. Those who lived under the protection of the nobility, and later those who lived in towns and cities, were seen as "civil," while those who hid in the extensive forests were "savage." The social construction of "savage" in Europe was also tied to some degree to racial, ethnic, and religious differences. Many of the peoples fighting the newly centralizing nation-states in Europe were pagans being "civilized" forcefully as well. "Savagery" also subtly merged with ethnicity, as, for example, in the case of the Irish, who saw the treatment of American indigenous people (genocide and war of extermination) literally being practiced on them at virtually the same time in the 1600s. It is, of course, difficult to disentangle racism based on skin color and other natural characteristics as a cause for hatred from the religious antagonism and social contempt based on different customs and norms within different cultures. In the case of attitudes toward American indigenous peoples, the latter is likely to have preceded modern notions of racism.

As Ward Churchill has noted, Protestant settlers went further than the Catholic Church in its conception of rights over the "non-human" (heathen) savages in the New World. While the popes had developed a complex system of legalities that was more honored in the breach than not,[7] English settlers asserted the "Norman Yoke" to justify their dispossession of native land. This principle declared that the only Christian and civil way to dwell in the world was to develop the land. Since English settlers maintained that the Indians "were [not] demonstrating a willingness and ability to 'develop' their territories in accordance with a scriptural obligation to exercise 'dominium' over nature," the Indians were forfeiting their right to land.[8] Of course, this entire construction would have been absurd if ever fully understood by indigenous peoples. First of all, they believed that *no one* could own any part of Mother Earth, be it land or water or the sky. Second, most Indians were part of hunting-gathering societies, and even where engaged in agriculture they had an entirely different system of division of labor, seasonal migration, and way of sustaining their societies than the way English settlers farmed their small plots of land.

The status of Indians as "lower" and "inferior" was further conceptualized in the nineteenth century as early anthropology arose. Lewis Henry Morgan, the influential anthropologist, proposed that all societies went through three stages of life: savagery, barbarism, and civilization. In his paradigm the Indian was "on his way" out of savagery and would eventually emerge as civilized. He was already far above the black man after all (in a dramatic self-fulfilling prophecy, Morgan and others held that Africans were obviously inferior to Indians since they were, after all, held as slaves in America, while the Indians roamed free!) But still, the Indians had to give up their religion, their style of dress, their land, their distinctive family and tribal relations, and, most of all, their communal ways. Without individual acquisition of land, complex machinery, and domesticated animals, no civilized society could emerge. John Wesley Powell, founder of the Bureau of American Ethnology and the US Geological Society, urged "the sooner this country [Western lands still under Indian ownership] is entered by white people and the game destroyed so that the Indians will be compelled to gain a subsistence by some other means than hunting, the better it will be for them."[9]

The construction of "Indianness" as "Otherness," "savage," and "heathen" from the time of the earliest American settlement was then the dominant motif in the altruistic mind as it dealt with this strange and foreign set of societies. While, of course, murderous Indian-hating settlers and armed cavalries would play a major role in eliminating millions of Indians, in some cases "Indianness" held more admiration among the wilder, "common" whites in America than within the educated classes. The frequent number of common whites who joined Indian tribes, the fascination with the captivity tale as genre (with much ambivalence about whether captivity was always involuntary or whether the subject captured had "gone native"), and strong links in some areas between traders and Indians suggest to author Richard Slotkin that a powerful attraction also characterized settlers' meetings with Indians. Those higher in social status such as missionaries and reformers feared that common whites would "go native" (actually joining tribes) or "act like Indians," taking part in the violent pursuit on the frontier or selling the savages alcohol or gambling with them and so on.[10] Hence, while missionaries and reformers generally favored a non-violent approach to Indians where possible, they also were extremely rigid about "heathenness" and "savageness" simply not being tolerable in a properly ordered Christian society.

## MISSIONARIES AS THE FIRST COUNTERINSURGENTS: CLEARING THE WAY FOR "PROGRESS"

As with other figures in American history, the role of religious missionaries has been sanitized and transformed to portray these struggling altruists as heroic and courageous, if a bit austere and old-fashioned for our modern tastes. Such portrayals, as exemplified in the powerful movie *Black Robe* (1991), have been criticized by Indian activists as racist and inaccurate.[11] In the film, the black-robed Jesuit Father LaForge is not only courageous but is the only figure shown as fully human. The "savages," particularly the Mohawks, who reject the missionary, are violent to each other as well as to settlers and engage in torture, rape, and other bestial acts. The viewer thinks, well it was a tough road, and too many people died, and so on, but the "good guys" did win in the end after all (perhaps the few "good" Indians as well as the whites).

While it is true that missionaries were often brave individuals, and a number even went "native" in taking the Indians' side against government policy,[12] for the most part American self-romanticism has totally transformed what missionaries were all about. What did the idealism of the missionaries behoove? What was their purpose? When King James I chartered the first colonies, he cited the obligation of "propagating the Christian Religion to such people, as yet live in darkness and miserable ignorance of the true knowledge and worship of God" and ordered "the savages bordering among them (the colonialists)" be converted. The Puritan leaders saw their "errand in the wilderness" as fulfillment of the Bible's Proverbs 25:25 "As cold waters to a Thirsty soul, so is Good News from a Far Country." Soon after the highly romanticized accounts of the Pilgrims and their Thanksgiving meal with Squanto, the Massachusetts' theocrats developed "praying communities" where they sought to "Wynn and incite" heathens "to the knowledge and obedience of the onlie true God."[13]

Of course, there was always some fascination among the Indians about Western religion, and many Indians (particularly in New England) did convert or simply complied after their societies were destroyed. But it was only by abandoning the "Indian way" for the white way that an Indian could be made over to a nonheathen and nonsavage. As Slotkin notes, "The Indian way and the Puritan way were, however, antithetical concepts. The Puritan way aimed at the creation of a sanctified civilization, a society ordered on rigid principles of divine authority. . . . *They prized cultivation: the bringing of wild man, wild passions, and wild nature under the check of order.* . . ."[14] From the Massachusetts Puritan theocracy of the seventeenth century all the way through the mid-twentieth century, as embraced by both government Indian policy and private religious and voluntary enterprises, terms for Indians' acceptance into "civilization" were the following:

- they had to give up their land base to white settlers;
- they had to accept farming (and later, manual labor) rather than hunting, gathering, and other indigenous technologies;
- they had to accept Christianity in *all* ways, including the Sabbath and blasphemy laws, with no trace of "paganism";
- they had to change their "savage," "half-naked" dress and look like white settlers;

- they had to significantly change their gender roles so women would not have to perform agricultural work and men would not be away from their wives on a seasonal basis;
- they had to change their sexual norms to display the purity and reticence supposedly characteristic of model European settlers;
- they had to develop their own private property and a respect for the settlers' private property;
- they had to accept in all ways Western law.

That this was a tall order for the Indians became evident early on in New England. Indians initially were friendly to Europeans. They had no concept of private ownership so could not conceptualize the colonialists' belief that they had "sold off" or given away their land base. They found the rituals of the Europeans interesting. Often they happily went into the white man's church. Yet by so doing they did not necessarily believe they were abandoning their own beliefs. Not monotheists, there was no reason for the Indian peoples to believe they were deserting their own beliefs by adding the "white man's God" to their prayers.

When wars broke out between Indian tribes and colonialists, the theocratic leadership of early New England was able to use religion to justify force. The Puritan leaders quoted Romans 13:2, "Whosoever, therefore resisteth the power, resisteth the ordinance of God; and they that resist shall receive to themselves damnation"[15] after the Pequot War of 1637. After a period of relative peace, the New England colonialists fought another series of bloody battles dubbed King Philip's War (1675–76) in which they killed thousands of Indians and destroyed most active military resistance in New England.[16]

Cotton Mather explained this bloody war as "God's speedy vengeance" on Indians for rejecting the gospel. The missionaries of New England society, in an early version of "better dead than Red," became convinced that there was no other way to bring the heathen to Christianity than by war. "The Indian's only access to heaven, they held, was through his adoption of the white Christian's culture. To remain an Indian was to ensure damnation."[17] For decades after the war, the severed head of the supposed leader of the Indian rebellion, King Philip, stayed impaled on the city walls of Plymouth as a warning of what would happen to resisters.

Other severed parts of his body were sent to other towns in Massachusetts for display. One must wonder "what's love got to with it" indeed.

If the events being discussed were not so tragic, they would almost be humorous: two totally different groups of peoples meet speaking different languages and adhering to different values, religions, and customs. Yet the Massachusetts Bay Colony law passed on November 4, 1646, reads, ". . . seeing the blaspheming of the true God cannot be excused by any ignorance or infirmity of humane nature . . . it is therefore ordered and decreed by this Courte . . . that no person within this jurisdiction, whether Christian or pagan, shall wittingly and willingly presume to blaspheme his holy name . . . they shall be put to death."[18]

Though New England's indigenous peoples could not have known the English word for God or what significance this held in Puritan religion, they would be held to this standard at the punishment of death. Lest all this seem too far in the past to be relevant now, Indian scholar Vine DeLoria in his well-known 1969 book *Custer Died for Your Sins* gives us several other sardonic tales of how little the religious missionaries and Indians (even Christianized ones) understood one another. Throughout the twentieth century, missionaries and charity workers always saw long hair as "uncivilized" and Indian-like. Ironically, DeLoria comments on how "after the tribal elders had been fully sheared, they were ushered into church meeting, (and) given pictures of Jesus and the disciples. . . . Looking down at the pictures, the ex-warriors were stunned to discover the Holy Dozen in shoulder-length hair."[19] Commenting on "missionary boxes" that were placed in churches throughout the Eastern US to "help the Indians," DeLoria comments:

> (White) people were horrified that Indians continued to dress in their traditional garb. Since whites did not wear buckskin and beads, they equated such dress with savagery. So do-gooders in the East held fantastic clothing drives to supply the Indians with civilized clothes. Soon boxes of discarded evening gowns, tuxedos, tennis shoes, and uniforms flooded the reservations. Indians were made to dress in these remnants so they could be civilized. Then, realizing the ridiculous picture pre-

sented by the reservation people, neighboring whites made fun of the Indian people for having the presumption to dress like whites.[20]

If the missionaries were guilty only of a sort of rigidity or profound misunderstanding, this would be regrettable. But as the justification Puritans made for killing Indians and the placing of the head of King Philip on their fortifications suggest, there is a far darker side. The missionaries, knowingly sometimes, unknowingly at others, were the cat's-paw of the military and gun-toting settlers. As DeLoria notes, Indian nations were destroyed culturally as well as physically to the same degree they had contact with the missionaries:

> Land acquisition and missionary work always went hand in hand. While the thrust of Christian missions was to save the individual Indian, its result was to shatter Indian societies and destroy the cohesiveness of the Indian communities. *Tribes that resisted the overtures of the missionaries seemed to survive. Tribes that converted were never heard of again. Where Christianity failed, and insofar as they failed, Indians were able to withstand the cultural deluge that threatened to engulf them.* [my emphasis][21]

Although many different experiences occurred between missionaries and Indian nations, and variations existed among Protestant denominations and between Catholic and Protestant missionaries, a general pattern emerges between King James' edict to convert the heathen and the final military defeat of Indians in the late nineteenth century. Missionaries (along with a few traders or prospectors) were often the leading element of white men entering a new territory. Indians were frequently friendly with them, with some converting to Christianity and others simply being fascinated with the missionaries. Usually one of two things happened: the tribes split between those members who Christianized and sought to curry favor with the Euroamericans, and those who clung to their ways; or some incident united a majority of a tribe or tribes against the missionaries and white power. In either event, once a missionary was threatened either physically or more figuratively, he sent for more white soldiers and settlers. Rarely did Indian nations ever go peacefully "into the night." Usually militia, cavalry, and armed settlers attacked the nations after an incident involving an "innocent" missionary and his wife or children or white farmers who lived near the missionaries.

An excellent example of the process of Indian removal by a powerful symbiosis between religion, the state, and settlers is given in Alvin Josephy's historical work *The Nez Perce Indians and the Opening of the Northwest*, which chronicles about fifty years (1830s through the 1870s) of conquest in what are now the states of Washington, Oregon, Idaho, and Montana. Although his focus is on the Nez Perce tribe, which for many years was allied with the white colonialists (only to end up being slaughtered in the 1870s), his work also covers approximately ten other tribal nations and bands living in the Northwest prior to white settlement.

George Simpson, the first governor of the Northwest territories (then organized as a trading company), sent for missionaries in the mid-1820s. Idealistic about converting the Indians and schooling them in English and farming, he wrote to the American Board of Commissioners for Foreign Missions (the coordinating arm of the Protestant missions), but warned that they would have to set up a mission in a protected village where "Indians did not roam" and in an area where they could put the Indians to work farming. The pragmatic link between religion, colonialism, and capitalism was illustrated in Simpson's letter to his trading companies, in which he noted that "the conversion of the natives might prove profitable to them, for it would place the Indians in greater need of white men's goods and thus increase company's profits."[22]

The first two missionaries sent to the area, despite the general openness of the Indians who welcomed them, were so alienated by conditions on the frontier and the "savageness" of the Indians that they ended up leaving. Jason Lee, a Methodist missionary, expressed "disgust" at "how much work needed to be done" and "how difficult it was to convert Indians in the wilderness" in comparison with the white-dominated Northeast. He prayed for divine help for the "degraded red man," but went into real estate instead.[23] Samuel Parker, a Congregationalist, replaced him, but he also did not remain. Parker felt continually undermined by the presence of white traders who mingled easily with the Indians.

Parker disapproved of the lower-class whites who "were leading a wild and wandering life and appear to have sought for a place where, as they would say, human nature is not oppressed by the tyranny of religion, and pleasure is not awed by the frown of virtue." He felt no progress could be made with the Indians because of the "demoralizing influence with the Indians (the trappers have) imposed upon them, in all ways that sinful propensities dictate."[24] Parker left to pursue the conquest of natives on the islands of Hawaii.

In the late 1830s, under the leadership of Henry Spalding, a stern Presbyterian minister, a mission was finally established. Spalding opened a school for Indians, converted a number of Nez Perces to Christianity, and, joined by a settlement of white farmers, put the friendly Indians to work farming. Although the Nez Perce nation developed strong ties to Spalding and to missionary Marcus Whitman, the goals of the missionaries were always unrealistic:

> [The] aim was eventually to make the Nez Perces into a nation of farmers, no longer anxious to leave their homes to chase buffalo on the plains, but settled happily around him [Spalding] and accessible to his religious instruction. . . . Ignorant of the Indians' deeply felt love of travel, adventure, hunting, and daring against enemies . . . he considered it his duty to get the Nez Perces collected and living prosperously on farms before they endured a tragic fate . . .[25]

It was not long, however, before Reverend Spalding began to alienate many Nez Perces and other neighboring Indians who came to the mission. His harsh regimen of enforced farming and laboring rankled many Indian men, as did his effort to impose a Christian commonwealth which banned even inappropriate language. Spalding also introduced the lash to punish Indian violators. This shocked the natives, who had never resorted to physical punishment in their own society. Adding insult to injury, Spalding ordered Indians to inflict the blows themselves on those who broke mission rules.[26]

It was only a matter of time before antagonism between the mission, on the one side, and a number of Indian groups egged on by white mountain men who also hated the missionaries, exploded.

One day two Indians insulted Spalding and demanded payment for their land, as they had heard was appropriate from other Indians and the white mountain men. After a bitter dispute, the mission's mill dam was destroyed. The mission was then surrounded by angry Indians, and only the arrival of government-appointed Indian agent Elijah White saved the lives of the missionaries and their allies. White hastily called a conference with the Indian nations. Using a combination of threats of force, on the one hand, and an appeal to the religiousness of some of the Indians on the other, White got the nations to agree to follow a set of Western-made laws on theft, private property, trespassing, and so on. The Indians, probably unknowingly, had accepted "the hangman's noose, the lash, and cruel imprisonment for the humane, ethical forms of social disapproval under which the Indians, without Christianity or civilization, had long maintained."[27] These laws, of course, were almost never used against white settlers who killed or injured Indians, raped women, and stole their land. The laws were enforced exclusively on Indians, many of whom were hanged for their crimes. Further, as was typical of Euroamerican interaction with Indians throughout the continent, they demanded that peoples who had lived without hierarchy (the Northwest tribes were organized as family bands with no strong centralized leadership) "for the first time in history, choose a single high chief of the tribe and acknowledge him as such by universal consent."[28]

By the mid-1840s missionaries Spalding and Whitman, despite their temporary victory, became less sanguine about their chances of success. In an area still isolated and populated mainly by "Indian-like mountain men," they felt that only the arrival of more pious white settlers would help win over the Indians. As Josephy summarizes the letters of the missionaries, "Christianity . . . required the disciplining of undisciplined Indians, something that could only be provided by the presence of a strong, civilized community that would force the Indians into a pattern of life which they had so far chosen to ignore or resist."[29]

In another letter, written to the Boston headquarters of the Protestant missions, an Oregon missionary captured the essence of how the missionaries hoped to lubricate the conquering of the Indians through Christianity:

> One thing is very certain, that the influence of the gospel will have the tendency to make them [the Indians] more submissive to the rule of the whites and will be the means of preventing them from wars with their new neighbors, and save them from utter extinction. It seems the only [way] they can be saved from being destroyed from the face of the earth is by their yielding to the control of the whites, and nothing will induce them to do this but a cordial reception of the gospel, and how can this be done without the labors of the Christian missionary.[30]

The missionaries were backed by new laws enforced by agents of the Northwest territory, and they got their fondest wish—a vast growth in white settlers heading to the Northwest in the 1840s and 1850s. The growth in white farmers led to continued splits in the tribes. A growing number of natives, even in the "friendly" Nez Perce nation, began to resent the religionists. Now more alienated Nez Perces saw friendly, Christianized Indians as "women," servants of the whites.[31] They also increasingly changed their mind about the missionaries. While initially the religionists had been seen as men of peace, like Indian shamans, by the late 1840s they were seen as "the men . . . bringing the whites from the East to take their country from them."[32] By the mid-1850s, faced with a decimation of their land base by encroaching white colonizers supported by church and state government, the Indian nations of the Northwest were given a choice: accept captivity within a small fraction of their traditional areas (a reservation) or face the use of force. The crisis for the Northwest Indians in the "interior wars" of 1855–58 was worsened by disunity wrought by the Christianization of some of the tribesmen:

> Although the Indians had no tradition of united action [across tribes] . . . all of them faced the greatest crisis in their history. There was no agreement on how to meet the threat. Some would fight with a patriotic determination to defend their homelands. Some would try to save their lives by submitting humbly, and some would try to buy their way to favor, and perhaps to new prestige and power for themselves, by taking the white man's side against their own people. It was the legacy of the division wrought by the missionaries and [Indian agent] Dr. White.[33]

Although one can speculate that the tribes would have been decimated by white settlers anyway, tribal division in the mid-1850s was a direct result of the missionaries' counterinsurgency work. White religious and government men, whether they intended a policy of "divide and conquer" consciously or not, enacted just such a policy. The nations of the Northwest were conquered one by one, and even the most loyal Nez Perces were subdued permanently in 1877 with no mercy given for their previous years of serving the whites.

As DeLoria argues, to the extent Christianity succeeded, it weakened Indian resolve and unity against colonialism. The missionaries disoriented Indians far more than any soldiers or settlers did. Here were white shamans preaching peace and love, but who brought with them the lash and other white man's harsh laws. They then brought more settlers and helped ease away the Indian's land. By the time angry Indians realized this, often, as in the case of the Northwest tribes, their people were already divided. Many now identified with Christianity and the white men's ways, and the base of their economy and tribal governance had already been destroyed by the success of the missionaries in converting some Indians to small farming and making them dependent on mission gifts of plows and other machinery.

While not all the results of the missionaries' actions could have been anticipated, the above account (particularly the quotes in their own words) suggest that the Jason Lees, Samuel Parkers, Henry Spaldings, and Marcus Whitmans *knew what they were doing.* They all would have preferred to see the Indians submit peacefully rather than all of the killing that ensued. But all envisioned a complete destruction of Indian "heathen" culture and religion and their replacement with American capitalist property relations, the nuclear family, Western dress, and Anglo law. If they meant "good," it was only within the repressive confines of their highly ethnocentric identification with Anglo-American Christian norms to the exclusion of all other ways of living and of knowing reality.

## KILLING THEM SOFTLY: PHILANTHROPIC "FRIENDS OF THE INDIAN"

By the 1870s, one chapter in the tragic story of Euroamerican conquest of the continent was complete: the indigenous nations had been militarily defeated and the number of "savages" who stood in the way of civilization vastly reduced. Yet at this time, the Indian nations in the West still held a large land base, maintained their culture as well as they could within their reduced enclaves, and held on to their kinship structure. This situation, oddly, might have been sufficient for military men and Western settlers. But it was not enough for Eastern reformers, philanthropists, and religious leaders.

Following the Civil War and Reconstruction, a large number of reformers who had been associated with abolitionism split between those who became radicals and a majority who embraced moral uplift. A few humanitarians would move on to causes such as women's suffrage, and a few became socialists and took up the cause of labor. But a large number of causes embraced by religious figures, humanitarians, and philanthropists from the 1880s through the first decades of the twentieth century would be viewed by today's standards as rather odd or quaint: the abolition of alcoholic drink (the temperance movement), the suppression of nude paintings and postcards (the vice and vigilance movement), and the repression of prostitution (the social purity movement). Many endorsed campaigns which, with contemporary hindsight, we might consider conservative; for example, the destruction of the power of immigrants through legislation against immigration, and "good government" reform to weaken ethnic voting power.

Like the other "humanitarian" movements, the "salvation" of the Indian became symbolic to churchmen and philanthropists in a way that combined sympathy with repressive benevolence. On the one hand, the movement for the Indian developed in cities like Boston as a result of outrage over the crowded and corrupt conditions reported on the new reservations. Frederick Hoxie's work on this period shows that the movement was clearly idealistic, beginning with mass meetings and engaging the likes of Oliver Wendell

Holmes and Wendell Phillips, as well as lesser names associated with abolitionism and suffrage.[34] There is no reason to question the "Friends of the Indian" movement's genuine sympathy and sincerity, and it isn't likely that its adherents would, retrospectively, have liked the results of all the actions they helped to stimulate.

But it is also true that the charitable acts of these "Friends of the Indian" led to the disenfranchisement of Indians from most of their land, to the removal of hundreds of thousands of children from Indian parents, and to the attempted destruction of Indian culture, language, and religion. Outrage about the reservation system never led reformers to ask the Indian nations what *they wanted*, nor did reformers ever urge the government, settlers, and missionaries to just *leave the people alone*. Quite to the contrary. The Yankee and Midwest reformers and benefactors manifested a noblesse oblige that held American Protestant social norms to be correct, and the imposition of these norms to be the solution to every social problem. The peaceful absorption of these norms by inferior peoples, who were considered as children, was held out again and again as the answer. Hoxie notes that throughout the nineteenth century, reformers foresaw peaceful assimilation as the vehicle to end Indian culture:

> While others glorified in the annihilation of tribal peoples, pious leaders from Thomas Jefferson to William Lloyd Garrison asserted that the Indians, once "freed" from their "savage" heritage, would participate fully in the nation's institutions. . . . National leaders expected that the destruction of "savagery" and the expansion of Christian "civilization" would convert individual natives into docile believers in American progress. With these ideas in hand, the future appeared predictable. On some future day, the Indians would be surrounded, defeated, and somehow rendered eager to join the dominant culture.[35]

Although in some ways the Indian aroused more sympathy at this time than African-Americans, Chinese immigrants or, in some cases, even Irish immigrants, the reformers' agenda for them was quite comparable to their prescription for other "non-civilized" racial groups in America at the time. They could be accepted *only* to the degree that they assimilated themselves into the dominant white Anglo-Saxon culture. Far from our post–civil rights era view of diversity, the "offer" of equal inclusion under civilized Christian standards was the benevolent, *liberal* position of the day.

The Indian Rights Association and other groups which arose from the furor of this period urged the government to "keep faith with the Indian" by providing for "civilization, Christianization, and enfranchisement" of the tribes. Indian associations also "undertook individual acts of charity such as supporting schools, providing funds for farm equipment, and marketing Indian handicrafts."[36] After the Civil War, religious groups successfully lobbied the federal government to have each conquered tribe assigned to a denomination. Hence the Lutherans sponsored one set of tribes, the Roman Catholics some other tribes, the Quakers some, and so on. This system of religious privatization by government continued through the mid–twentieth century.

Beginning in 1883 the major religious, political, and charitable leaders associated loosely as "Friends of the Indian" began a series of annual meetings at Lake Mohonk, New York. The recommendations and platforms advanced at Lake Mohonk were extremely influential on government policy between 1883 and 1933, and most Commissioners of Indian Affairs (the Bureau of Indian Affairs [BIA] under the US Department of the Interior) came either directly from the Friends of the Indian movement or were appointed on their recommendation, shaping the policies of Presidents Cleveland, Harrison, McKinley, Roosevelt, Taft, Wilson, Harding, Coolidge, and Hoover. While government policy toward the Indians has been sharply criticized over the years, it was greatly shaped and even implemented by America's churches and missionaries.

The first impact of their program was the eradication of the tribes' communal land base. Reformers considered this a "good thing" because only by becoming owners of private property and farming could the Indian be made "civilized." As prominent "Friend of the Indian" Dr. Merrill E. Gates, then-President of Amherst College, reflected in a speech:

> To bring [the Indian] out of savagery into citizenship . . . we need to awaken in him wants. In his dull savagery, he must be touched by the

wings of the divine angel of discontent. . . . Discontent with the tepee
and the Indian camp . . . is needed to get the Indian out of the blanket
and into trousers — and trousers with a pocket in them, and with a
pocket that aches to be filled with dollars! Here is an immense moral
training that comes from the use of property. Like a little child who
learns the true delight of giving away only by first earning and possessing what it gives, the Indian must learn that he has no right to give until
he has earned, and that he has no right to eat until he has worked for his
bread. Our teachers upon the reservations know that frequently their
lessons . . . are effaced and counteracted by the [Indians'] old communal instincts and customs. We have found it necessary, as one of the
first steps in developing a stronger personality in the Indian, to make
him responsible for property.[37]

The most prominent "Friend of the Indian" was Massachusetts
Senator Henry Dawes. Dawes' visits to several reservations convinced him that the communal ties and collective property rights of
the Indians stood in the way of their "advancement" to civilization:

The head chief told us that there was not a family in that whole nation
that had not a home of its own. There was not a pauper in the nation,
and the nation did not owe a dollar . . . Yet the *defect* [my emphasis]
of the system was apparent. [The Indians] have got as far as they can go,
because they own their land in common. . . . There is no enterprise
to make your home any better than that of your neighbor's. There is no
*selfishness* [my emphasis], which is at the bottom of civilization. Until
this people consent to give up their lands and divide them among their
citizens so that each can own the land he cultivates, they will not make
much progress.[38]

Dawes and his religious and reform allies got their way with the
passage of the Indian Land Allotment Act of 1887 (the Dawes Act).
Although complex, the act's basic thrust was to eliminate tribal
ownership of land by "allotting" each adult male "ready for responsibility" a portion of land as an individual small property. In
theory, such decisions were to be made by tribal vote whenever
they "wanted civilization." In practice, pressure from a combination of settlers, charity and religious organizations, and the BIA on
the one hand, and an increased assimilation and desire for profits
on the part of some Indians themselves on the other, made the land
offer hard to resist. Many "elections" for allotment were also boy-
cotted by traditionalists, so even if only a tiny fraction of the tribe

wanted allotment, BIA-staged elections usually came up with positive results. The paternalism of the allotment of individual plots of
land over the course of the fifty-year period is illustrated in the so-
called *last-arrow ceremony*, a pageant run by the BIA as "civilized"
Indians "graduated" to private land ownership:

> These proceedings always began with an order to the entire reservation
> to assemble before a large ceremonial tipi near the agency headquarters.
> The crowd would look on while their "competent" brethren were sum-
> moned individually from inside the lodge. The candidates for land titles
> were dressed in traditional costume and armed with a bow and arrow.
> After ordering a candidate to shoot his arrow into the distance, the re-
> siding officer, usually the agent, would announce "You have shot your
> last arrow." The arrowless archer would then return to the tipi and re-
> emerge a few minutes later in "civilized" dress. He would be placed be-
> fore a plow. "Take the handle of this plow," the government's man
> would say, "this act means that you have chosen to live the life of the
> white man — and the white man lives by work."[39]

Why did this plan, ethnocentric and paternalistic as it was, fail
so miserably even on its own terms? By the 1920s a large percentage of formerly Indian-owned land had fallen into the possession of
either individual Western landowners or large companies. The
idea of "allotment" was flawed in a number of ways: small plots of
land were hardly profitable for cultivation in many areas of the
West, but often more suitable for grazing; in some cases rich min-
eral and other resources made the land far more attractive and profitable to corporations; Indians lacked the experience and, in most
cases, the desire to be farmers; and, because Indians were unaccus-
tomed to Western capitalism, large numbers of unscrupulous
whites were able to buy up thousands of these individual Indian
plots. In some cases, perhaps a decision to sell was advantageous to
an Indian owner, but in most cases white ranchers and businessmen intentionally kept Indian farmers in debt until they had to sell
their land, or supplemented their monetary offerings with large
amounts of alcohol until a poor deal was made.

Concurrent with the critical loss of the Indian land base, educators and government policy worked to wipe out native culture and
language. Indian education was aimed at eliminating the Native

American tongues and banning the use of Indian languages and tribal rituals such as dances. Indian children were believed to be appropriately trained only for menial positions as unskilled laborers or semiskilled vocations. Thomas J. Morgan, a Baptist minister who came out of the "Friends of the Indian" movement, served as BIA commissioner from 1889 to 1893. His view of education for the Indian was that "it should seek the disintegration of the tribes . . . they should be educated, not as Indians, but as Americans. In short, public schools should do for them what they are so successfully doing for all other races in this country—assimilate them."[40] "The Indian teacher must deal with the conditions similar to those that confront the teacher of the blind or the deaf. She must exercise infinite patience," said Estelle Reel, commissioner of Indian education at the turn of the century.[41]

Perhaps most tragic was the BIA- and religious missionary-imposed system of Indian boarding schools to remove children from their parents and homelands. Indians were systematically seen as unfit parents, and thousands of Indian children were placed in white American homes. As Ward Churchill sums up:

> Between the 1880s and the 1980s, more than half of all American Indian children were coercively transferred from their own families, communities, and cultures to those of the conquering society. This was done through compulsory attendance at remote boarding schools, often hundreds of miles from their homes. Native children were kept for years and systematically "decultured": indoctrinated to think and act in the manner of Euroamericans rather than as Indians. It was accomplished through a pervasive foster home and adoption program—including "blind" adoptions where children would be permanently denied information about their origins—placing native youth in non-Indian homes. . . .[42]

Of course, it would be inaccurate and ahistorical to blame religionists, philanthropists, and reformers for *all* the consequences, some obviously unintended, of the cultural genocide inflicted on Indian peoples since the end of the Civil War until it gradually ended under the tumultuous protests of native groups in the 1960s and 1970s. But the humanitarian movement *did* advocate full and complete assimilation, and its imperialistic ventures into the lives and structure of Indian culture were far more extensive than advocated by many laissez-faire politicians of the nineteenth century or by many white generals and settlers. While most colonizers wanted the Indian's *land*, the repressive philanthropists also demanded their *souls* and their *culture*. Without the "Friends of the Indian" movement and the massive investment of all Christian churches in Indian resocialization, the BIA may have been a different instrument of power. The mantle of "doing good" enabled the imposition of a series of actions against the Indians that, if advocated by generals or Western settlers, would probably have been rejected by the governments of the late-nineteenth and twentieth centuries and would have received serious opposition from at least some voters.

## THE RELEVANCE OF INDIAN REPRESSION TO THE AMERICAN HISTORY OF CHARITY

Although the history of Euroamerican oppression of Indian societies is well known to most scholars and in a vaguer way to the American public, the relationship between these events and how social welfare developed in the United States is generally not explored. Accounts of American charity stress the development of a public sector, from the old English Poor Laws to the eventual passage of legislation such as the Social Security Act of 1935. Yet there are two important ways in which the battle against indigenous peoples and "Indianness" greatly affected American social welfare history.

First, if the history of the seventeenth to early nineteenth centuries is well understood, we can see that Western rejection of the Indian social organization did not proceed all at once nor was it ever total. Gradually, through political and social processes, Indian forms of society were stigmatized and villainized, and its attractions were overcome by a combination of force and Christian and patriotic ideology. In this process the Indian form of social organization, which would have made the practice of charity quite irrelevant, was eliminated as a possibility for the society as a whole.

Secondly, there is at least some historic connection between the experience of the missions and its early efforts to convert Indians, and the growth of philanthropic societies to work with others, including "whites."[43] The objectives the philanthropists hoped to achieve with Indians were not entirely different than the objectives they hoped to achieve with "ruffian" or "lower order" whites.

The economic organization of indigenous societies was a dramatic contrast to the way English settlers organized their own society. As opposed to the hierarchical dominance of a landowning class that ruled over a large number of tenants, indentured servants, and paupers (and in the South over slaves), Indian societies had no poor, no almshouses nor economic inequality. As DeLoria notes, "In the old days a tribe suffered and prospered as a unity. When hunting was good everyone ate, when it was bad everyone suffered. Never was the tribe overbalanced economically so that half would always starve and half would thrive. In this sense all tribal members had a guaranteed annual income."[44]

As I have already noted, the fact that Indian society was more *advanced* in many ways did not go unrecognized by some white settlers. Thomas Morton's colony of "New Canaan" in the early years of Massachusetts illustrated the appeal of a utopian society to some white settlers. Puritan leaders looked with such askance at whites mixing with Indians and reveling together at the maypole that Morton was arrested, tried, and deported to England. Many others were attracted to Indian ways, so much so that New England colonies began to legislate against intermingling of the races. Connecticut colonial laws, for example, imposed three years in jail, fines, and whipping for those who chose to "departe . . . and joyne or settle with Indians."[45] Even so, the appeal of Indian society remained. Henry Timberlake, a prominent Virginia lieutenant who served as a negotiator with the Cherokees, declared Indian society superior to the white one (he mentioned their lack of a dole and almshouse) and considered their offer to live among them.

But most deemed going native a major problem. William Smith, a prominent member of Philadelphia's elite and author of *Historical Account of the Expedition against the Ohio Indians* written in 1765, saw whites crossing the line as a major social problem of the time. Unable to understand this attraction except in terms of moral deviance, he attributes its appeal to the poor morals of lower-class whites:

> For the honour of humanity, we would suppose those persons to have been born of the lowest rank, either bred up in ignorance or distressing penury, or who had lived with the Indians so long as to forget their former connections. For, easy and unconstrained as the savage life is, it could never be put in competition with the blessings of improved life and the light of religion, by any persons who have had the happiness of enjoying, and the capacity of discerning, them.[46]

Given the attraction that some whites had for Indian society, it is not impossible to believe that aspects of native societies (including their economic organization) could be appealing and even be copied by colonialists. While this may seem difficult to contemplate today, American revolutionaries did copy Indian political forms in the Articles of Confederation and our Constitution, particularly drawing on the Iroquois confederation's political organization.[47] It is not inconceivable that, without the severe repression of the intermixing of whites and Native Americans and the later development of a populist anti-Indianism (particularly led by Andrew Jackson), white people, particularly the poor and indentured, might have copied Indian economic organization. The religious-legal-political attack on Indian life reinforced private property, class divisions, and the English method of dealing with poverty and other social problems. If changing the organization of settled society was irreligious and "Indian-like," this left only palliative remedies for social inequality available even to reformers. That is, to the extent the Indian societies were regarded as "communistic," white settled society invariably defined itself in opposition to such "savage ways."

Secondly, the moral technology of the missions to the Indians had an important symbiotic relation to other early American charitable endeavors. English settlers arrived with their own set of laws and institutions related to the dole, the Poor Laws. But the Poor Laws were public aid, often inspiring anger and parsimony among colonial settlers and politicians. At best, the Poor Law administration grudgingly accepted some, such as widows or the elderly, to receive aid, but as with modern welfare benefits they also aroused anger, directed particularly at strangers, transients, and those regarded as "undeserving poor."

In sharp contrast to public relief, the possibility of morally converting those who lacked the status and "civilization" of the elite by visiting them inspired great rhetoric and even excitement among churchgoers from the early days of America. Cotton Mather argued that New Englanders had an obligation far beyond the Poor Laws, because alms were not a solution, only spiritual help was. Mather popularized the notion that men and women should engage in voluntary organizations in "a perpetual endeavor to do good in the world." Drawing on the early experience of proselytizing among the Indians, he noted, "Always bear in mind that charity to the *souls* of men is the highest form of benevolence. Send preachers, Bibles, and other books of piety to heathens at home and abroad; support the Church, and keep a watchful eye on the spiritual health of the community." The mission to the poor at home was similar to reaching out to heathens in the New World or overseas, because "the poor [too] need admonitions of piety quite as much as alms." Mather warned against relying only on material aid. "Cannot you contrive to mingle a spiritual charity with your temporal bounty?" he asked, advocating extreme care in the bestowal of alms. He noted that "giving wisely was therefore an even greater obligation than giving generously; and withholding alms from the undeserving as needful and essentially benevolent as bestowing them on the deserving."[48]

Moving benevolent operations to frontiersmen and their families who—like the Indians—were also regarded as unsettled, uncivilized, irreligious, and uncivil, was a natural progression from the civilizing efforts aimed at Indians. Historian Conrad Wright notes how the dramatic rise in charitable enterprise in New England by the late eighteenth century grew out of earlier missionary activities. The Boston Missionary Society, for example, had been working for many years fruitlessly trying to convert Indians on the New York frontier. Failing in these goals, the society and others like it began to shift their work to the white pioneers, also regarded as pagans. There is a "great dissoluteness of morals prevail[ing] in many places on the frontier where all religious institutions [were] neglected."[49] By the second and third decades of the nineteenth century, a major social movement of the time was the organizing of Bible tract societies and other missions to help civilize lower-class whites.

The construction of the poor as "savage" closely resembled some aspects of Indian savagery: men without work (even during depressions) were guilty of sloth and seen as failing the obligation of the "Norman Yoke"; people without a permanent residence were seen like Indians, as immoral and disreputable; and those whites who failed to accept legal and religious norms suffered repressive treatment and categorization as "undeserving" as well. Women were "immoral" if they did not accept patriarchal gender roles or were sexual outside of marriage. Men and women could be cast as immoral as Indians by their coarseness of language, blasphemy, intemperance, Sabbath breaking, or engaging in other vices.

Of course, a combination of periodic unrest among the white poor as well as the critical fact that poor white men gained the right to vote in most areas of America by the mid-nineteenth century made reformers' actions against them less than fully comparable to the genocide of the Indians. Social mobility in the United States, though overrated by some historians, made the conditions of whites different from those of people of color. Interestingly, however, links between the behavior of transient whites and Indians were made as early as the mid-eighteenth century in New England. Colin Calloway, an expert on the diaspora of Indians in New England after their military defeats, shows that "Indians who maintained more traditional lifestyles found themselves harassed as 'vagrants' and 'transients'" and were seen as part of the "wandering poor" (a term usually associated with poor whites).[50] Jean O'Brien, exploring a similar period in the history of Indian women in New England, also found an official tendency to lump "the wandering Indian" with the "strolling poor" as a social problem.[51] I shall explore in the next chapter how the distinction between "civil" and "savage" carried over from Europe affected poor and "deviant" Caucasians in ways that paralleled the treatment of Indians.

# 2—Charity and the Poor: "Not Alms, but a Friend"

*Government welfare [is] the least desirable form of relief because it comes from what is regarded as a practically inexhaustible source, and people who once receive it are likely to regard it as a right, as a permanent pension. . . .*

Mary Richmond, a founder of social work[1]

*It seems often as if charities were the insult which the rich add to the injuries which they heap upon the poor.*

Josephine Shaw Lowell[2]

There is little to be proud of in the American treatment of poor people. In particular, those deemed the "undeserving poor" (a term that at times encompassed the majority of non-aged men who were unemployed and not visibly disabled, and most women who were single, separated, or not part of a traditional family constellation) were treated extremely punitively well into this century. The English colonial heritage, shaped by harsh versions of Protestant moralism, may have sometimes taken on a meaner spirit in the New World, where fear of the unknown and potential violence on the vast forested frontier reinforced the "civil" versus "savage" distinction. Both the early public sector represented by town and local officials who enforced the Poor Laws, and the charitable sector, from religious leaders to early charitable missions, can be faulted for enforcing a harsh vision of social control. The punitive measures that are perhaps most shocking to today's consciences include:

- forcing the poor to wear the letter 'p' on their clothes in some colonies to intentionally stigmatize those who received aid;
- the use of the lash to punish a wide variety of offenses, including pauperism;

CHARITY AND THE POOR — 47

- the forcible taking in the dead of night and "dumping" of some poor people, particularly the mentally ill, in order to place them in other towns and thus avoid relief costs;
- the auctioning off of the poor and often young orphans or mentally retarded people to private parties, usually to the low bidder, inviting vicious exploitation by nonpoor families;
- the use for two centuries of the workhouse and poorhouse (dubbed "indoor relief") to house large numbers of poor people in conditions that were often degrading and harsh. The strongest fear of many working-class people, as late as the middle of this century in some areas, as well as those on relief was the specter of ending up in the poorhouse;
- the use of the treadmill in some workhouses to inflict maximum punishment and pain on the "inmates" convicted of no crime but poverty.[3]

As with the tragic story of genocide against the Indians, it is too easy to adopt a retrospective feeling of superiority over our ancestors. The treatment of the poor reflected the widely held belief that poverty is a moral flaw essentially characterological in nature that's only worsened by providing material aid, for example, alms, or as it came to be known in colonial and nineteenth-century America, "outdoor relief" (as distinguished from aid in a poorhouse or workhouse, where recipients gave up their freedom as a condition of "help"). This view was shared by so many people throughout American history that it can be considered a cultural norm. Despite the tendency of some social welfare historians to portray US history in a progressive fashion, many Americans still display these beliefs. Nor have our social policies changed as dramatically as some optimists imply. Some argue cogently that the poorhouse of old has been replaced by homeless shelters, group homes, and correctional institutions, that the forced work of the workhouse is now renamed "workfare," and the war against "outdoor relief" is now a war on welfare. Rather than a progressive view of American history, a more accurate framework treats social policy as cyclical. When social disorder empowered groups of poor people or economic depressions placed large numbers in need, political conditions changed and social welfare benefits rose. Conversely, when poor people and related groups of advocates were weak, repressive policies have dominated.[4]

This chapter will suggest that in a parallel to the treatment of the American Indians, leading philanthropic, reform, and charity agencies engaged in repressive benevolence towards the poor of all races by defining poverty as reflecting sin and moral fault and by seeking its "solution" through moral reform efforts. At least until the late nineteenth century, charitable leaders condemned giving material aid to the poor, particularly government relief. Charity leaders, paralleling the missionaries' approach to the Indians, accented a strategy of resocializing the poor by offering them visitation and counseling, advice, friendship, and role-modeling to "proper" upper- and middle-class modes of living. The phrase made popular by the Charity Organization Societies (C.O.S) during the late nineteenth and early twentieth centuries, "Not Alms, but a Friend," represents the fervent belief of charity leaders that money, food, or fuel were *not* the answer to poverty, but only "a friend" from the upper or middle classes was. How "friendly" these counselors were will also be explored in this chapter.

It is critical to recognize that despite the complexity of American history, as a general rule the common people favored material aid, and gradually many public officials found that giving baskets of food and wood to the poor and working class, particularly in urban areas, was not only fair and just but quite beneficial to themselves politically. Over the course of the nineteenth century, large numbers of working-class people and particularly those unemployed during the century's periodic depressions came to oppose punitive treatment, and began to demand material aid as their *right*. This is not to say a majority of people (except at very exceptional moments) supported radical measures of income redistribution. But it is accurate to state that only pressure from the crowd, often composed of poor urban immigrants, and from emerging proponents of socialism, populism, and radicalism helped develop a minority viewpoint among Americans that poverty was an economic and political issue, not a moral failure. While local officials who administered almost all aid (there were no federal provisions for aid then) inherited a repressive system for dealing with poverty, gradually, due to the growth of universal white male suffrage in the nineteenth century, they had to reach certain accommodations with the voting public. As the working class and poor gained political strength, particularly through the urban machines, public officials had little choice but to expand "outdoor relief" programs. Elected and appointed officials, particularly in the developing cities of America, often resisted reformers' calls to cut off public aid because they knew firsthand the suffering of their constituents and feared the unrest that such cuts could spark. Public officials, particularly in large cities such as New York, frequently endorsed public works jobs for the unemployed as well.[5]

Within this context, the "reformers" of the middle and upper classes, charitable and voluntary agencies to "assist" the poor, and even early social workers were the most conservative groups. Perhaps surprising to modern readers who would expect these groups to be liberal, fairly consistently in American history between the 1700s and at least the early twentieth century, charity leaders argued for "indoor relief" (the poorhouse or workhouse, the orphan asylum, institutions for "fallen women," etc.) rather than "outdoor aid" (relief given without surrendering one's autonomy and living in an institution). By the post–Civil War period, when population growth made some forms of institutionalization of the poor logistically unrealistic, philanthropists urged that assistance be given only through a system of surveillance and scrutiny over the poor through visitation that would shape and mold their behavior rather than merely provide material aid.

In order to understand the perspective of religious leaders, secular charitable leaders, and early social workers, we need to review the prevailing idea held by these comfortable reformers that poverty was usually a moral flaw, not an economic one, and that the best solutions were assimilation, education, rehabilitation, and, in extreme cases, punishment. Like the Indians, the poor were seen as undisciplined children. This analogy—the poor and the savages—was frequently made, as in this popular 1854 book about poverty in New York City by the Reverend E. H. Chapin:

> No one needs to be told that there are savages in New York as well as in the islands of the sea. Savages not in gloomy forests, but under the strength of gaslight . . . with warhoops [sic] and clubs very much the same, and garments as fantastic, and souls as brutal, as any of their kindred at the antipodes, China, India, Africa, will you not find their features in some circles of the social world right around you?[6]

## THE EMERGENCE OF THE
## CHARACTER REFORM STRATEGY

Charitable institutions in America emerged from religionists who had fairly harsh views of life, and charitable ventures were led (as often they still are) by the most affluent people in American society. Colonial and early American theologians did not support modern liberal notions of equality, much less a provision of aid as an entitlement of citizenship. John Winthrop, the early Puritan leader, supported charity but did not think that God meant "the great ones" to be equal to "the poor and inferior sort of men." The poor "should never rise against their superiors," although he admitted that the "mighty" had some (unspecified) obligation to the poor. Even the most liberal of the Protestant sects, the Quakers, urged a submissive attitude on the poor and saw charity in terms of noblesse oblige. In the words of William Penn "God had not placed men on the level, but has arranged him in descending orders of subordination and dependency; due respect for these God-ordained differences required Obedience to Superiors, Love to Equals . . . Help and Countenance to Inferiors."[7]

Although most ministers and philanthropic leaders accepted the existence of a group of "deserving poor"—widows and orphans, the elderly, those ruined by flood, fire, or illness[8]—they found that for most of the poor, *immorality* and *irreligion* were the chief problems. For both theologians and affluent reformers, it was far more important that a stern morality be enforced than a poor widow or orphan be assisted. Benjamin Franklin, for example, who vehemently opposed the English Poor Laws as being too liberal and hence promoting sloth and bad morals, noted, of England "There is no country in the world in which the poor are more idle, dissolute, drunken, and insolent. The day you passed that act you took away from before their eyes the greatest of all inducements to industry . . . repeal that law and you will soon see a change in their manners. . . ."[9]

Benjamin Rush, the prominent early American physician, signer of the Declaration of Independence, and noted reformer of the late eighteenth and early nineteenth centuries, advocated that

Philadelphians not get carried away with the newly developed medical dispensary. He urged them not to exhaust benevolent funds on medical aid to the poor, but rather to promote a religious, deference-supporting education for them "since their morals are of more consequence to society than their health or lives."[10]

Poverty, unemployment, and other social concerns were seen not as issues of economics or politics but of morality. Charitable leaders (at least until the late nineteenth century) usually failed to endorse social or economic reforms. Rather, charity had several moral functions: one, to help settled citizens (particularly the affluent) meet their own Christian duties (see chapter 3); second, to shape and maintain the morals of others, particularly the poor; and third, to protect the commonwealth against the dangers of pride, rebellion, or social distance. Both church and political leaders feared the poor, particularly immigrants, as a destabilizing force. Alms, if they must be given, were only incidental to the basic charge of character reform.

Although Protestant clergy and organized congregations would always play important leadership roles in charity, the organization of philanthropy was increasingly secularized. Charitable groups were organized as fiduciary bodies as early as the late eighteenth century and resembled today's voluntary agencies in structure. They featured corporate liability from lawsuits, boards of trustees, and in some cases even hired staff. Conrad Wright points to the formation of as many as two thousand local voluntary organizations in New England between 1790 and 1830, ranging from missionary societies to Masonic lodges to orphanages. Although many groups retained obvious religious and moral connections—the names of some groups include the Boston Society for the Religious and Moral Improvement of Seamen, the Massachusetts Society for the Suppression of Intemperance, the Connecticut Society for the Promotion of Good Morals, the Society for Discountenancing and Suppressing Public Vices (Bath, Maine), and the Society for Discountenancing Vice and Immorality (Concord, N.H.)—they were not led by clergy and claimed a broader secular mission.[11]

As historian David Rothman has so well described in his classic book, *The Discovery of the Asylum*, charity also was revolutionized with the early nineteenth-century religious revival movements and the Jacksonian period. Leaving behind the somewhat static social views of the colonial period, these new reformers claimed a "utopian flavor." The new philanthropy aimed at "reform[ing] the deviant and dependent and . . . serv[ing] as a model for others." The decades of the 1820s through the 1850s, for example, featured the massive building of new institutions—almshouses and workhouses, mental hospitals, prisons and penitentiaries, orphanages— presented to the public as dramatic positive reforms. It was, as Rothman puts it, a period "at once nervous and enthusiastic, distressed and optimistic."[12] The idealistic fervor of America impressed the world, including the famous French visitor Alexis de Tocqueville, but American utopianism also developed a kind of intrusiveness which reflected a moralistic version of social control, much of which we would now look upon as punitive, undemocratic, and repressive. Today it is quite hard to believe that our ancestors saw the poorhouse and the mental asylum, the orphanage, and the prison as the solution to most social problems, including simply having a low income.

Fear of the mob no doubt also combined with the utopian moral aims of this period. Voluntary organizations in the nineteenth century unabashedly explained their missions in terms linking immorality with the "dangerous classes." Lyman Beecher, the prominent minister from Connecticut who established the Society for the Suppression of Vice and Promotion of Good Morals in the early nineteenth century, expressed alarm at "the moral trends" in society including "public inebriation, profanity, [and] Sabbath desecration." Without vigorous countermeasures, he warned, the hordes of urban poor would soon "swarm in your streets, and prowl about your dwellings." Reacting to the recent introduction of universal male suffrage which was then challenging elite power, Beecher insisted that new institutions were necessary to control the mob:

> Local voluntary associations of the wise and the good must step in to exert a moral force distinct from that of government, independent of popular suffrage, superior in potency to individual efforts, and competent to enlist and preserve public opinion. Such associations—a sort of

disciplined moral militia—would discountenance individual vice and bring collective pressure to bear against evil.[13]

Ironically, although many social scientists praise voluntary organizations as the epitome of "civil society," Beecher and many of his nineteenth-century colleagues developed them as vehicles to bypass public government and the suffrage of the "mob."

Historian Paul Boyer has traced the story of moral movements in the nineteenth and early twentieth centuries and suggests that most voluntary organizations founded by middle- and upper-class Protestants were a response to the perceived threat posed by immoral, lower-class immigrants. The founding of the Young Men's Christian Association in the mid-1850s was directly linked to such class fears. The Reverend George W. Bethune addressed the New York YMCA and compared the "social threat of the city's 'lowest order' to that of an armed uprising" and cast the young men of the YMCA in the role of defending soldiers, "calm, resolute, armed, drilled, and prepared for the fight, taking their positions as guardians of the city."[14] After the draft riots of the Civil War and the mass strikes of the 1870s, such fears of mob agitation became even more intense. In founding the first Charity Organization Society in 1877 (the forerunner of today's United Ways), minister S. Humphreys Gurteen recalled in horror the image of the New York draft riots in 1863:

> Five thousand men, women, and children sweeping down the leading avenue of the city in the darkness of night, the lurid flames of a hundred torches disclosing a scene of wild license scarcely surpassed by any single incident of the French Revolution: women, and mothers at that, with their bare breasts exposed to the winds of heaven, brandishing deadly weapons and uttering foul and loathsome language . . . while the very air as they passed was polluted by their drunken breath. . . . we shall have only ourselves to blame if the poor, craving for human sympathy, yet feeling their moral deformity, should some fine day wreak their vengeance upon society at large.[15]

In an editorial after the Paris Commune of 1871, the *New York Times* noted with trepidation that "Every great city has within it the communistic elements of a revolution." However, the *Times* felt that revolution was unlikely in the United States, since "the industrial school and the children's charities are transforming the youthful Communists into industrious, law-abiding, property-earning citizens."[16]

While this moral view of poverty and fear of the dangerous mob meshed well with dominant class interests throughout American history, it is not necessary to see American philanthropic character reform *only* as a form of social class repression over the lower classes by the upper classes. Ideas and beliefs have autonomy, and shape attitudes toward life that are not necessarily consistent with self-interest. Clearly, at many points in American history, the moral mission of charity has been widely supported among all social classes. Through a variety of mechanisms — church sermons and Bible tracts, temperance plays, early school texts like the McGuffey's Reader, pledges demanded by fraternal organizations — proper-thinking respectable citizens developed a view of correct behavior which placed the poor, particularly immigrants and people of color, women without husbands, and men without visible means, into the categories of deviant, dangerous, or immoral. These beliefs take hold even (and sometimes most intensely) among those just above the lowliest status, or those who themselves have had firsthand experience with poverty.

The characterological view of poverty both reassures and challenges. The reassurance comes from the idea that no matter how much the "respectable" citizen has to struggle in life, he or she is always above the most degraded. As Reverend Samuel Prime put it in his 1847 book about the notorious Five Points slum area of New York, "Wherever sin is, there is misery. One fact . . . is a consolation to a man who tries to do the right things. It is, that the willful vices of the inhabitants of these refuges of the poor have reduced them to this condition."[17] But an active Christian could not accept this situation with equanimity. Rather, such conditions did not mitigate the duty to help change these victims of character flaws. As put by Charles Loring Brace in his famous book *The Dangerous Classes of New York* (1872):

> Those who have much to do with alms-giving and plans for human improvement soon see how superficial and comparatively useless all assis-

tance or organization is, which does not touch habits of life and the inner forces which form character. The poor helped each year become poorer in force and independence. . . . *Christianity is the highest education of character. Give the poor that, and only seldom will either alms or punishment be necessary.*[18] (My emphasis)

American character reform was both stern and repressive as well as idealistic and optimistic. Its dramatic difference from a theoretical laissez-faire ideology was in its active involvement and care about those in poverty as well as a host of other issues (alcohol, prostitution, child welfare). Yet, as with the Indian experience, such active intervention may have done more harm than "good."

## CHARITIES AGAINST THE POOR I: ENDING "WELFARE" AS THEY KNEW IT

The repressive benevolence of the charity leaders was apparent throughout the nineteenth century in their constant war against "outdoor relief," the only form of material aid available from public sources at a time long before Social Security or unemployment insurance. These campaigns are too numerous to review here, but peaked in two time periods: the Jacksonian period, when efforts to eliminate outdoor relief succeeded in New York, Massachusetts, Pennsylvania, and as far west as Illinois,[19] and in the last three decades of the nineteenth century, when ten major cities including New York, Brooklyn, Philadelphia, Baltimore, Washington, St. Louis, and San Francisco cut off outdoor aid.[20]

The three parties to the battle included the poor and working class on the one hand, the affluent charitable reformers on the other, and on the third side, local officials, who found themselves in the middle. Three instances of conflict in New York City perhaps best illustrate the nineteenth-century battles over welfare. As a key center of developing industry and immigration, it is not surprising that New York would figure prominently in class battles throughout the century.

In the 1850s the combination of the incipient organization of Irish laborers along with periodic depressions (1854–55, 1857) led to both organized pressure for assistance and bread riots. In response, New York's leaders, notably Mayor Fernando Wood, responded by initiating reforms which included not only increased alms but public works jobs to help the unemployed. The largest charitable group in New York at the time, the Association for Improving the Condition of the Poor (AICP), attacked Wood's "welfare schemes" and suggested that such "indiscriminate giveaways" cultivated in workers and the poor the idea that relief was a "right." They counterposed their method of visiting the poor (see below) as "scientific charity" which would "stimulate incentives for saving and industry" rather than engage in "demagogy" and "indiscriminate philanthropy."[21]

Although charity leaders failed to end outdoor relief (and, paradoxically, many volunteers of the AICP came to support at least some social reforms by the 1860s), in the 1870s a virulent new campaign against outdoor aid began again. The relief rolls had swollen with the depression of 1873 and with the pressure of workingmen's demonstrations and riots. As Michael Katz has well documented, in the battle over relief in Brooklyn (then a separate city) reformers and charity leaders saw the city as a "pauper's paradise." Citing not only the high cost but municipal corruption,[22] reformers found a champion in Mayor Seth Low. Katz comments, "There is no mistaking the class character of the campaign (against outdoor relief), with its wealthy patrician leadership on one side and its political machines with their working-class constituencies on the other." To Low as well as the affluent reformers, including the AICP, public relief was "superfluous, wasteful, and corrupting." Public officials, deprived of authority by 1876 to offer anything but coal, found themselves surrounded by poor people that winter. As their offices were attacked by the poor, officials released food from storage. And yet by 1878, the "reformers" had won again, and outdoor relief was abolished in Brooklyn (and later New York City as well).[23]

Perhaps most astounding from a modern point of view was the opposition in the late 1890s in New York by a host of reformers, including the leaders of the Charity Organization Society and its famous social workers such as Josephine Shaw Lowell, Edward

Devine, and Fredric Almy, to the mothers' pension (the forerunner to Aid to Families with Dependent Children, or AFDC). At that time, single or separated poor women (mostly widows) who could not pay their bills routinely had to surrender their children to a poorhouse or orphanage in return for aid. Following the depression of 1893 and the beginnings of what would become the Progressive movement, a variety of thinkers and reformers observed that the huge cost of housing children in orphanages could be saved if poor mothers were given minimal financial support. The idea of retaining family unity also came into social and cultural prominence for the first time in this period, with removal of children from their parents for no cause but poverty becoming a subject of public debate.

Yet in New York, charities vehemently opposed mothers' pensions. Influenced in no small part, according to historians David Schneider and Albert Deutsch, by the huge amount of public funds they received from the city for maintaining orphanages, juvenile homes, and other institutions, the charities waged a major campaign against the measure. Some referred to the bill derisively as "the shiftless fathers' bill," claiming it "would encourage irresponsible fathers to desert their wives, since public support would be given to their offspring." Charity leaders won the battle and kept the provision in the New York City charter that banned outdoor relief, at least technically (it was violated in practice), until the Great Depression. Years later, New York and some other cities and states did provide mothers' pensions. In New York City they were able to do so only by contracting the provision of aid out to charities, leaving them to police mothers' morality and habits.[24]

Although the above examples reflect only one city and set of leaders, it is indicative of charity's role in nineteenth-century American history as an opponent of government entitlement programs. Campaigns against welfare hardly began with the likes of Newt Gingrich. Rather, calls to end "welfare" and instead place people in institutions and orphanages was a view shared by many upper- and middle-class people in the nineteenth century as well as today.

## CHARITIES AGAINST THE POOR II:
## "FRIENDLY" VISITING

If political change, economic or social justice, even public works jobs or alms could not relieve poverty, then what was the solution? For much of the nineteenth century charity leaders stressed the poorhouse as the answer to poverty. But population growth and the limits of popular tolerance for removing the poor from their own homes by force made such a strategy unrealistic. Rather, reformers began to rely on visiting the poor in their homes, assessing their moral characteristics, and offering advice. Such strategies are as old as church missions to the poor. In part they derive from European experiments in dividing up cities and towns into districts, where church and later public officials could distinguish between applicants for aid as "deserving" and "non-deserving."[25] But American charitable leaders developed and tested this strategy far beyond the European example, helping to move it from its obvious religious heritage to a more secularized and (eventually) professionalized form.

Visiting the poor at their homes to judge their character had goals similar to the poorhouse: in both cases the aim was not to bring assistance of a material nature but to affect character change or rehabilitation which would come from modeling of proper work habits, temperance, and propriety. But "friendly visiting," as it came to be known by the late nineteenth century, had several advantages over institutionalization. It provoked less hostility from the poor and allowed for more long-term follow-up over time of those families being "helped." Vicious paupers or immoral women could simply leave the poorhouse unredeemed and resume their deviant ways, but (assuming the person remained in the same neighborhood) community visitation would enable the upright citizens to gauge the change, if any, in the habits of the poor.

Two early experiments combining relief with moral uplift were run by and aimed at women. In the late eighteenth century, the Ladies Society for the Relief of Poor Widows with Small Children began in New York City, and investigated "the means, character, and circumstances of each applicant . . . with minute care. . . .

Help was denied to widowed mothers who failed to meet the strict moral standards set in the Society's by-laws."[26] At the same time, Quaker women in Philadelphia through the Female Association of Philadelphia practiced a similar version of moral uplift: "[they] visited the home of each applicant to examine particularly into her moral character, her situation, her habits and mode of life, her wants, and the best means of affording relief, so that assistance may not be extended to the vicious, and idle, when it is due only to the honest and industrious suffering under sickness and misfortune."[27]

Although a number of experiments in the first half of the nineteenth century centered on visiting and attempts at character reform, it was the great philanthropic movements of the late nineteenth century—the charity organization societies and the settlement house movement—that serve as a key bridge between the older charities and today's social service agencies. Most important, what the theorists of C.O.S. and the settlements hoped for was not only that charity could be detached entirely from *giving alms*, substituting advice and consolement for the need for money, food, or housing, but moreover that visitation or social settlements would allow the different classes (ideally the affluent volunteer and the poor) to meet in a *relationship*, not in the conflictual harshness of one taking another to the poorhouse. The notion of the unimportance of alms when compared to relationship therapy was stressed by Gurteen, a major theorist of C.O.S.:

> The chief need of the poor to-day [is] not alms-giving, but the *moral support of true friendship* [original emphasis]—the possession of a real friend, whose education, experience, and influence, whose general knowledge of life, or special knowledge of domestic economy are placed at the service of those who have neither the intelligence, the tact nor the opportunity to extract the maximum of good from their slender resources.[28]

The famous Charity Organization Society motto "Not Alms, but a Friend" contained the very contemporary idea embraced by a wide variety of professions, political, religious, and civic groups that advice, counseling, education in skills, and character change benefit the poor most, not money or employment. Even the social settlement movement, often contrasted with the C.O.S.'s stinginess, primarily differed from C.O.S. in its acceptance early on in its history that some alms or certain social reform measures were not inimical to relationship therapy. Their chief aim was still, as Mina Carson's insightful history notes, to give "not money, but themselves." She quotes settlement pioneer Samuel Barnett as saying "money would never be enough. The rich owed the poor their *real* [original emphasis] 'wealth': the knowledge, the character, the happiness which are the gift of God to this age."[29]

Both the C.O.S. and the settlement movement agreed that the wealthy were the best role models for the charitable relationship. Gurteen insisted that "the personal intercourse of the wealthier citizens with the poor at their homes" would bring together "the extremes of society in a spirit of honest friendship." The point of the friendly visit was to "impart to the cheerless tenement or the wretched hovel, [a] little of their own happiness."[30] Octavia Hill, the British settlement leader, assumed the more affluent would be able to ". . . enter into their lives, their thoughts; to let them enter into some of your brightness; to make their lives a little fuller, a little gladder. You who know so much more than they, might help them so much at important crises of their lives . . . you might teach and refine and make them cleaner by merely going among them."[31]

As critical thinkers could predict, however, the "friendly visitors" never overcame the condescension and paternalism of their origins—not to mention the hostility they evoked among socialists, unionists, and others who believed that social justice, not visitation, was needed. Even though it was not so much wealthy as middle-class women who entered the slums, and even though charities (over protest) came to be forced into giving some alms, the ideas of character reform and control of subordinate classes would always undergird their actions. French writer Jacques Donzelot argues that in the early twentieth century, some degree of aid to the working classes came to be accepted throughout Western society only in exchange for what he calls "mandatory tutelage," in which "submission to instruction and surveillance by social personnel" is required, and "thus the denial of the prerogative to freely choose habits, associates, and pleasures."[32] As we shall see below with the visitors' actions, the bestowal of some private charity in exchange for meekness and deference was not so terribly different from how the missionaries were willing to "teach" the Indians and even supply them with clothes and food in exchange for them giving up their own culture.

Case records of friendly visitors during the first three decades of the twentieth century suggest that Donzelot's characterization is not merely hyperbole. While poor people who meekly complied with visitors' requests and dictates were sometimes "rewarded" with aid, a complex of moral, sexual, and vocational standards had to be adhered to as well as a stance of deference to those of higher breeding. In the absence of these conditions, not *only* could relief be denied but children could be taken away from the family, uncooperative adults placed in the workhouse, recalcitrant children placed in juvenile homes, and access to employment or other services blocked by harsh reports made about a family.

Beverly Stadum's review of the case of a "Mrs. Pernet," who sought aid from Minneapolis Associated Charities from 1910 to 1922,[33] reveals a number of the problems with the "friendly" visitors. Actually, Pernet never asked the agency for help but circulated a letter to her neighbors because her husband lay dying with heart disease, and she was destitute with her three children. Rather than praising such self-help, when the Minneapolis charity heard of it they went to her home and confronted her. They informed her that such letters were not proper and not to be repeated. After a relationship of sorts was formed with the agency, the visitor made clear that they disapproved of her plans to rent to a male boarder after her husband had died (a frequent practice at the time). Visitors argued throughout the summer with Mrs. Pernet about the impropriety of male boarders, although taking in a boarder would add fifteen dollars a month to her income. Mrs. Pernet also ran afoul of the visitors—now officially social workers—when her work record as a domestic did not come up to snuff:

> In one home where she did day work, the lady discovered doilies missing, accused her of theft, and called [the charity agency]. Another employer found her bringing her own belongings to wash along with the

assigned laundry. The social worker announced that with the reputation
she was building, no more referrals for employment would be given her.

Already viewed as uncooperative, and possibly barred from certain
areas of work by agency reports about her, she also ran afoul of the
agency for possible alcohol abuse:

> In the summer of 1915 a caseworker stopped by unannounced to witness
> one of the sons carrying in a pail of what looked like beer. Mrs. Pernet
> claimed it was milk; the agent was skeptical as milk already was sitting
> on the counter and no creamery operated nearby. The worker called
> again in the evening and found Mrs. Pernet 'neatly dressed in light col-
> [ored] cotton dress, beads, and several articles of adornment. Her
> breath was strong with liquor.'

Whatever Mrs. Pernet's faults or the idiosyncrasies of the Minneapolis agency, other records confirm the visitors' intrusiveness, acceptance of anecdotal evidence they then used against
poor families, and their tendency to mete out punishment to those
who violated middle-class standards of dignity, work conduct, and
morals.

Fragments of case records from Connecticut's friendly visitors[34] confirm how powerful the influence and judgments of charity workers were over the poor and how moralistic the visitors
were. Strong conservative norms about women's behavior colored
almost all "aid." For example, in one case, the charitable association declared, "Woman voted unworthy of help as she is too flash-
ily dressed." In another, with surprising candor the records
indicate that the "Treatment plan [was to] get Mrs. C to be more
moral." Visitors assumed the right to police sexual relations and
even the propriety of marriage as the following entries indicate:

> Visitor called on girl at the restaurant where she was working but she
> was rude and refused to discuss her illegitimate baby.

> Discovered woman's plan to marry. She begged worker to make no in-
> quiries about man, as former matrimonial venture nipped in bud by
> worker's predecessor. Worker wangled man's address, talked to his
> landlady, [and] instructed Mrs. T not to marry him.

Some of the case notes would be amusing for their naked intrusiveness and attempts to run others' lives if their negative outcomes for

poor women were not so poignant. For example, "Dr. reported woman very ill with TB and [she] should be placed in a sanitorium. Worker explained that [the] woman had run gamut of misconduct and if cured would surely return to an immoral life. Conference had voted, in view of the record, not to recommend treatment."

For poor men and women, a rigid work ethic not only focused the advice given ("Suggested that Mrs. P. make it so uncomfortable for Mr. P. at home that he would have to go to work.") but was used to assess intelligence ("Woman may have mental defect. For example, she cannot line a coat."). Moreover, the price for being out of work was high; as is still often the case in contacts between the unemployed and their service workers, an early-twentieth-century unemployed worker could not understand why he had to surrender so much information and pride to get relief: "He was loath to give names of all his relatives and became extremely upset when worker insisted. [He] Asked why they all had to be visited just because he wanted to work."

But what appears as most striking in the records—beyond the well-known enforcement of middle-class morality on poor families—was the visitors' insistence on poor people's deference and submission. In the following case records, threats and intimidation are used against the noncompliant:

> Threatened Mrs. G. that relief would be discontinued if she does not do exactly as she was told. [Visitor] Explained that when she accepted charity, she gave up right to make any decisions.

> Woman was entirely without fuel but refused to give information about her relatives. Worker told her that if she got cold enough, she'd do as she was asked and give early history.

> Conference voted [the] family be threatened with having their children removed—then following up with friendly visit.

When visitors were called into situations in which they *did not* have such power, they complained, "They [family] are a difficult problem because entirely self-supporting and therefore cannot be forced to follow suggestions made for their own good." Finally, those families who were compliant got descriptions such as "a fine, meek family," or family members were judged separately as to their compliance: "Mrs. G. is always appreciative of the things that are given her but the children would like to be dressed like other children and their attitude is not admirable."

I have gone into some detail over these records not because every friendly visitor or early social worker practiced their benevolence as harshly as in the examples above. Some in fact resisted agency dictates and took money out of their own pockets to aid the poor. Nor do I mean to suggest that families and individuals were not helped by many visitors. As Linda Gordon and others have pointed out, women and children sometimes gained protection from the visitors and charitable agencies against abusive husbands and boyfriends.[35] And for men as well as women, the simple need for some charity at a time when there were no Social Security pensions, unemployment insurance, or Medicare and Medicaid was too overwhelming to not accept the loss of pride and privacy that went along with a "visit." However, to acknowledge these facts only serves to buttress the argument that charity seems of value only in the absence of any publicly provided social aid. Beverly Stadum's history of the Minneapolis charities points out the aid some women secured by contacting outsiders to intervene in their families. Yet she also concludes that "client resistance and antagonism towards workers were more apparent than any substantive improvement in family life arising from agency intervention."[36]

"Friendly visiting" and the charity workers of the period were not seen as altruistic by radicals, socialists, trade unionists, and immigrant organizations. Rather, some recent revisionist histories can only praise these philanthropists by ignoring the political spectrum of the time—as if the proponents of charity and even more conservative forces represented the only choices. Melvyn Dubofsky's history of labor at the time quotes workers who noted that "social workers [were] people peeking through your window, seeing how you live and what you are."[37] Sam Gompers, head of the American Federation of Labor, warned, "Let social busybodies and 'professional morals experts' reflect upon the perils they rashly invite under the pretense of social welfare."[38] The radical John Reed in his introduction to the 1917 book *The Crimes of Charity* captures some of the contemporary extreme distaste towards "charity":

Every person of intelligence and humanity who has seen the workings of
Organised Charity, knows what a deadening and life-sapping thing it is,
how unnecessarily cruel, how uncomprehending. Yet it must not be
criticised, investigated or attacked. Like patriotism, charity is respectable, an institution of the rich and great—like the high tariff, the open
shop, Wall Street, and Trinity Church . . . industry grows bloated
with it, landlords live off it; and it supports an army of officers, investi-
gators, clerks and collectors, whom it systematically debauches. Its giving is made the excuse for lowering the recipients' standard of living, of
depriving them of privacy and independence, or subjecting them to the
cruelest mental and physical torture, of making them liars, cringers,
thieves. The law, the police, the church are the accomplices of charity.
And how could it be otherwise, considering those who give, how they
give, and the terrible doctrine of the 'deserving poor'?[39]

## CHANGE AND CONTINUITY

This chapter has suggested that, like the action of the church
missionaries and "Friends of the Indians," the development of
charitable institutions to assist the poor in America combined benevolence with repression. Charity's focus was hardly on social,
economic, or political change but on character reform. Its key
achievements were the elimination in many cities of the small
amount of local funds that went for public "outdoor relief," and
the development of an intrusive and sometimes punitive system of
friendly visiting. As friendly visiting eventually developed into
modern counseling and social work, it has obviously undergone
important changes. Professionalization has changed the moralistic
vocabulary and many of the more quasi-religious aims of the visitors. In part, there has been genuine change for the better; certainly
a combination of civil rights and civil liberties laws now protect clients from the worst forms of maltreatment. Perhaps even more important, many clients of social service agencies from mental health
centers to family agencies today are truly voluntary, and, in fact, as
we shall discuss in chapter 5, are more often middle-class than
poor.

Many social welfare experts and historians emphasize the positive, consistent with their progressive, teleological view of history.
It is true that historically the visitors who went out to reform the

poor's character did sometimes come to support reforming the system; this was true of the AICP to some extent, the C.O.S. to some degree, and, of course, the settlement house activists to the greatest degree. Hence, read backwards, the Braces, Gurteens, Hills, Lowells, Richmonds, and so on are a kind of bridge to an eventual better way. Of course, it is not an irrelevant fact that people and institutions change for the better. But the point is that benevolent middle-class charity leaders, like Lowell (as in her quote at the chapter's heading), could come to this point *only* by criticizing and repudiating their past and changing their view toward public social welfare reform. In moving away from the charitable paradigm, the more praiseworthy historical figures end up endorsing a view that's opposite from where they started: supporting social movements to improve conditions for the disadvantaged (not charity!).

The most salient fact is not that a number of middle-class philanthropists changed their position, but that social movements and political pressure from the 1890s on changed the environment in which charity operated. Populism, militant trade unionism, socialism, syndicalism, and other movements between 1890 and World War I forced middle-class and upper-class leaders to accommodate social reform as a compromise with more radical possibilities. And, of course, in the depths of the Great Depression, with a quarter of Americans out of work, the old conventional wisdom about the character of the poor being at fault briefly collapsed. The Depression, combined with widespread unrest, led to an opening for America's mini-version of the welfare state with the passage of the Social Security Act in 1935.

However, historians and other observers tend to overestimate the changes brought by the 1930s and subsequent legislation that did provide critical aid to groups of people who needed it. History is contradictory, not simply forward-moving. While some forces in American society—the labor movement particularly in the 1930s and 1940s, and the civil rights and other social movements of the 1960s—came to embrace redistributive policies, they were arguably always in a minority. Perhaps only in the case of the elderly can we see a long-term secular trend towards a cultural norm that material aid is acceptable. Yet, as I write, even this is debatable, as benefits are being challenged.

Moreover, reforms in aid for some of the poor (such as the passage of AFDC as part of Social Security in 1935) did not change the character reform components of "welfare" and its disapproval of unwed mothers or its discrimination against racial minorities.[40] It is not only that the "undeserving poor" have always been treated harshly, but that repression and character reform have remained at the fore of the business of human service work throughout the twentieth century. Hence, when the forces that favored the welfare state weakened, it was not such a dramatic change to see the correctional and therapeutic stance of services once again come to be the dominant motif.

For most of the twentieth century, liberal-minded observers have seen the work of reform as merely left to be done; the next bill or act would help those left out. But the fate of the "welfare state" in the last two decades suggests another possibility. Rather, specific legislation aside, American social policy remains strongly grounded in the Anglo settler mentality and has remained committed to repression, while giving some aid. The balance between repression (private and public) and popular movements for public benefits, of course, constantly changes with social and political events, but it is not so clear that the underlying nature of repressive benevolence has changed that much.

Have things changed totally? Students who read the old Connecticut case records often tell me that these accounts are not *all that* different from what they are asked to do in their social work field placements. Today, seminars on "resistant" clients analyze as "borderline personalities" those who refuse to be meek with their human-service professionals; workers police alcohol and drug use, sexual activity, and household management, and can take children away from families who engage in misbehavior, although extensive due process rights have been added. Usually, of course, workers don't refer to "immorality" but to "addictions," or to "immature" or "antisocial" personalities, or simply to the catchall word "dysfunction." Interestingly, students' *primary* response to the Connecticut records is that, of course, the same feelings and actions exist today among service workers but are revealed only in the back rooms of agencies, mental health clinics, and welfare offices. Students express surprise mostly that visitors and charity officials actually *wrote down* these comments. Today, with more open client access to records, charges of immorality or subjective reports about poor families are possible subjects of a lawsuit, and hence comments are made discreetly.

In sum, while there have been some major improvements since the days of the friendly visitors, the glorification of "charity" allows for a lack of clear accounting of how different today's social workers, student volunteers, community police officers, big brothers and sisters, and religious missions *really* are. The agencies of the nineteenth century are still with us: the YMCA and YWCA, the Salvation Army, the Boy Scouts, the United Ways (heirs to the Charity Organization Societies), Catholic Charities, and family service agencies (descendants of agencies like the Associated Charities of Minneapolis). To discuss their histories may lead to uncomfortable questions about the present and what the project of charity is all about. Many groups, such as church officials, heads of middle-class professional and civic organizations, political leaders, and even some liberal historians, wish to gloss over these events or present them in a more positive light. In contrast to the lack of any defense for past actions taken against the Indians, some conservatives have actually supported returning to the nineteenth-century model of charity, while some liberals have also sought to minimize charity's negative features.[41] How charity has kept its sentimental halo and noble reputation intact despite its history will be our next subject.

# THE SURPRISING

# SUCCESS OF CHARITY

# AS SYMBOLISM

*The time is not far off, apparently, when private charity . . . will be al-most obsolete. . . . Surely that is natural and normal in a nation dedi-cated, as a nation, to the life, liberty, and happiness for all its people.*

Gifford Pinchot, New Deal reformer[1]

# The Surprising Success
# of Charity as Symbolism

As I write, charity once again is taken for granted as central to our national values and character. Obviously, if charity is meant only as neighborly "goodwill" in which each of us helps the other through a personal crisis or sickness, there can be little question that we will always need charity. However, I use the word "charity" as it came to be defined in Western theology, and later by government and formal nonprofit enterprises, to refer to a set of institutions and a specific form of social action. Yet not only did organized charity arouse considerable antagonism among the poor and some social critics until recently, the growth of public sector entitlement programs in the United States during the 1930s led some observers like New Deal reformer Pinchot to predict the eventual demise of charity altogether. Pinchot's prediction, interestingly, proved to be correct in describing the future of many European societies; while some charities, particularly religious ones, continue to exist, the "social security" of citizens as understood in a broader sense in Europe flows from government programs. The demise of charity has not only not occurred in America; if anything, support for *private* social welfare is now broader than ever and enshrined in social policy. In order to analyze the resilience of charity in a meaningful way, we need to briefly address what alternatives to private aid exist and why they have failed to gain much ground.

The reliance on large-scale charitable enterprises to attempt to ameliorate social problems assumes a form of social organization in which sharp economic inequality exists and, with it, accepts (sometimes even glorifying) the fact that there will be those who are impoverished and needy. Only two major alternatives to the charitable project exist. One is to completely transform our social organization into a more egalitarian society in which poverty does not characterize large parts of the population. Such alternatives have, of course, been proposed by socialists, communists, anarchists, some feminists, and ecological activists, and indeed practiced by many indigenous peoples throughout the world.

These alternative discourses have almost always existed in America, although they sometimes remain hidden. Howard Zinn's *A People's History of the United States* offers a few examples of this hidden discourse, which existed even in the absence of words like "socialism" or "anarchism." For example, Zinn quotes a "Privates Committee" of American militiamen at the beginning of the American Revolution who opposed the "great and overgrown rich men" and drew up a bill of rights that included a call for a redistribution of property.[2] A century later at mass meetings in New York, workers passed resolutions that supported limiting the total ownership that any individual would be allowed.[3] While such discourses about altering the system of ownership and wealth have a long history in America, they have been repressed in historical memory and/or associated with dangerous "isms" that Americans understand as "foreign" and "bad," often without being able to even elucidate what is "foreign" and "bad" about them.

A second discourse, usually framed as the dominant alternative leading to an improved society, is a reform approach that accepts the outlines of a capitalist system but seeks to limit the excesses of a free market by providing a welfare state. Many social movements have come to understand government welfare programs as well as limitations on private power (minimum wage laws and other labor legislation, civil rights, environmental, and other regulatory laws) as representing the alternative to untrammeled free market capitalism. To the extent viable models are available, Sweden, Holland, and other welfare states have sometimes been held up as alternatives. While American society has been altered in the twentieth century by reforms resulting from social movements in the '30s, '60s, and '70s (Social Security, labor legislation, civil rights measures), the weakness of genuine reform efforts in America is striking. Not only is it true that a totally egalitarian program has rarely captured mass support in America, it is also arguable that the reform alternative that relies on state power as advocated by liberals has also failed to become very popular. This is not only the case in the last two decades. Even during the periods of liberalism's greatest success (the New Deal, for example), Americans accepted state-sponsored reform grudgingly and only when justified as temporary and emergency measures. In the 1960s, reform succeeded only with the assurance that the costs would be kept low and that emphasis would be placed on work and character-building rather than on wealth redistribution.[4]

In Part 2 of this book I will try to tackle the question of how and why charity has retained its dominant position both in the American pantheon generally and in the practice of social welfare. I will suggest that charity's success is not based on any empirical evidence of real effectiveness, but on its symbolic importance. Charity is a *moral enterprise* with a clear social script. It produces heroes and model citizens who give, and deferential and meek citizens who accept. It delineates society with a clear boundary between moral and immoral. Such a script makes more sense to most Americans than the other two alternatives. Secondly, the provision of aid as a *right*, through government programs or other less "personal" and visible methods, conjures up the idea that areas of private giving may be foreclosed. That is, if aid to the elderly, the poor, and people with AIDS is taken care of more fully by government, where would the Christian (and the philanthropist and the professional) practice generosity? On whom would Christian sympathy fall? Liberals or other supporters of social welfare often dismiss such concerns, stating there is plenty for the charitable-minded to do. But this begs the question; if a more egalitarian society emerged, it *might* leave less room for individual moral heroics because need would be fulfilled more routinely and automatically. Charity has tremendous symbolic appeal as an enterprise, based on deference on the one side and heroics on the other; it is probably true that a check in the mail from the government cannot touch this type of symbolism.

In the following chapters I will trace the historic success of charity both as an American ideology and a set of institutional arrangements. Beginning with its religious roots in Christianity, philanthropy in America came to be a province of the rich and powerful. In the twentieth century—particularly in its last half—a huge apparatus of ostensibly caregiving institutions and organizations has arisen and been glorified as "nonprofit." Though founded by wealthy sponsors, nonprofit organizations have been severed from these origins in the public mind. And despite the religious origin of charity and nonprofit organizations, the ideology of voluntarism and personal service has also been secularized and separated from its historic roots.

# 3—The Symbolic Appeal of Christian Charity

*I felt that charity was a word to choke over. Who wanted charity? And it was not just human pride but a strong sense of man's dignity and worth, and what was due to him in justice that made me resent, rather than feel proud of so mighty a sum of Catholic institutions.*

Dorothy Day, Catholic worker[1]

*The clergy should discontinue occasional and paternalistic charity as a habitual form of action; the members of the clergy should concentrate their efforts on preparing members of the laity to transform the temporal structures from the ground up and thus attack the origin of social problems.*

Camilio Torres, radical Colombian priest[2]

Knowing about the Christian tradition of charity is clearly central to understanding how most Americans think about issues of altruism and social welfare and how American institutional culture has incorporated charitable principles in secular forms of philanthropy and social service. Not only do most Americans claim to be practicing Christians, churches still receive two-thirds of all private donations. Moreover, any examination of charity must note its religious connections: the cross in the Red Cross, the "C" in the YMCA and YWCA, the fact that Catholic Charities is the largest social service provider in the US (outside of government), that Thanksgiving attracts the most volunteers of any one day of the year, and that the Christmas season accounts for the most private donations. Secular fundraising often strongly evokes (consciously or unconsciously) religious symbols and sacred imagery. Whether it is a United Way poster displaying a poor mother and child, harking back to Madonna and child, or a call for a noble "crusade" against hunger or disease, deeply evocative symbolism going back to religious zeal is an integral part of today's nonprofit world.

Interpretation of scripture is a subject of historical and continued dispute. Summarizing the vast differences in religious practice in Christianity is equally as complex. Some religious radicals lay claim to Christ as a revolutionary while, as we have seen, the dominant Protestant beliefs in the first centuries of America were often harsh and illiberal. I will argue that on the whole the biblical heritage (as historically interpreted by Western churches and parishioners; we can't know exactly what authors of either the Old or New Testaments had in mind) is neither conservative nor radical, but symbolic. While some biblical quotations—"the meek shall inherit the earth," "it is harder for the rich man to enter heaven than for a camel to fit through the eye of a needle"—have been widely used by radical movements of the poor around the world, it is generally the case that the normative Christian tradition mandates a *sympathetic* attitude and practice towards the poor, disadvantaged, or diseased. There is nothing in the Bible resembling advocacy of material redistribution of resources, much less social or political revolution. The poor, the ill, the imprisoned, and the weak are to be treated with kindness and love, but the Bible deals with this as a matter of personal sentiment and moral obligation. The Bible *never* addresses problems such as lack of money, employment, housing, and political power—unless one is to infer from the many verses of the Bible which support submission to authority and secular power that the status quo should be supported. When any political position can be gleaned from church history (as opposed to scripture), it has most often been the acceptance of such status quo, whether those arrangements were the slave societies of Rome, the feudalism of Medieval times, or the capitalism of modern times.[3]

This chapter will suggest how the symbolism of Christian charity has shaped the Western approach to altruism, as developed further in the succeeding chapters. I will note how three strands of Christian thought helped structure the nonprofit world: the primacy of sentiment and sentimental attachment, the emphasis on donorship, and the creation of a sacred sphere conceptualized as separate from the market and politics. As Christianity became an institution in Europe it spoke for a mass of faceless poor and disadvantaged, but it also singled out the donors—individual lords, landowners, and later merchants and the rich generally—for special recognition; and while it created a sacred sphere for charity, early Christianity left a considerable realm "rendered unto Caesar," and eventually much of the non-spiritual realm was completely left to the economic and social forces of the marketplace.

## THE PRIMACY OF SENTIMENT

Perhaps no figure represents the cultural infatuation with religious sentiment more than the world-renowned late Mother Teresa. It is not clear whether a majority of people selected randomly on a street corner could actually tell you much about Mother Teresa's concrete accomplishments, much less her political or social views. Yet she is a morally cherished figure for having journeyed to the far-off slums of the world, where she lived humbly and ministered to the sick and suffering, the poor and the disadvantaged. But what social advice or political views did Mother Teresa impart? In a 1981 visit to Washington, D.C., Mother Teresa was confronted by African-American activists about the need for jobs and housing in their community rather than charity. She responded with a vague answer: "First we must learn to love one another." Upon further questioning about her mission, she promised only to bring "the joy of loving and being loved." At a press conference she noted that, "I think it is very beautiful for the poor to accept their lot, to share it with the passion of Christ. I think the world is being much helped by the suffering of poor people." In 1995 the elderly nun was quoted as saying that people without money or power could make the world "a better place" by smiling more.[4]

Mother Teresa's platitudinous answers and complete lack of interest in changing the status quo of the poor cannot be dismissed as idiosyncratic, since to a large extent they do seem to represent the position of Christ, Paul and the other apostles, and the Christian saints. As summarized by the well-known sociologist of religion Ernest Troeltsch: "The aim of charity was not the healing of social wrongs, nor the endeavor to remove poverty, but the revelation and the awakening of the spirit of love, of that love, which Christ imparts and in which He makes known to us the attitude of God Himself. Above all else, the Church desires to show love and to awaken the response of love. The relief of distress which she actually achieves is the result of this spirit, not her first intention. . . ."[5]

Indifference to conditions of inequality in the actual world—as compared to the Kingdom of God—allowed a variety of injunctions to come from the apostles that strongly support inequality and oppose rebellion. The famous "rendering unto Caesar" has always had the direct effect of allowing current social arrangements to stand in exchange for tolerance of the church by civil authorities, a pattern established since the early Christian church first compromised with the Roman emperor Constantine. In turn then, St. Paul argues, "You were a slave when called? Never Mind." (1 Cor. 7:21), and St. Peter (2:18–3:7) intones, "Slaves, be submissive in all fear to your masters; . . . Likewise wives, be submissive to your husbands."[6] The notion of equality was even further from the mind of Protestantism's founder, Martin Luther. He replied with rancor to the radical Anabaptists and the peasant rebels of the sixteenth century, also quoting Paul, ". . . make all men equal and so change the spiritual kingdom of Christ into an external worldly one! Impossible! An earthly kingdom cannot exist without inequality of persons. Some must be free, others serfs, some rulers, others subjects. As St. Paul says, 'Before Christ both master and slave are one.' "[7]

The mission of the apostles and saints both past and current (as Teresa awaits her inevitable sainthood) was to be *among* the poor and sick and suffering, promoting joy, not social change. Being "among the poor" serves several purposes: it recreates the dramatic symbolism of Jesus dwelling among the poor and downtrodden, it provides solace to those who suffer, and it reflects the message of love that symbolizes Christianity. In fact, many theologians argue that it is not at all the material help that Christianity brings, but its spiritual help, which enables the poor to endure and await the better life of the future. As one minister says of St. Vincent de Paul, "He dealt first with the souls of men, and although he never lost sight of the physical need and the physical remedy, he made it clearly second. He left many a happy man in a loathsome prison, and he made many a galley slave contented with his unchanged conditions . . ."[8]

None of the above is meant to minimize the powerful symbol of the Christ story. That Christ was pictured as poor and nearly naked, entering towns as a humble man on a donkey, is a powerful symbol, one that served to secure a noble place for the poor for a millennium-and-a-half in Western society prior to the rise of modern capitalism. Such imagery still allows for what sociologist Max Weber called a "salvation religion": It gives the lower classes symbols in which they can see the possibility of a radical overturning of the powerful (perhaps in the next world), or at least a populist hostility to the rich and powerful.

Yet despite these hopes of the poor, Christianity's historic organized role as *Church*[9] has been more to substitute charitable sentiment and legitimize social structures than to overturn any of them. Moreover, sentimentalizing everyday acts, the church obscures the need for rational inquiry into the causes of society's problems and deeper efforts at changing social structures. Christian charity emphasizes the *intent* and *purity* of the giver above notions of efficacy and actual social change.

Contrast the offer of a "smile" and "love" by Mother Teresa with the way modern American society treats other problems. For example, the dangers of precipitous stock market plunges which threaten to injure the rich have been debated by government and media, and sets of regulations developed to protect stockholders from harming themselves. Low corporate profits provoke weighty policy discussions of tax breaks, deregulation, or concessionary labor contracts by workers. Events that threaten the middle class similarly provoke policy debates of rational alternatives. Military base closures have, in another example, almost always been accompanied by a discussion of policies to secure new businesses, jobs, training, and relocation for people negatively affected. The point here is not to argue the appropriateness of these policies. What is noteworthy is the *lack* of moralistic sentimentality in these debates. Ultimately the companies, citizens, and communities will demand to know what money, what jobs, and what profits will be gained or lost.

Can you imagine the US government or press advocating to Wall Street bankers or major companies on the brink of failing, or to anxious soldiers and military base employees, the dispatch of a large team of nice people who bring advice and maybe some soup and food to help? Would politicians intone, "We realize that you have problems, we share your pain. But we trust that with some smiles, love, and prayers, all will be well." Obviously, this type of response would be laughed at on Wall Street or Main Street. Yet it is ultimately the "solution" that satisfies many people of all parties and political persuasions when issues of poverty and other social and human service issues are brought into the public discourse. It is not simply that business or upper-class or middle-class people have more power than the poor or other marginalized people and can therefore demand more of government. While that is true, it is a superficial analysis of how such a cultural consensus is achieved. Talk of soup kitchens, volunteers, religious missionaries, food baskets, and charity fundraisers carries enormous weight with the public outside of any rationalistic framework of business decisions, scientific explorations, or public-policy debates (all of which require at least a pretense of rational discourse). Charitable discourse, on the other hand, is primarily sentimental and symbolic. It is meant to center on emotions and expressions of appropriate caring. When poverty, illness, or disability is concerned, very ordinary acts have been historically sanctified and charged with meaning. This cultural heritage is almost exclusively the result of the influence of Christianity, which romanticizes sentiment toward the poor, ill, distraught, and suffering.

Christian notions of charity—from primitive Christianity to Medieval Christendom to Calvinism to current liberal notions of most mainline Protestant churches and official Roman Catholic thought—have always supported a dualism that separates economic and political life and their *outcomes* from a personalistic religious expression of good will or the *intent* of the giver, which is sanctified. While religion has sometimes sparked radicalism, it does so *only* to the extent that it can overturn charity as a central paradigm and replace it with secular and political content, usually drawn from other social movements. Yet most Christian charitable efforts (even some labeled as "radical") lack any rational ways to judge efficacy. For example, the Catholic Worker movement is sometimes described as "radical," but its adherents describe their philosophy as seeking no more than to take seriously early Christianity's call for hospitality and corporal acts of mercy to the poor.[10] The difficulty is, despite its good intentions, the sharp contrast that these religionists imply in how their work should be evaluated compared with other pursuits in life.

That is, the "personalism" of Christianity even in radical form is taken to mean living among the poor or disenfranchised, learning from them, and working with them to meet their basic needs for food and shelter. The presumed nobility of such ventures is divorced, however, from any particular outcome. This stress on intent and simply "being with" the poor (or other groups) leaves unanswered questions about whether the poor will ever get decent jobs, education, or homes, whether the ill can be healed, or whether the underpaid will get a living wage (if such questions are entertained at all). It substitutes means for ends.

Charity belongs to a totally different class of social action than economic or political action. It is symbolic and relies on charisma rather than rationalistic standards. We are comfortable praising the volunteer who enters another's life because we understand such action to be in the (idealized) realm of personal communication between giver and receiver, and in the presumed personal sacrifice of the giver. Such acts are not considered to be of economic, political, or social importance, but rather in the spiritual realm of life. Like romantic love or personal heroism, charity is personal, it can't be imposed, evaluated rationally, or held to the same standards as other activities. All charity is good, just as all love or heroism is held to be good.

## TO THE GREATER GLORY OF THE RICH; THE FOCUS ON DONORSHIP

Of course, it is not enough just to talk sentiment. Christianity early on insisted that material goods needed to follow good intentions.

While social historians Phillipe Aries and Georges Duby note that charity, in the sense of civic notables giving a certain amount to their cities, was present in pagan Rome, they point out that "the idea of steady giving, in the form of alms, to a permanent category of afflicted" originated with Christianity.[11] The ancient Church became a central social welfare institution following the granting of the right to receive bequests by Constantine and the subsequent sponsoring by the church of the rituals of life from birth to death. As early as the fourth century, the exchange of money for an expiation of sins was becoming common; as Bishop Cyprian of Carthage put it, charity was "a great comfort of believers . . . a remedy for sin . . . by which the Christian . . . accounts God his debtor." As one observer comments, Christianity now became an exchange: "The almsgiver could now become God's creditor. Faith had become a financial transaction. Indeed, poverty [can be argued] as a socioreligious necessity: if there were no poor, what would become of charity and how could the fortunate buy grace?"[12] Later St. Eligius said it more elegantly: "God could have made all men rich, but He wanted there to be poor people in this world, that the rich might be able to redeem their sins."[13]

During Medieval times, almsgiving became so obsessive and ostentatious that a comparison with the tribal potlatch is not out of place. Whether it was political opportunism, "hedging one's bets" for the afterlife, or out of true religious conviction, giving to the church became a competitive venture for centuries among nobility, officials, and later traders and businessmen. In what historian Bronsilaw Geremek cites as a not unusual example of the ostentatious nature of Medieval charity, one well-to-do townsman in Lubeck left instructions upon his death to donate alms among 19,000 people in the town (out of about 22,000 to 24,000 total inhabitants).[14] Historian R. H. Tawney recounts an example of how the sin of usury (then a serious sin) was successfully atoned for by a merchant who agreed to build Notre Dame cathedral when the bishop of Paris was short of funds.[15]

For a better part of a millennium the poor, the sick, and the outcast would surround the gates of monasteries, manors, and later cities with hands out, awaiting the distribution of alms. Although complex, it can be argued that in many ways the poor were treated better and far less stigmatized than in later days due to their somewhat protected status as serfs and even wanderers under the church (and within feudal society generally).[16] In feudal France, for example, every aristocratic residence was expected to have an accredited representative of the local almoner, who was responsible for visiting paupers. The aristocrats were obliged to provide food and lodging. Their residences' "gates were open to the poor, who were admitted to receive, as in Lazarus' house, the crumbs from the Lord's table; it is a blessing for the master and his entire household to submit to this necessary and ritualized despoliation."[17]

Even if charity was more redistributory in Medieval times than in the five hundred years since, charity's ritualized process ironically glorified the rich. The poor were after all just a "mass," a crowd. They took on no special individuality much less any social status. The poor, in fact, owed the rich their prayers, and as time went on supplicants were also expected to exchange submission and obedience for their alms. The status of giving, not receiving, was key, as theological historian Boniface Ramsey suggests:

> Almsgiving . . . [was] characterized less as a work whose motivation is the alleviation of social ills than as a profoundly spiritual exercise. So it is that its thrust is rather heavily donor-centered: it confers benefits on relationship to Christ, makes Christ his debtor, opens heaven to him, and earns him the prayers of the poor. Regularly the value to the giver is emphasized. . . . They exist [the poor] for the sake of the rich, to offer them opportunities for beneficence or to test them. . . . One might suggest that the very concept of the identification of Christ and the poor, at least as some of the Fathers develop it, tended to work against the poor by wallowing them up in him. . . .[18]

Along with the patronage of the wealthy came a legitimation of the dominant system. Those who give create a society after their own image. They build not only a large retainer of supplicants but are able to dominate the physical and social landscape first, of the feudal, and later the capitalist order. As Aries and Duby note, almsgiving exalted the rich:

> The civic ideal that the great were under an obligation to give largesse . . . implied that largesse made manifest the right of the power-

ful to control their community. After all, few basicilas would have been built without such a reflex. The most spectacular were gifts of the emperor or leading clergymen. They were acts of men who had every intention of making it clear, in the old-fashioned way, that they were the ones who had a right to nourish, and so to control, the Christian congregations who assembled in them. The names of those who brought offerings to the altar were read aloud in the solemn prayers of offering . . . frequently these names were acclaimed. . . .[19]

This glorification of the rich to poor continues today. The rich donate in their beneficence, and the poor should be thankful. Charity by the affluent was discussed quite openly in the nineteenth century as a "Christian alternative to socialism." The intelligent and judicious process of charity which demanded meekness from the poor while upholding social inequality was heralded by religious figures as an antidote to the communism or socialism being preached by the irreligious. Father William G. Byrne of Boston explained in 1880 that, "It is through . . . alms-giving on the part of the wealthy and . . . gratitude on the part of the poor, that we are saved . . . the dry rot of communism or a war of classes." Similarly, John Roche, an editor of the *Boston Pilot*, a Catholic paper, affirmed, "Alms-giving brings out the best in the haves and prevents the have-nots from embracing an irreligious and destructive socialism."[20] As a response, lower-class people and social critics, as we saw in chapter 2, often came to be alienated from the Church. A historian of late-nineteenth-century Boston noted that members of trade unions applauded when Jesus was mentioned at their meetings, but hissed at any reference to Christianity and its ministers.[21]

Despite the dramatic changes in Western society, I will develop how the same philanthropic glow continues to shower the rich and famous today. In a donor-donee or patron-client relationship, it is never the poor, the ill, or the suffering who stand out. Indeed usually they stand with downcast eyes and submissive looks while waiting in lengthy bread or soup lines. Not only are there too many millions of them for any to stand out as individuals, they are not, after all, the heroes of the Western social script. They are by definition the passive recipients of charity. Rather, it is the rich philanthropist or generous corporation that gains the power and recognition of the observer. The Ted Turners of the world can insure that their names are known through the power of generous gifts. American Express or the Sprint company can pledge a percentage of their new sales and gain public acclaim. In a sense, the process is self-reinforcing: the mass is anonymous, the recipient of unasked-for largesse, a passive lump. The cultural heroes—the business-people or rich and famous—are active and bold; even taking from their own pockets to insure social justice. No one looks too hard into the coffers of American Express, Sprint, or organized corporate charities like Second Harvest because we all understand implicitly that equity or actual income redistribution to remove poverty is not the point; it is profound symbolism so the rich can bestow their wealth, no matter how small a percentage of their net profits.

## CREATING A SACRED SPHERE

Modern Christianity constructs a separate sacred realm away from the everyday mundane concerns of life; part of the appeal of sacred rituals, symbols, and folkways are their ability to help us cope with the unknown, difficult, and complex nature of life. However, Christianity has not always, in every form, been an "otherworldly" religion: to take only a few examples, many of the early Christ cults, and continuing through the early monastics of the Medieval times, embraced a more totalistic form of Christianity as did the millennial religionists of the Medieval world, as do American religionists today from Protestant fundamentalists to Catholic liberation theologists. While some moments in religious history have sought to bring together the sacred and secular world, generally speaking, modern Christianity reinforces the split of sentiment, symbol, and the triumph of good from the secular world of the marketplace.

This history is useful in analyzing how the modern nonprofit sector arose. As long ago as early Medieval times, radical idealism was separated from the institutional church. To make peace with the society it found itself in, the Catholic Church as an institution was conservative, supporting the nobility and monarchy, as well as the institutions of serfdom, slavery, and warfare. Yet for many young men who rejected vassalage or were able to run from their status as serfs, monastic living became a counterculture. Troeltsch notes the more "radical visions of Christianity continued in monasticism [as] a safety valve." But its very isolation led monasticism to have "no clear and logical relation to the church" as a whole.[22] In many ways, the tradition of private charity and nonprofit organization continues such a split between the profane and the sacred. As the major institutions—business and government— comprise the power structure of society, some idealists are allowed and even encouraged to work in small outposts of the empire to feed the homeless, care for the sick, and minister to the wounded. The more idealistic and different from the dominant organizations a charitable group is (such as the few self-proclaimed "radical" nonprofit organizations), the more likely its workers are to be poorly paid or serve as volunteers and be furthest from any power, prestige, or real decisionmaking.

But if Medieval times had already pioneered a separate sacred sphere for "doing good," the rise of capitalism clearly demarcated the role of Christianity from the marketplace much further. The Catholic Church of the Middle Ages had for centuries sought to limit the excesses of trade through prohibitions on usury and concepts such as the "just price." Its interference, in fact, with both economics and politics was a major factor in the rise of Protestantism. Protestantism (and eventually modern Catholicism) discarded the traditional suspicion that existed in the church toward moneymaking. As R. H. Tawney explains, "Puritanism in its later phases added a halo of ethical sanctification to the appeal of economic expediency, and offered a moral creed, in which the duties of religion and the calls of business ended their long estrangement in an unanticipated reconciliation." The rise of Protestantism and capitalism forced a new vagueness concerning what charity could do or even what an ethical approach to the marketplace could be. As Tawney says, "Naturally, therefore, they [theologians] formulate the ethical principles of Christianity in terms of comfortable ambiguity, and rarely indicate with any precision their application to commerce, finance, and the ownership of property."[23]

Gradually over time, although churches made known their political and economic policies in broad and vague statements, the separation of church from the economy and church from the state defined a separate sacred sphere. If the church was to stay out of state power and out of the marketplace, what role could it play? Here Tawney identifies charity

> as the sphere [in which] only those parts of life which could be reserved for philanthropy, precisely because they fell outside that larger area of normal human relations, in which the promptings of self-interest provided all-sufficient motive and rule of conduct. It was, therefore, in the sphere of providing succor for the non-combatants and for the wounded, not in inspiring the main army, that the social work of the Church was conceived to lie. Its characteristic expressions . . . [were] in the relief of the poor, the care of the sick, and the establishment of schools.[24]

Max Weber, the foremost thinker on the rise of capitalism and Protestantism, suggests that this was the natural progression of the sacred sentiment under capitalism. Weber spent much of his career arguing that "rational economic association" simply cannot be limited by any kind of sentiment or a "charitable orientation." As capitalism arises:

> There is no possibility, in practice or even in principle, of any caritative regulation of relationships arising between the holder of a savings and loan bank mortgage and the mortgagee who has obtained a loan from the bank, or between a holder of a federal bond and a citizen taxpayer. Nor can any caritative regulation arise in the relationships between stockholders and factory workers, between tobacco importers and foreign plantation workers, or between industrialists and the miners who have dug from the earth the raw materials used in the plants owned by the industrialists. The growing impersonality of the economy on the basis of association in the market place follows its own rules, disobedience to which entails economic failure and, in the long run, economic ruin.[25]

In other words, "business is business" becomes the impeccable logic of modern society, particularly when reinforced by the individualist notions of Protestantism. This creates a sanctified sphere of sentiment that is extremely vague, even irrelevant to daily life, because it is at such a high level of abstraction.

In this context, the notion of "Not Alms, but a Friend" fits extremely well. The Catholic Church, as noted, had glorified alms-giving. But early Protestantism rejected the great pageant of alms-giving as practiced in the Medieval church, holding that the new "stewardship of wealth" entailed a different obligation for the rich. Whereas Medieval charity emphasized the symbolism and senti-ment of giving, not amelioration of the receiver, the new stewards of wealth (often as both private figures and officials of local govern-ment) would emphasize the *obligations* of those receiving aid. The duty to be charitable was no longer unconditional; early New En-glanders, for example, were urged to be "preferential in your char-ity." The simple glory of bestowing alms was replaced by conditional aid related to the acceptance of behavioral norms, now rigidly applied so that distinctions between "deserving" and "un-deserving poor" were emphasized with an insistence that he who would not work would not eat, and that those not exhibiting proper morality or deference should not get aid.

Although vast change has taken place since the early days of American charity, the emphasis on sentiment delivered through a separate set of voluntary organizations continues in today's love af-fair with the "nonprofit." Although some organizations bring food, shelter, or other tangible goods, most often, as I discuss in chapter 5, they deliver advice, consolement, rehabilitation, and education. These nonmaterial benefits fit much better into the moralistic guid-ance the settlers brought to this country and hold less threat to the competitiveness of the capitalist market.

# 4—Philanthropy: For the Greater Glory of the Rich

*Perhaps the most overrated virtue in our list of shoddy virtues is that of giving. Giving builds up the ego of the giver, makes him superior and higher and larger than the receiver. Nearly always, giving is a selfish pleasure, and in many cases is a downright destructive and evil thing. One has only to remember some of the wolfish financiers who spend two thirds of their lives clawing a fortune out of the guts of society and the latter third pushing it back. It is not enough to suppose that their philanthropy is a kind of frighted restitution, or that their natures change when they have enough. Such nature never has enough and natures do not change that readily. I think that the impulse is the same in both cases. For giving can bring the same sense of superiority as getting does, and philanthropy may be another kind of spiritual avarice.*

John Steinbeck[1]

Although it is true that Christian charity's focus on the donor has linked a "halo effect" to philanthropy, during a number of periods in American history and for some social observers it seemed the height of absurdity to assign the virtue of generosity and goodwill to the rich and powerful. How has it then happened over time that wealthy businesspeople and corporations are sanctified in our culture as being caring and socially responsible? This chapter will suggest how a series of social, legal, and economic developments have separated the role of the wealthy as accumulators of fortunes from their role as givers, severing the logical connection between making a profit and disposing of small parts of it.

By reifying wealth into philanthropy, a successful social script has been created that replaces in modern society the hegemonic role of the church in earlier centuries. Although the rich actually give no more of a percentage of their income to charity than do the very poor,[2] considerable sums of money are given. Perhaps more important, the rich are highly visible in the money they do give, and a great deal of time and effort is expended by corporations in organizing volunteering by their managers and employees and in promoting various causes to the public.

### HOW AMERICA'S RICH BECAME HEROIC

American society obviously could not honor its rich in the same processional and grand fashion as Medieval society feted its feudal lords or powerful clergy. After all, US society is presumably committed to democracy, an end to the visible differences of caste and status that existed in late-eighteenth-century Europe and to some degree of secularism. Early in American history, such prominent figures as Cotton Mather and Thomas Jefferson insisted that charity was an obligation of all, in fact, and required no great wealth or power. Yet historically, as capitalism developed as an economic system, a variety of new organizational vehicles provided an arena to glorify the wealthy donor.

Moving quickly and admittedly incompletely over American history, it is of interest to look at several examples of these organizational vehicles. The four discussed below: trusteeship, foundations, the federated–community chest–united way structure, and corporate cause-related marketing, have come, despite earlier controversies, to be widely accepted in American life.

### The Boston Brahmins, "Trusteeship," and the Domination of the Nonprofit World

In the early days of the republic, no clear lines differentiated between "for-profit" corporations and what would come to be understood as "not-for-profit" or "voluntary" sector organizations. Nor was there a clear line between public and private. Harvard University, now perhaps America's most famous nongovernmental institution, was founded as a public institution and supported by tax funds for nearly two centuries. Many colleges, libraries, historical societies, and missionary societies, but also banks and stock holding companies, were publicly chartered, and, as historian Peter

Dobkin Hall notes, regarded as properly subservient to the political will of the people despite having boards which oversaw their administration.[3] For those wealthy enough to leave bequests and establish new institutions, the resultant ambiguity was quite problematic. As early merchants and powerful New England families began to accumulate wealth, they wanted to invest their money where they saw fit and leave their own legacy to the future rather than see their wealth placed in the hands of the public (including the newly emergent political parties).

The Federalist Party, as the representative of America's elite at the time, came to support the maximum flexibility possible so the wealthy could use their money as they saw fit. The Jeffersonian position in the first decades of the nineteenth century opposed these efforts. It sought to limit the ability of the wealthy not only to make bequests but to accumulate corporate property. The Jeffersonians did not see the accumulation of property and wealth through colleges, mechanics societies, or even hospitals or museums as being terribly different from the incipient accumulation of private wealth in early forms of stock companies.

Courts in the first half of the nineteenth century developed a clearer legal concept of trusteeship, gradually favoring the Federalist, elite position over the Jeffersonian one. The famous Dartmouth College case, which reached the Supreme Court in 1818 and was argued by Daniel Webster, came about when a Jeffersonian legislature in New Hampshire reorganized the college so that it more clearly became a governmental unit, to which, of course, the previous board members objected. Webster conceded that the college was chartered by the state but argued that this did not diminish the private character of the donated money. "The gifts were made to the trustees and, as such, constituted private contracts between trustees and donors," he argued. On the other side was the view that Dartmouth was a public entity created for the public, and not subject to private whims. The Supreme Court ruled with only one dissent that Dartmouth was indeed "private."[4] Peter Dobkin Hall comments that had the ruling not gone in this direction, not only would we not have our modern American "nonprofit" sector, but the gradual development of law supporting for-profit corporate organization would also have been affected. Today, we assume that no matter what the *public impact* of corporate action, if the money is not raised through taxes or direct government fees the organization is private; but this was not always the dominant view.

Still, the absolute power of the wealthy to leave their property to descendants and have trustees manage it was not acknowledged by all states. For example, New York state placed all charitable and educational organizations under a Regents, a public authority. In an important court case in 1844, Pennsylvania challenged the will of Stephen Girard, a wealthy Philadelphia merchant who left seven million dollars to start a college for orphans. Again, despite state history, the courts ruled that the wealthy have the right to transmit their wealth however they see fit. Connected with the issue of bequeathing property was the question of what actual rights and duties trustees should hold. In simple wills, trustees are usually restricted to a time-bound act of carrying out the wishes of the deceased. But was a trustee of an ongoing organization (a charity, mission, college) simply to represent the deceased wishes' only? Or did he or she represent their own interests? And what was the organizational interest, short-term gain or long-term survival?

Anthropologist Clifford Marcus notes that Massachusetts was the place where these issues were most closely tested through extensive litigation. An 1830 case (*Harvard College v. Armory*) established the "prudent man" rule, which gave wide latitude to trustees in determining investments and the future of the institutions they managed.[5] This was significant not only because it boosted a private, voluntary sector apart from state control. It also helped complete what was coming to be a link between private capital and benevolent ventures, what Marcus calls the "Boston model." This model, which was well in place by the 1840s and 1850s, was dominated by the Brahmin leadership of Boston. The Boston upper class, one of the first concentrations of significant wealth in the US, feared the impact of growing universal suffrage, not to mention the mob of immigrants landing on American shores. Trusteeship, or what some authors call the "fiduciary model,"[6] allowed the linking of elite trustees who sat on banks, insurance companies, and stock ventures with the literally dozens of new "charitable" groups that came to control Boston (from Massachusetts General Hospital to the Humane Society to Boston Mechanics Institute to the Boston Society for the Prevention of Pauperism). A sort of private government could now function independently of popular sovereignty. Writes Hall:

> The wealthiest and best-supported institutions were tightly interlocked, not only with one another but also with the central economic enterprises of the region . . . they served as capital pools, for example Massachusetts Hospital Life Insurance Company, a for-profit subsidiary of Massachusetts General [Hospital], was a large source of investment capital and tightly interlocked with textiles and real-estate development and railroads. . . . The Brahmins, acutely concerned with the problems of establishing and maintaining leadership (and being worthy of it), had created a network of educational and cultural institutions whose purpose was to train, test, and sort out the young, promoting the most able to preeminent positions as trustees of the central organizations that defined the Brahmins as a class.[7]

The Brahmin model—linking powerful private interests through a large array of boards of both capitalist and "nonprofit" organizations—would expand throughout the country, although not without some resistance and alternative models. For example, a strong preference for a public sector model existed in the Midwestern states throughout the nineteenth and even twentieth centuries (hence the dominance of public universities in the Midwest, for example). The lack of democracy in a wide range of American institutions—hospitals, colleges, charities, and social service agencies—would again become an issue in the US nationally, especially in the 1960s and 1970s. But for my purpose, what is so interesting is the relative ease with which the legal and historical construction of trusteeship (or directorship) allowed for a privatization of our institutions with an almost completely upper-class leadership. This is true to a degree strikingly different from other nations where (except for religious organizations) one does not expect to see large numbers of private schools, colleges, hospitals, orphanages, day care centers, or museums.

By the late nineteenth century, whether it be a local charity, a library, a museum, an opera, a symphony, a college, a manufacturers association, or a bank, the same or similar faces were present on the boards. To this day the rich control and dominate the boards of major nonprofit organizations. Of course, the most elite cultural settings (ballet, opera, symphony, art museum) have board members who are highest in social status; but even within human service organizations, as a recent study shows, business executives, lawyers, and financial managers still dominate the boards, representing corporate interests within their local areas.[8] It is even more ironic that at a time when approximately half (or by some estimates more) of all nonprofit funding actually comes from taxpayers, this sphere running parallel to government — an estimated 1.2 million nonprofit boards[9] — is privately controlled and technically not responsible either to the public at large or to their presumed beneficiaries.[10]

### The Robber Barons Cleanse Their Reputations

Perhaps few historical developments would more shock an industrial worker or populist of the turn of the last century, who Rip-Van-Winkle-like awoke in contemporary times, than to find the names of robber barons like Carnegie and Rockefeller associated with large, progressive foundations and philanthropic giving. Equally jarring, at least to some elderly CIO and New Deal activists, must be the association of a name like Ford (previously associated with anti-Semitism and the belligerent antiunionism of the first Henry Ford) with philanthropy and thoughtful innovation and policy development.

The creation of what were initially called "charitable trusts," and, later foundations, helped along this startling turn of events: the conversion of vast amounts of wealth accumulated during America's "Gilded Age" by conservative, antilabor, laissez-faire businessmen into "clean money." There was vehement opposition during the Progressive Era and again to some extent in the 1930s and 1960s. In one of the most dramatic early examples of this opposition, Social Gospel minister Washington Gladden in 1895 raised the issue of "tainted money" soon after John D. Rockefeller bestowed a large sum to help establish the University of Chicago. Attacking the robber barons as "Roman plunderers," "pirates of industry," and "spoilers of the state," Gladden urged every institution to ask itself of contributions, "Is this clean money? Can any man, can any institution, knowing its origin, touch it without becoming defiled?"[11] Andrew Carnegie, despite his unusual personal background as a Scottish Chartist who genuinely seemed to be uncomfortable with his vast wealth, was remembered by unionists and socialists as the bloody murderer of the Homestead Strike of 1892, which dramatically crushed an effort to organize the steelworkers union. In response to Carnegie's efforts to provide Wheeling, West Virginia, with a library, Wheeling unionists called him "the greatest of oppressors," a man "who gave with one hand and took away with the other." They charged that accepting the free library building would be a "disgraceful monument" to "a cold-blooded outrage."[12] And indeed, Wheeling was one of several American communities to reject Carnegie's money.

As late as 1969 populist Congressman Wright Patman of Texas held dramatic hearings in Washington attacking foundations. For Patman

> the economic effect of great amounts of wealth accumulating in privately controlled, tax-exempt foundations. . . . [is] the problem of control of that capital for an undetermined period—in some cases in perpetuity—by a few individuals or their self-appointed successors; and . . . the foundations' power to interlock and knit together through investments, a network of commercial alliances, which assures harmonious action whenever they have a common interest.[13]

Yet, as with many ingenious inventions of American capitalism, the foundation has succeeded to a remarkable degree over a relatively short historical period in sanitizing wealth and honoring, as in the Medieval pageantry of charity, the wealthy donor as hero.

While the idea of a foundation goes back to ancient Rome, at the turn of the previous century such forms were still of questionable legality in the United States. Certainly wealthy people did make large contributions to churches, charities, libraries, museums, or specific ventures, but the idea of a large sum of money being specifically set aside for "the general well-being of mankind" was not clearly lawful.[14]

Carnegie and Rockefeller were quite forward-looking in constructing the foundation as institutional form. First of all, as noted, the robber barons' gifts were controversial, at least from the 1890s through the second decade of the twentieth century. By developing a separate organizational vehicle (the foundation) to administer the wealth and over time more quietly and judiciously give some money away, the donor would enjoy greater social peace and legitimacy. Secondly, what united the very different world-views of Carnegie, a secularist who felt obliged to not turn his heirs into spoiled, wealthy kids, and Rockefeller, a profoundly religious man who felt God was acting through his wealth, was their realization that America was changing and that self-made millionaires like themselves were no longer the future:

> The insight that Rockefeller and Carnegie had was that the society was not going to be managed any longer by Scottish immigrants who go into steel mills or by Ohio accountants who become millionaires. Their insight was that the society is going to have to be managed by somebody else, and what they were doing was to create a system whereby such managers could be trained.[15]

More specifically, they understood that wealth needed to be professionally managed, and that simply because some people were good at business did not mean they understood or had expertise in charity, education, international affairs, and so on. Further professionalism, of course, provided a strong buffer between the origins of the money in the schemes of oil consolidation or big steel monopolies, and those representatives who would appear before the press and public to announce new grants or research studies. Rockefeller's 1909 musings were quite prescient in calling for a division of labor between the wealthy and a professional philanthropic staff:

> We cannot afford to have great souls who are capable of doing the most effective work slaving to raise the money. That should be a business man's task, and he should be supreme in managing the machinery of the expenses . . . [yet] You would not place a fortune for your children in the hands of an inexperienced person. . . . Let us be as careful with the money we spend for the benefit of others.[16]

The professionalization of charity, of course, would occur through a number of changes between 1900 and 1930. These include the formation of a number of professions (social work, public administration, social planning, accounting, management) and the increasing consolidation and rationalization of "charity" into a corporate entity through federations and community chests. The foundation was key in helping wealthy donors to legitimize their wealth. In some instances foundations even made their names synonymous with liberal social change. Donors also found a way to perpetuate their family wealth legally while saving fortunes in taxes. The largest growth in foundations was clearly related to the latter objective.

The high taxes of the Roosevelt era played as large a role. In 1934, calculating that his tax bill could rise from the 12.5–16 percent range in the twenties to as high as 63 percent that year, Rockefeller moved a huge amount of his wealth to nontaxable charitable trusts held by his advisers and family.[17] Often motives of personal and political legitimation *and* tax avoidance worked in tandem. For example, the Sloan Foundation, originated in 1937, the year that General Motors chairman of the board Alfred Sloan fought one of the most dramatic labor disputes of the century, was also revealed in the press to have avoided $1.9 million in taxes over the previous three years. At the end of the year Sloan moved $10 million of his wealth into a foundation that he and his wife controlled.[18]

As philanthropic critic Ferdinand Lundberg pointed out some time ago, the accomplishments of the wealthy through foundations are "an intellectual sleight of the hand" since these fortunes of the rich could be taxed and used instead by the public sector:

If the Fords, now, should achieve something humanely tremendous through their foundation they would not achieve it with *their* money but with *our* money . . . [if] it is nevertheless insisted that all this foundation effort represents philanthropic activity, then it is governmentally coerced philanthropic activity, under the threat of taking the principal in taxes if the income is not devoted to narrowly applied good works. The government, in brief, forces the rich to tend to their own plantation.[19]

What Carnegie and Rockefeller could not foresee was how the foundation as form would come to share with other mechanisms of the "nonprofit" world the rather amazing accomplishment of allowing the public to see *their* money spent by private parties as a *positive* feat. While charity is acclaimed, the government sector is seen as negative and harmful as exemplified by programs such as welfare or by "faceless bureaucrats" managing our lives. While not necessarily the key issue at the time of the invention of various mechanisms discussed in this chapter, the antigovernment mantra has been consciously reinforced over the century by the very rich. At a major celebration of the "Rockefeller Century" in the 1980s, David Rockefeller intoned the glories of philanthropy while gloating at the poor fate of government as an institution:

> Now the message of limited government is spreading all around the world. I hope that with this recognition comes a positive global understanding of the real role and function of an independent nonprofit sector. Such an extension of the real legacy of my grandfather on the worldwide basis would provide his most lasting monument and most important profit.[20]

Indeed, David is quite right that the first Rockefeller would be pleased not only at the acclaim of the Rockefeller name but the bad stead that public aid and entitlement is now held in.

### Militant Civic Boosterism: Community Chests and United Ways

Power in twentieth-century America has greatly shifted in all spheres of life from wealthy individuals and families to organizations, namely corporations and large bureaucracies. While conspicuous giving, attending charity events, and sitting on elite boards continue to play a major role in many upper-class individuals' lives, the imperative toward active civic boosterism and charity has also moved firmly into the corporate ranks, becoming virtually a job requirement for middle and higher level managers. The Charity Organization Society (described in chapter 2) as early as the 1880s attempted to consolidate the many charities and bring "scientific methods" and "trustification" to the world of charity. By the time Rockefeller wrote in 1909 about creating "benevolent trusts," his thoughts were hardly original; coordinated drives had begun in some cities under the control of chambers of commerce and boards of trade.[21]

A major turning point in securing greater corporate control over American life was the manner in which Woodrow Wilson managed the domestic political front during World War I. Moving away from a public sector model even in wartime, Wilson staffed the war effort with a host of ad hoc boards and agencies whose staff were primarily corporate chieftains, with some representation of the AFL. Under the leadership of the War Council with J. P. Morgan as chair, the largest mobilization in US history included a massive charitable solicitation at home, leading to the development of three hundred community "war chests" and the raising of an unprecedented $200 million. Somewhat coercively mandating that all charities work together and support the war effort with donations, the war chests used the militant patriotism and antiradicalism of the war to engage in a forced voluntarism. Historian Roy Lubove comments: "It took a courageous man to refuse to subscribe in view of the social pressure and stigma of disloyalty to the war effort. Some cities maintained investigation departments with paid employees to follow up delinquent pledges, and in Albany a 'Loyal Legion' pursued slackers. In many cities pledges were deducted from the pay envelopes. . . . To insure that labor turnover and mobility did not obstruct chest collections, factories in Youngstown, Ohio, deducted the unpaid pledge remainder from the departing employee's paycheck, and in Detroit, factories were asked to underwrite employee subscriptions."[22]

War mobilization seems to have wide appeal among the population throughout American history. But while obviously patriotic appeals envelop the entire nation, corporate leaders often gain the most. Freed from the restraints of government regulations and fed by huge production needs, corporations have boomed during wars. Moreover, residues of anticorporate sentiment are diminished by war fervor.[23] In the post–World War I period of labor unrest and anti-immigrant raids, the "militant civic patriotism transcending race, class, and religion" appealed to business (and many citizens) at a time when socialism, syndicalism, and mass strikes were not yet history but a current preoccupation. It was in this context that business sought to make the war chests permanent as "community chests." Despite the noble words of William Procter—of Procter & Gamble—who described the chest movement as "the agent of brotherhood which embodied the great impulse of the war period,"[24] the community chests simply established coordinated giving on a local level. The forerunner of the modern United Way, the chests served to place charity on a businesslike corporate model with efficient collection of funds. They also established the principle that only certain respectable agencies got the money. Of course, as with the development of the trustee model and foundations, the community chest movement was not without its opponents. Lubove reports that plenty of "critics accused the chest of being a menace to the survival of private, voluntary welfare or a conspiracy of businessmen to save money and bother," and prominent figures in early social service, particularly those who had stood for reformist social action or were active in the settlement house movement, often opposed them.[25] After World War II the chests changed increasingly to a company-wide rather than a community-wide solicitation, becoming in turn the United Fund and finally today's "United Way."

The success of the chests-funds as a corporate priority is fascinating because, unlike the power of bestowing money directly, which the rich exercise through their roles as charity fundraisers or as creators of foundations, the rewards of federated fundraising for corporations are more subtle. That is, when a Rockefeller or Turner give a large sum of money directly, gains in status and legitimacy are clear. Yet corporate embracement of a complex system of charitable giving by its employees is less easy to explain simply. Certainly a great deal of corporate support for chests and united ways is ideological. In the 1920s, corporate welfarism became a major business strategy, and popular leaders from Henry Ford to Herbert Hoover were prime promoters of preventing more government intervention with voluntarism. When in the midst of the Great Depression, Congress appropriated $25 million to help the

Red Cross cope with the emergency, it turned down the money, winning the praise of Hoover who asserted the superiority of private charity to any type of public assistance.[26] Two decades later in an in-depth study of community chests in the nation's heartland, a group of social scientists reported that among "Hoosier businessmen support for voluntarism was greatly motivated by a vision of a highly centralized and highly income-equalizing alternative system" that might occur in the absence of their charitable efforts.[27]

But ideology or latent purpose is not a full explanation either. Corporate leaders, like most Americans, came to believe that they have certain moral duties. Eleanor Brilliant, a historian of the United Way, notes that "mythmaking" plays a large role to this day in the minds of the staff, executives, and thousands of volunteers across the nation who make these huge fundraising campaigns work. The "mythmaking" Brilliant notes is the belief that the limited charity of payroll deductions will solve large social problems, and that corporate executives and employees represent the entire community by dominating the boards that solicit charity. To those who volunteer their time and to the many executives who are "loaned" out to direct parts of United Way campaigns, charity work is just a natural good part of American life, a job obligation, and a pledge of caring about America's social ills. Yet as Brilliant and others note, the "grass roots" quality of the chests (and United Ways) which they never tire of promoting is unreal unless one believes that corporate officials are the "grass roots."[28] Controlling the leadership at the national level and almost always on local committees are corporate managers and executives. Of course, labor union staff, public servants, social workers, even some housewives and average workers are represented, but they are in a minority.[29] As one critic characterized the theory of federated campaigns:

> Motivated by the remarkable theory that the immediate desires of the businessman coincide with the long-range needs of everyone else, the numerically insignificant but economically formidable sponsors of united funds have appointed themselves stewards of our philanthropic outlook, custodians of some of our most important philanthropic organizations, and bursars of their funds.[30]

Beyond the ideological commitment of corporations and the raw social power they gain in the community, four other specific functions can be seen as consequences of the corporate leadership of the annual rites of voluntarism. First, these campaigns have come to serve as a free testing and training ground for young executives and managers. Less risky than early promotions within actual corporate profit centers, potential executives can be tested in a range of interpersonal, financial, and leadership skills in the highly regularized and routinized world of United Way drives and committee work. Second, as large non-local firms emerged as dominant throughout the century, their isolation from the local community could be mitigated by heavy involvement in the local chests (later united ways).[31] We are "local" after all, even a chain store like Wal-Mart can claim, because our managers sit on the city's board of the United Way or chair one of its prominent committees. Thirdly, federated fundraising, in a sleight of hand, presents the company as generous, often without the company *itself* making major cash contributions. When Totalmax Company gains great public relations for raising $2 million this year, placing second in the community or exceeding its goal by 20 percent or whatever, the implication for local citizens is what a wonderful thing Totalmax has done! But the money collected is from *the employees* of Totalmax, *not* the corporate coffers nor even from its upper echelons. Brilliant suggests that in part the development of the idea of intensive workplace solicitation after World War II was a successful strategy to shift corporate fundraising from its own deep pockets—which with the high tax rate helped the companies avoid taxes during the war—back onto its employees.[32] "Corporate rhetoric is not entirely clear (on who the giver is)," notes Brilliant, "and the corporations seem to like it that way."[33]

Finally, social control over employees must be mentioned as a latent function as well. Avoiding multiple solicitation or the possibility of a union organizing employees as a result of charitable or other causes gaining access to plants was a clear corporate concern behind the idea of forcing "one big drive" rather than having many charities active in the workplace. Additionally, once the United Way was established, employers used it (at least until court cases and political opposition in the last two decades) as a test of lower level employee loyalty as well as managerial performance. Many corporations would fill out the pledge cards for their employees in advance, and new employees were warned of repercussions if they resisted giving. A utility chairman observed, "We want to participate in the community, and a man is not intelligent if he won't pull his load." This executive "regard[ed] the United Fund pledge cards circulated to his employees as intelligence tests."[34]

Even in the 1980s, 100 percent participation was important enough in some companies for supervisors to cover for noncontributing employees by giving a dollar or other small amount in their name.[35] Employee compliance with the donation process became one measure of how loyal the employee was in general to the company. Beginning in the 1960s and 1970s, the opposition of minority groups, congressional investigations, and court cases began to question coercive charity. Yet for most corporations, complete support of the United Way as the sole charity admitted into the workplace continues. Even after some companies have now consented (after court decisions and considerable political agitation) to allow alternative fundraising, and the United Way itself has moved to "donor choice" to mitigate controversy, the fundamental issues remain. Just as corporate offices were measured by their profit margins, United Way participation is still an index of community and employee loyalty.

### The Corporation is Your Friend: "Cause Related Marketing"

Despite the growing corporatization of American life, until the last several decades or so business control over philanthropy usually remained hidden from public view. True, the CEO of Prudential might head up a major public board, the CEO of Ford Motor Company might sit on ten major nonprofit boards, the Mellons may have had a great deal of control in Pittsburgh through their many foundations, and other CEOs dominated the national and local United Ways. But they did all this ostensibly in their role as beneficent citizens, presumably without the intention of directly benefiting their corporations' profits. Nor, at least until the late 1960s, were corporate ties a fact that would be publicized by nonprofit organizations or government. Like doctors or lawyers advertising, there was a certain noblesse oblige about service that made wide publicity for companies (as opposed to individuals) undesirable. In other words, while contributions from a Nelson or David Rockefeller were certainly seen as heroic, it was still viewed as somewhat bad taste to praise Standard Oil Company as a donor.

Interestingly, this began to change with the social unrest of the 1960s and 1970s. Unlike the anticapitalist movements earlier in the century, many of these later social movements, while critical of companies, were not essentially anticorporate. Harsh rhetoric aside, they often aimed more for inclusion or reform. For example, the civil rights and women's movement pressed for equal employment, corporate investment in the ghettos, equal pay for equal work, and so on. One key turning point in the relation between this unrest and corporations was the beginning of strong involvement by major companies in the racial crisis during and after the major urban riots of the 1960s. Particularly influenced by government jawboning and the obvious dangers to their legitimacy and sales in the major cities, a number of more forward-looking companies increased training, community and economic development, and minority hiring. They also created a wide variety of nonprofit boards, task forces, and committees where luminaries like Henry Ford II and David Rockefeller sat down (to the great fanfare of the media) with civil rights and community leaders. Similarly, the agitation of the environmental and consumer movements in the 1960s and 1970s against corporate excesses tested the legitimacy of corporations.

Many major corporations made donations to community groups or foundations as part of this sort of "enlightened self-interest" before the mid-1970s, but the 1970s added the buzzword of "corporate social responsibility." As one author notes, while enlightened self-interest suggested a *permissible* activity because it advanced the company's own welfare, corporate social responsibility went further by saying that the corporations had a *duty* to participate in efforts to solve social problems and advance the welfare of the nation.[36] What is ironic about the corporate social responsibility movement[37] is that neither pressure from the Left on companies, nor exhortations from the Right—for example, rhetorical appeals by Presidents Reagan and Bush in the 1980s and 1990s for companies to do more to replace public sector cutbacks with private funds—has actually increased corporate donations very much.[38] Rather, the main impact of these pressures has been a highly open and visible corporate presence in almost all areas of charitable and service fundraising, often as part of a successful marriage between marketing and "social responsibility."

Cuts in public spending in the 1980s vastly reduced government expenditures for programs such as the arts—including Public Broadcasting and the National Endowment for the Arts (NEA)—and slashed social service spending on welfare, health, job training, those with disabilities, and housing. As agencies receiving government money through contracts faced severe cuts, many feared extinction. Corporations—pressed by the idea of voluntarism, but also more and more approached by nonprofits of all kinds themselves for funding—sometimes found that "charity sells." Higher profits as well as positive community relations combined to sell many corporations on the idea of being responsive to this new range of appeals from politicians, nonprofit and service leaders, their own fellow board members in the organizations they were involved in, and, in some cases, even from social movement activists concerned with issues such as poverty or homelessness in the 1980s and 1990s.

"Cause related marketing" is a new form of charity, in which a corporation adopts a particular cause or package of causes and is able to expand its market and profits while supporting these worthy aims. In one example of cause related marketing, companies find that sponsoring orchestras, symphonies, operas, and museum exhibitions is a good way to reach upscale consumers without the high cost of advertising broadly. For example, SCM Company, which sponsors museum exhibitions, admits that it would cost $51 million per year on advertising for five years to reach the customers it now does on $200,000 a year. In another strategy becoming increasingly popular, corporate giving is conditioned on numbers of units sold, so the charity gains as the company expands markets. Pioneered in the early 1980s by American Express, which contributed two cents to charity for each new cardholder, other examples include American Airlines giving the Dallas Symphony five dollars for every passenger who flew their newly inaugurated Dallas-London route, and another three dollars to the Fort Worth Symphony for each new route segment; and Chesebrough-Ponds which pledged five cents to CARE for every customer coupon redeemed during a special newspaper promotion. McDonald's reports that for every Ronald McDonald House it builds, sales in that particular market area jump, evidently indicating a new direct link between consumer spending and a warm fuzzy feeling.[39]

The most prominent "cause related marketing" has involved highly touted national campaigns such as the sprucing up of the Statue of Liberty for its 1983 anniversary (initially also sponsored by American Express), the Hands Across America rallies in 1986 (with Coca-Cola as the initial sponsor, but with other corporations joining in), and Second Harvest, a program which provides the homeless and poor with surplus food and involves Kellogg, Kraft, Stop 'N Shop, McDonald's, Monsanto, Procter and Gamble, Beatrice Foods, and the Grocery Manufacturers of America. The possibility of corporate abuse beyond profit-taking is illustrated by Second Harvest. SH not only saves companies millions of dollars by providing them with large tax breaks, it has sent out spoiled, damaged, and unsellable goods to soup kitchens and shelters that found them to be inedible or unhealthy. Yet these companies are protected from lawsuits by Good Samaritan Laws. Critics such as Theresa Funiciello further charge that the tax savings are intentionally inflated since the companies list as tax deductions "fair market value" prices on goods that can't be sold and often arrive even further damaged or inedible.[40]

While corporate cause related marketing has soared, suggesting that the public has little problem with it, a number of criticisms have emerged. Philip Morris and other tobacco companies have, of course, been virulently attacked for their aid to minority communities as an advertising ploy and a way to co-opt opposition. Many have criticized corporate grants to schools that have often been conditioned on forms of advertising, both subtle and not so subtle, as an unfair influence on young students. As one social service official quipped about a variety of corporate sponsorships "If your image is bad, [now] you buy Shakespeare!"[41] But beyond co-optation or legitimation as a corporate motive, some nonprofit observers have other fears; since giving is not going up as a whole, they worry that firms that do cause related marketing may reduce their total giving to charity by tying their entire "social responsibility" program to such causes.[42] Shell Oil, for example, handles social responsibility as a "performance center," just like it would any other strategic management operation. With corporate officials engaged in goal setting and strategic planning, companies not only can avoid unpopular or controversial causes, but they can also avoid *any* charity that doesn't add to the company's investment potential or improve its customer base. If Big Food Company in the past has given to, say, the American Cancer Society and the Red Cross, but now sees more profit in giving only to, say, the local homeless shelter if and when it sells new food products, total giving is down in two ways. The old charities are excluded completely, but the new charity also gets its loaves of bread *only* if and when Big Food Co. has good sales. The biggest irony then about the new popularity of corporate charity is that it may undermine the very nonprofit philanthropic sector shaped in large part by the business world itself throughout the nineteenth and twentieth centuries. After all, if social responsibility (or whatever we call the motivation for corporate giving) can be done entirely "in-house" through corporate departments, then the future of foundations, united ways, and other organizational vehicles we have explored could eventually come to be anachronisms.[43]

## THE MAKING OF THE PHILANTHROPIC SCRIPT

*Turning Money to Status and Immortality*

In the review above of some organizational vehicles of philanthropy, I have discussed the less than completely altruistic motives for these endeavors. Critics of American philanthropy have cited a combination of financial self-interest, legitimation of the capitalist system, and perpetuation of dynastic wealth as key motivations for giving. Yet as important as these motivators are, there is a tendency on the part of many critics to sometimes emphasize economic self-interest to the exclusion of the "irrational" or symbolic appeal of charity. Philanthropy, while self-interested, follows the social script of donorship, bringing with it the promise of honor and immortality to the rich as it did in earlier millennia. Further, charity finds a place in upper-class sociability patterns and pressures on the wealthy to conform and compete.

As important as economic and ideological motives are, they are insufficient in capturing completely the motivation of wealthy giving. A sole emphasis on these factors, would, for example, fail to explain why in gross percentage terms giving by the rich and corporations has remained fairly stable over the last three or four decades despite sharp differences in the political climate (the 1960s versus the 1990s, for example) and substantial changes in tax laws over this time.[44] The reason is that many of the actions taken by the wealthy are not strictly rational. For example, the history of large foundations in the US, at least for the first seven decades of this century, was full of odd assortments of missteps, family lawsuits, corruption, and organizational failure so severe that in some cases the foundations never made grants at all or had boards that never met. Waldimer Nielsen notes that otherwise extremely "rational" businessmen simply did not act that way when putting their money into a perpetual trust or charitable forms. Often they failed to consult the usual financial advisors and failed to do research, simply not believing that these decisions had the import of their business dealings. Nielsen reminds us that ". . . the creation of a foundation is a particularly personal, even egotistical act. It tends to be performed either by a person in middle age, riding the crest of financial success or by someone at the end of a long and successful career, faced with death and destiny . . . the usual forms of organizational rationality do not govern the intense and intimate act of creating a foundation. . . ."[45]

Moreover, although the federated-community chest-united way structure came to have many functions for business, the embrace of these forms can be explained only partly as a result of a rational self-interest. Can all companies really justify the large amount of time their executives spend in lengthy meetings for the United Way or other time-consuming nonprofit boards? Perhaps in some cities and with some companies this pays off, but probably many of these activities are not profitable in any quantifiable business terms.

We need to look back at the religious and cultural imperatives that reward the wealthy for donorship and stewardship. As noted earlier, large sums of money create both opportunities and burdens on the superrich. One of the opportunities is to gain power, status, and even immortality from their money in a fashion similar to the lords, monarchs, and clergy of the Medieval era. But as in those days, wealth holds its burdens, including guilt for some people. Others worry about their fortunes being wasted by spendthrift relatives. Most commonly, rich people seek to avoid having their money "eaten up" by government. The social script of philanthropy allows wealth to be ceremonially and publicly displayed while simultaneously protecting the family (or corporate) name and power over the use of the money. As Clifford Marcus notes: "Nonprofits [are] one arena of legitimate and public identity in which otherwise very private fortunes and families can establish an enduring interest. In the form of universities, medical research centers, hospitals, museums, art collections, and the like, the nonprofit sector, protected by tax exemption, is the permanent home of organized old wealth in American society."[46]

Both Carnegie and Rockefeller were not only prescient in a political and social sense, but both became emotionally convinced that their lasting contribution would be through donorship. Early on in Carnegie's career of giving away libraries, he wrote to his wife: "Yes, life is worth living when we call forth such works as this! I saw many people standing gazing and praising and the big words CARNEGIE FREE LIBRARY just took me into the sweetest reverie and I found myself wishing you were at my side to reap with me the highest reward we can ever receive on earth, the voice of one's inner self, saying secretly, well done."[47]

John D. Rockefeller similarly noted that there is only so much one can do with money; nice clothes, the best food, cars, and mansions simply did not eat it all up. But more than this, in his view, a wealthy man's major satisfactions could not come only from owning material goods or enjoying business success, but from "a taste for giving where the money may produce an effect which will be a lasting gratification," assuming such giving was done in the proper way.[48]

Just as donated basilicas and cathedrals, elaborate stained glass windows, and statuary reflected the pride, power, and hoped-for immortality of elites of earlier times, the names Carnegie and Rockefeller evoke now, a century later, their public giving: Rockefeller Center, Rockefeller University, Rockefeller Foundation, Carnegie-Mellon University, the Carnegie Corporation, the Carnegie Institute. Perhaps to a majority of schoolchildren if not the adult public, these names evoke only status, education, and public importance, not the image of wealthy businessmen.

The focus on donorship as power and as Christian duty continues to be a major script today in many (though, of course, not all) moneyed families, as evidenced by studies of the wealthy done by Theresa Odendahl and Francine Ostrower in the 1980s and 1990s. One donor told Odendahl frankly that his giving was motivated by the thought that, "I want the sons of bitches to know who I was." More subtly, other of Odendahl subjects saw philanthropy as a mark of refinement, indicating that their family was of "old" wealth and could afford to give up some money and forgo some ostentation for the obligation of not only donorship but for board membership, charity events, and other nonprofit work which usually comes with donorship. Just as giving was the noblesse oblige of Medieval times, giving today becomes (in the words of Paul DiMaggio and Michael Useem), "a ritual of class solidarity."[49] A prominent dinner table at a benefit for the Metropolitan Museum of Art or Lincoln Center symbolizes that you have arrived, but better yet, a dedicated wing at the museum or at the symphony hall suggests the family name will remain into posterity.

As with other forms of ritual and social script, the imputation of power, pride, religiosity, or altruism is complicated by pure rote conformity. One donor told Ostrower that being on a nonprofit board was a mandatory "accoutrement." He said, "I am a trustee of a hospital. You *have* to be a trustee of a hospital if you're wealthy. It's required. . . . But I know nothing about hospitals."[50] Another millionaire told Odendahl, "We pretty much give to the same things, the safe things. . . . It's a club. What is the phone company giving? What is the bank giving? And everybody else falls into line, in proportion."[51]

The charitable script then is about more than self-interest and legitimation. As power was symbiotically held in Medieval times by feudal lords and the church, today for the truly wealthy, charitable work is part of the exercising of power as well as an obligation deeply embedded in their religious or secular moral principles. The hope that future generations will remember the family (or corporation) name as a force for good instead of money hoarding or evil deeds lies behind many gifts and campaigns.

### The Substitution of Means for Ends

Viewing philanthropy as occurring within this highly idealized realm helps explain why American charity is so often irrelevant to the needs of its recipients, or as recounted in chapters 1 and 2, even hostile to the interests of the poor or disenfranchised. Critics of reliance on philanthropy have generally stressed two issues: one, that charity is insufficient to meet the social welfare needs of the American people compared to more widespread public provision, and second, that American charity has helped legitimize a highly individualist, anemic welfare state as opposed to more advanced European social welfare systems. Both of these critiques are supported by this work, but I suggest that as true as these points are, they are insufficient as a critique of charity as a cultural enterprise.

As noted earlier, charitable work is enshrined in a donor-focused realm essentially concerned with sentiment, not improving social reality. The famous phrase "beggars can't be choosers" is an important cultural truth; as we saw in chapter 1 with the Indian experience and in chapter 2 with the treatment of the poor throughout American history, recipients have often not been consulted by the givers. For while public entitlement—whether for a motor vehicle or fishing license or for a Social Security or veteran's benefit check—can be contested and fought for as rights, voluntary aid is just that. If it is unsuitable or irrelevant, if it is harmful, well, after all, "beggars can't be choosers." This is why the used tuxedos and evening gowns sent to Indian reservations are a startling but apt example of how little utility or rationality has to do with philanthropy. Charity gives donors opportunities for redemption, coping with guilt, and showing off. Once the latest campaign is over, concern with the issue at hand often fades. In the example of the campaigns to "help" the Indians, when the clothes were rejected as condescending, other goods were sent, and finally the issue of the reservations themselves simply faded to other causes. The wealthy in the East who organized aid to the Indians did not mean ill, but they had little knowledge of or interest in Indian culture much less an inkling of their desire for independence.

Today's charitable industry, in contrast to its earlier history, certainly practices seeking community input and often includes (sometimes tokenistically) some actual recipients of social services on their boards. Yet it often still fails to respond at the level of deeper, structural concerns. When homelessness arose as a major issue in the late 1970s and 1980s, for example, it was defined primarily by social service, mental health, and church and voluntary leaders as an issue of sympathy and help. Then a whole new industry was created: shelters and soup kitchens; mental health and substance abuse counseling aimed specifically at street people; and "Hands Across America" rallies, and Second Harvest food collections. The result of this well-intended philanthropic sentiment is to a large extent as Dickensian as the nineteenth century: the homeless are given bread and some soup, a cot, and some slips of paper with potential job referrals. Of course, advocates and movements among the homeless themselves as well as a number of radical critics have raised more structural issues: deindustrialization and the need for good jobs, the housing crisis, the need to restore and improve social benefits, and so on. But none of these issues are very amenable to charitable intervention. It is not only that the issues are too big for the private sector (even the largest churches or charities can't build affordable housing), they also require a different set of means and ends than that of charity.

Philanthropic endeavors are aimed at *process*, not social or economic accomplishment. Even when charitable workers and volunteers agree with a more structural interpretation of homelessness and poverty, for example, they are less interested in social movements or political changes that could help end poverty than in the process of charity.[52] What they become expert at is raising money, publicizing and advertising a cause, setting up committees, boards, and task forces, and planning speeches and praises to their own goodwill. Some of these skills are excellent to have, but they are not relevant to all problems. As Mark Twain said, "If a person owns only a hammer, he tends to see all objects as nails." This obsession with fundraising and committee meeting suggests to this writer that it is the *symbolism* of helping that appeals to many people rather than any actual accomplishment. So, for example, ending homelessness would require massive social and economic changes, not continued shelterization.[53] But accomplishing this would require a strong social movement or at minimum a large-scale political mobilization that charity leaders, service workers, and volunteers have little interest nor expertise in. Hence, although ten other soup kitchens may exist in a neighborhood, often planners and committee members assemble again to start another one — perhaps this one will have fresher food or be open longer. A consumerist mentality develops in the nonprofit world as well as in business; if we collect more money, how do we expand the kitchen? Can we serve kosher or vegetarian food? There would be nothing wrong in this if all the money in the world were available or if soup kitchens actually related to the real problems underlying homelessness. Instead, simple expansion, even enjoyment, of the planning and process of fundraising replaces the original idealistic goals that brought many originally into social service work.[54]

If charity pleases its recipients, of course, the givers are happy. It is also true that if enough protest or antagonism is raised as a

result of insensitive gift-giving or sympathy seeking, givers sometimes will respond and change the process a bit. Whether it be
scandal (for example, the United Way of America) or actual rejection (one thinks of the protests against Jerry Lewis' telethon and
his "kids" by disability rights activists), charity can become controversial. Mostly though, charity is a ritual, unconcerned with its effects and almost never examined.

## Accepting the Gift

Finally, I need to briefly return to the issue of the public's view of
wealthy philanthropy since I noted that at several points in American history, businessmen and corporate elites were viewed more
negatively than today. Theresa Odendahl is correct when she
stresses the legitimation that giving brings, and the fascination that
the poorer have with the acts of the rich: "Fundamentally, the ideology of the elite . . . depends on this perception of the middle
and working classes—that the wealthy deserve their status. Conversely, the belief of the mass of citizens that a special minority
must have special authority depends on the elite maintaining a pos-
ture of noblesse oblige. The complementary ideologies help explain the perennial fascination with wealth and the wealthy that is
so notable a part of the attitude of the American people."[55]

Yet it is possible to overstate the legitimacy argument and the
reciprocity of the rich and poor. There are urgent material reasons
for poor people to accept crumbs from the rich. Even in the heyday
of anticorporate sentiment in the 1900s and 1910s, most cities and
towns accepted Carnegie's libraries, and most churches, charities,
and universities accepted Rockefeller's money. Again in the Depression and at the height of the 1960s unrest, few organizations or
political groups "looked gift horses in the mouth." The reality is
that it is not necessarily ideology or politics that determines
whether to accept a gift. Rather under capitalism, money rules and
few have the luxury of refusing it.

A very small minority of people in capitalist society make decisions about money based on pure principle, and they probably
were only slightly more numerous in 1900 or 1935 than they are
today. Many poor people understand that philanthropic funds

come to social agencies with strings attached and hidden motives. And, academics, researchers, and other middle-class professionals also have critical thoughts about foundations, institutes, and other funding sources. Yet, neither the poor nor upper-middle-class person refuses offers of grants very often.

This is not to minimize the principled agency some people or groups can have, such as when Washington Gladden attacked "tainted money" or the Wheeling workers rejected Carnegie's donation. However, what I am saying is that these are rare instances, and we should not conversely take acceptance of money as full legitimation either. At times the donee can come around and "bite the hand" that feeds. For many groups of people, particularly those near the bottom of society, there isn't much choice about taking money. The alternative may be simply starving. After all, a panhandler really doesn't legitimate the person who hands over a dime. At the bottom of society, the sources of funds may all seem equally evil or perhaps equally benevolent.

Further, most people understand that there are sanctions for those who refuse money and act out of pride or political motivation. The benevolence of charity does not like rejection. Turning it away, too noticeably anyway, challenges the idealized realm of giving. Reminding donors that there are actual *subjects* upon whom their charity is bestowed creates severe problems for the charitable script.[56]

# 5—The Sanctified Sector: The "Nonprofit"

*If there was not a nonprofit community out there . . . I do not think we would still be a democratic country. This may be exaggerated, but the public demand for the government to do this, that, and the other would be [so great]. . . . We would probably be a huge big government doing all these things—Socialistic!*

A businessman quoted in the book *Charity Begins at Home*[1]

*The question is, who do you want to put your trust in: an agency replete with champagne fund-raisers, political deal making, and its own bulging belly to fill, or a mother who is directly responsible for feeding, clothing, sheltering, acculturating, and, yes, entertaining her children?*

Former welfare mother and welfare rights organizer Theresa Funiciello[2]

## AN AMERICAN LOVE AFFAIR

There is little question that the oft-quoted Alexis de Tocqueville was right about America being (then and now) unique in its vast proliferation of voluntary organizations and institutions. Politicians, of course, have frequently pointed to the existence of the charitable sector to argue against governmental programs. As President Franklin Pierce warned in his famous 1854 speech vetoing a proposal by Dorothea Dix to set aside federal land for mental hospitals, "[If] Congress is to make provision for such objects [of charity], the fountains of charity will be dried up at home."[3] Indeed, in an example of a self-fulfilling prophecy nearly a century-and-a-half later, polls suggest Americans think private charity does a better job at helping people than do government programs.[4]

The contrast between government and the private voluntary sector is not only misleading because, as I shall discuss, the latter is now greatly funded directly and indirectly by the former. It is also unfair because it compares a sacred sphere with a profane one. As we have seen, the origin and deeply embedded symbolism of the nonprofit institution have Christianity and thousands of years of history standing behind them. To retain their mythical sacred status, the institutions of the nonprofit sector—described in the literature as the "independent sector" or the "third sector"—actually must obscure their almost complete reliance on government on the one hand, and their resemblance to the profit-making sector on the other. Descriptors like "independent sector" involve a kind of logical jujitsu, since institutions that fall between business and government often *do* make large surpluses *and* cost taxpayers considerable money as well.

It is true that the popularity of the sanctified sector may be in part a result of the historic antipathy of Americans for big government. But it could also be argued that the enormous appeal (particularly since the 1960s) of adding the prefix "non" to "profit" may also reflect suspicions of the profit-making sector or capitalism in general. Both of these strands play a role in the vast expansion of nonprofit organizations, but neither is as central as the popularity of ritualized action which combines sanctified heroism with fun and entertainment. "Doing charity" arguably is another American quest for self-fulfillment, and one which—unlike self-help groups or astrology, collecting sports memorabilia, or other pursuits—sparks little complaint from family, friends, or teachers. One can do almost anything in the US as long as it is *for* charity: play golf, listen to rock 'n roll, climb a mountain, run for miles, jump from a plane. After such rituals are over, whether it is a charity walk in one's community or a huge music benefit like Farm Aid or Live Aid, few people concern themselves about what was actually done with the money collected. This seems almost besides the point. The following sample of March of Dimes events across America in the late 1950s reflects to what degree daily life's more pleasurable attractions—heroic athletics and sports, amusements, fashion, salesmanship, and entertainment—are embedded in the charitable pursuit: "Skindivers cut a hole in the ice at Gardner, Massachusetts, and dove for contributions thrown from the shore. Temperature: two below zero. Hot rod races at Helena, Montana, raised

$1,500; the tenth annual March of Dimes spaghetti dinner raised $2,864 in Cleveland; a corn sale brought almost $1,000 in Carver County, Minnesota; a radio auction netted $1,207 in Puyallup, Washington; an outdoor auction raised $1,250 in Payette County, Idaho; a balloon sale netted $4,556 in Abilene, Texas; a Chicago fat man sat on an oversized apothecary scale until 77,200 dimes balanced his weight; a New York disc jockey stayed awake for two hundred hours; a St. Louis telethon brought in $100,000, and one in Broome County, New York attracted $11,784; it cost $150-a-table to attend a fashion show in Midland, Texas; Pittsburgh raised $4,800 with a teen fashion show, and Denver pocketed over $25,000 with its annual fashion show, one of the big social events of the local season; thousands of dollars were raised with 'airlifts'— airplane rides at a penny-a-pound."[5]

Unlike politics, which many people consider "dirty" and boring, and unlike business, whose motives are suspect, even when its products are not, raising and giving money to nonprofits appears to be both fun and self-fulfilling insofar as these activities combine sincerity with plain old amusement. Charitable ventures also provide a noble image of equality. Major sports and entertainment figures often volunteer their time in a high-profile way, and the rich may attend and sponsor charity balls and benefits. But, as shown in the example above, everyone can support charity because the ideology of charity rests on the notion of every penny counting, and each person giving what they can (and achieving acclaim in proportion to their means). In a sense, to compare the mythology of charity to government is like asking Americans whether they wish to watch "Seinfeld" or a political debate of gubernatorial candidates on television. Except at times such as war or similar public mobilizations (and possibly sexual scandals), government activity is simply just less compelling to Americans than charity.

## THE REALITY BEHIND THE ILLUSION

While most people associate the words charity and nonprofit with providing social services, these activities constitute only a small portion of nonprofit giving. "Nonprofit" is a legal status; it does not mean that the organization does not accrue a financial surplus. While most people conjure up a noble image of nonprofit institutions, the public might regard many of them as being quite self-serving. In addition to the thousands of educational, health care, arts and cultural, religious, research, civic, and membership organizations in the nonprofit world, one finds, for example, the Best Western Hotels International (an association of hotel owners), the Christian Broadcasting Network (CBN), CNN's C-Span network, the Educational Testing Service (ETS) that administers the Scholastic Aptitude Test and Graduate Record Exams, the National Collegiate Athletic Association (NCAA), even defense contractors like the Mitre Corporation in Massachusetts.[6] In fact, nonprofits own a trillion dollars in assets and account for 10 percent of America's gross domestic product. They have grown four times faster than the overall US economy since 1970, and now employ one in nine Americans.[7] In the Northeast the top one hundred nonprofits employ more people than the top hundred leading private companies, in Atlanta their expenditures are four times larger than those of the city and in San Francisco they are twice as much as the municipal budget.[8] Nor does it take much to be a nonprofit (the IRS approves over 95 percent of those that apply). Many people are ignorant of what a nonprofit organization is. While a for-profit business is defined as an entity whose surpluses are either kept by a private owner or distributed to stockholders through dividends, a nonprofit entity not only may make a "profit" as commonly understood, but, as a *Philadelphia Inquirer* study in 1990 found, major nonprofits that year had a 9 percent average surplus, far higher than Fortune 500 companies.[9] Another study looked at two different years of IRS returns during the 1980s and found that (respectively in the two years) 85 percent and 86 percent of nonprofits ran fund surpluses which ranged from 2.7 to 3.4 million dollars on average per organization for each of the years.[10]

How is this possible? The law requires only that nonprofits follow the "nondistribution principle," that is, that no individual takes the surplus as "profit." However, there are many other ways to dispose of surpluses. Of course, a great deal of money is saved as a hedge against hard times and goes directly into investment port-

folios, endowments, or bank accounts. Most major nonprofits—
from hospitals to universities to big health charities like the Red
Cross to the American Cancer Society—have large endowments
and investment portfolios. In major cities of the nation, the greatest
landlords are even nonprofits. In New York City, for example, the
Catholic Church is the biggest landowner in Manhattan, followed
by Columbia University, and then by the huge hospital/health care
enterprises. Large nonprofits commonly own fleets of cars, purchase luxury hotel accommodations, pay for expensive flights for
its officials—flights on the Concorde figured in the United Way of
America scandal—and provide princely salaries and golden para-
chutes to its executives. The widely-publicized scandal surround-
ing William Aramony of the United Way of America differs only in
degree, as pay and benefits for nonprofit executives generally mirrors the corporate world.

But fund surpluses may well go for other uses. Most boards of
directors of the largest organizations are composed of business executives, many of whom sit on multiple boards. Nonprofit expert
Bertram Weisbord, hardly a radical observer, notes:

> When men or women who are associated with private firms sit on board
> of directors of nonprofits, they can and often do see to it that the orga-
> nization purchases services from the proprietary firms they represent.
> When nonprofit and proprietary organizations are controlled by the
> same people, inputs that are used jointly by the two organizations can be
> accounted for in ways that load costs onto the taxed firm and revenues
> onto the nonprofit, thus permitting higher aggregate salaries to be paid,
> at the expense of tax collections.[11]

In simple cases of "self-dealing," a banker on the board of directors gets the organization to take out its loans and keep its money in
his or her bank, the real estate developer builds or improves the
charity's buildings, the auto executive handles its fleet, the phar-
maceutical supplier gets the hospital business, and the computer
company executive sells the university its new computers. Little
here is illegal unless restraint of trade can be shown, which is unlikely since the FTC rarely polices the nonprofits. A more complex
form of "self-dealing" that Weisbord refers to in the second part of
the quote above, and which is becoming increasingly common, is

for-profit subsidiary spinoffs of nonprofits. A majority of the large nonprofits now have for-profit subsidiaries that make money in unrelated areas. Under pressure from Congress and small business, the IRS does tax what it calls "unrelated business income" (UBI). The standard of the UBI itself is actually quite generous, since if one can show the profit had anything to do with the *usual* business of the tax exempt organization, one doesn't have to pay taxes. A university or hospital making money from its cafeterias, bookstores, or fitness centers will generally find that these profits are tax exempt. But, as they make more lucrative sums from scientific patents and computer software, for example, the IRS may tax these profits. Among the difficulties with this system is the opportunity to move money around to avoid taxation while maximizing profits and minimizing adherence to regulations. For example, Pat Robertson's nonprofit Christian Broadcasting Network (CBN) launched the Family Channel, which paid off handsomely to the tune of $211 million in 1995. Although the Family Channel did have to pay taxes under the UBI clause, Congress and the IRS have investigated how monies are moved back and forth between Robertson's profit and nonprofit entities.[12]

Perhaps the reader will view all this as being uncharacteristic of the local charity they know and contribute to. It is true that the word nonprofit covers a multitude of types and sizes of organizations. Just as the ideology of free enterprise and capitalism rests on the image of the corner grocery store and small auto repair business as emblematic of the free market, rather than on the image of Exxon or Philip Morris, the ideology of "charity" is meant to conjure up in people's minds the small neighborhood church with its basement bazaar, the local homeless shelter, or a volunteer friendly-visitor-to-the-elderly program. The difficulty with this outdated image—as with the image of the free market—is that the small local charity with no ties to a major national organization is becoming less and less common, just as Wal-Mart or Home Depot are replacing many local small businesses.

The "diversity" and "pluralism" of American voluntarism so often touted is also more mythical than real. First, many people are unaware, because of the multiplicity of agency names and the complex labyrinthine nature of our fragmented human services system, that the organization they are giving to or even are a client of is affiliated with a broader organization such as the Federation of Protestant Welfare Agencies, Catholic Charities, or the Jewish Philanthropies. Secondly, funding contracts by government with nonprofits and allocations from sources such as the United Way require not only organizational and financial stability, but demand that agencies meet certain uniform standards in everything from their level of professional staff to methods of fundraising. Contracts from government or annual funding allocations from the United Way have come to be seen as guaranteed income by the largest human service agencies. As a number of experts point out, there is a great deal of rhetoric in the United Way about how important the process of "planning" and "allocations" is. These are often the most prestigious committees of local united ways. The irony is, though, that each year the United Ways continue to give most of their money to the mainstay "established" organizations: the Red Cross, the YMCA and YWCA, the Girl and Boy Scouts, the Salvation Army, the family service agencies affiliated with the Family Service Association of America, and Catholic Charities.[13] The myth of diversity and the complex skills needed to assess social agencies become a bit less arcane when one realizes that the same agencies over and over will receive funds.

To be fair, loss of a government contract or a reduction in United Way allocation could force some of these agencies to cut their services. Because of the commitment of both the United Ways and most governments to the survival of noncontroversial agencies, the "regulars" get money while new or more innovative organizations are forced to the rear of the funding line. But my key point is that the big nonprofit agencies receive a huge amount of funding, which is simply not evenly distributed. As Funiciello points out, New York City's total contracts with its private human service sector were above the federal share of Aid to Families with Dependent Children (AFDC) in the early 1990s, and 90 percent of such funds went to only one-fifth of New York's agencies.[14] The "mega-charities" as she calls them center comfortably on or near Park Avenue (not exactly where poor people live) and include Catholic

Charities, the Federation of Protestant Welfare Agencies, the Jewish Philanthropies/United Jewish Appeal, the Community Service Society, and the Childrens Aid Society.

An organizational life cycle study of the nonprofit world would, I believe, find a similar pattern to that of the life cycle of small businesses. Many small nonprofits are founded annually, particularly since the explosion in public contracting to the private nonprofit sector began in the 1960s. The IRS approved 40,276 applications in 1994 for tax exemption, mostly from the religious and charitable sectors.[15] And, of course, among these are many small, low-budget agencies such as shelters for battered women, centers for teens, and soup kitchens for the homeless. Each year, however, a large number of them close down: for example between 1987 and 1989, 40,762 tax exempt organizations folded.[16] Like small businesses that find themselves unprofitable due to competition, lack of a viable product, or pressure to merge or be acquired, a large number of nonprofits fade from existence in a fairly short time. A close look at the most long established agencies, even so-called "grassroots" ones like settlement houses or community centers, will find that either the organizations are under the umbrella of a broader national group or have moved to finance themselves through fees and business subsidiaries rather than private donations. Occasionally, we might find a shelter or community center reliant primarily on public funds, but the politics of the new "contract state" mitigate against this. In part due to government cutbacks but also to a great extent because of the unstable partisan nature of service funding at all levels of government, few organizations rely on the largesse of city hall, the state house, or even the White House and Congress as their main source of funds.[17] Rather, the main source of nonprofit funding now is *neither* private donations *nor* direct public grants, but *fees for service*; either through health insurance (Blue Cross–Blue Shield and other private insurers, Medicaid, and Medicare), per capita government fees (such as for children in foster care or group homes), or through actual fees-for-service paid by the consumer (costs to attend entertainment events, private pay for psychiatric counseling or drug treatment, tuition for nonprofit schools and universities).[18]

Lester Salamon, an expert on nonprofits, fears that the fate of charities may parallel the history of nonprofit hospitals. Way back in the first decades of the century the nonprofit hospital was a small, local community institution. Its doctors often knew their patients personally, and hospital trustees made decisions (often on a case-by-case personal basis) about admitting charity cases.[19] Today the big nonprofits — like Massachusetts General or Columbia–Mount Sinai Medical Center — are no more characterized by these personal relationships than the large for-profit health chains like Humana. Salamon fears that all nonprofits may be following the lead of the hospital in undergoing a comparable "transformation involv[ing] a switch from small community institutions to large bureaucratic organizations staffed by professionals, supported by fees, [and] oriented to paying customers." Cautiously he wonders "whether other segments of the nonprofit sector will join hospitals in becoming 'once charitable enterprises,'" and admits that "the pressures in that direction are unmistakable."[20]

## THE GENTRIFIED Y

Although no one organization can capture all the variations within the sanctified sector that span huge chasms of size, bureaucracy, and wealth, the transformation of the YMCA from a nineteenth-century evangelical organization into a provider of health fitness for the affluent (or as one businessman put it, "The Yuppie Men's Cash Association")[21] highlights two salient issues in American social welfare policy: Who should benefit from public money, and what do we mean by "charity" or "need"?

As noted in chapter 2, the YMCA was founded in the 1850s in England and later America as an evangelical Protestant men's organization to socialize predominantly middle-class employees who were new to urban areas, thus protecting them from intemperance and the irreligious mob. Like other nineteenth-century organizations that survived into modern times — for example, the Girl and Boy Scouts — the genius of the Y was its eventual secularization, and its switch from imposing character reform through Bible classes and moral lectures to a health and fitness program, educational, and club focus. Sociologists Meyer Zald and Patricia Denton note that the Y developed an "enrollment economy" run through locally autonomous chapters, which paralleled the capitalist economy. If the public wanted swim classes, they got them; if they wanted outdoor clubs, they got them.[22] Not surprisingly, by the mid-twentieth century paying customers got preference at most Ys. When government and critical social welfare experts attacked charities in the early years of the War on Poverty for not serving the poor or inner-city residents, the Y along with a large number of other nineteenth-century moralistic charities-now-turned-enterprises were among their targets.[23]

The Y's transformation began before government contracting of public services, the rise of the health and wellness craze, and the privatization of much of the social welfare sector. But, critics in the 1960s would not have expected that only two decades later many Ys would often abandon providing the few services, such as lodging, which previously were associated with lower-status consumers (the popular Village People song about "staying at the YMCA" notwithstanding!). In Philadelphia in 1985, for example, the Y sold off its residence hall for $13 million to a large commercial developer, evicting the hall's three hundred residents. According to the president of the Philadelphia Y: "The sale will allow the . . . YMCA to get out of the shelter business and to pour millions of dollars into renovation of the Central Branch's athletic and office space. . . . Renting rooms is no longer part of the Y mission. Our emphasis today is health enhancement."[24]

Similarly, in Dallas, Texas, the Y withdrew from an older facility and redirected its resources toward higher-income neighborhoods as it sought to attract "a predominantly white, middle- and upper-class clientele."[25] In Washington, D.C., a magazine article reported that 80 percent of the Y's members there were in the highest income brackets, one-third of them lawyers. Not surprisingly, the D.C. 'Y' offers, in addition to the most fancy and up-to-date health equipment, financial planning classes with topics such as "Our Changing Tax Laws," "Building your Estate," and "Preserving Assets."[26]

Of course, lawyers have the right to play raquetball and accountants to lift barbells, but the broader issue is why they need public support to do so. Because nonprofits are exempt from all federal, state, and local taxes, they are subsidized institutions; further, they also receive many public grants and subsidized loans. When the Y in Washington, D.C. sold its building for $5 million, it paid no taxes on its gains, and when it subsequently raised another $700,000, this sum was also untaxed. The Los Angeles Y received a $1.5 million federal grant and a $3 million federally guaranteed low-interest loan for investments in new equipment. In Baltimore, the Y financed its growth with a $480,000 HUD grant, a half million dollar revenue bond from the city, and an additional $1 million in federal funds. But even when the Ys don't receive special grants, for-profit physical fitness centers complain of unfair competition since the Ys can offer lower membership fees because they pay no taxes, have lower postal rates, often enjoy free advertising, and even are exempt from many government regulations. Indeed, a survey of eighteen metropolitan-area Ys revealed that "YMCAs and [private] health spas provide essentially the same services, at approximately the same costs, through similar promotional vehicles," yet the Y is tax exempt while other health clubs are not.[27]

Lest the Y be seen as idiosyncratic, direct public funds as well as indirect subsidies (tax exemptions, for example) go to major nonprofits for all sorts of luxuries: travel and fine dining for executives, champagne and lobster fundraisers, new gyms for universities and hospitals, glossy mailings for self-promotion, expensive lounges, restaurants, and even getaway lodges for physicians and other highly paid employees. Nonprofit entities have built stadiums in many cities, later turning them into profitable ventures. New facilities in many nonprofits are striking: the new Methodist Hospital in Houston has valet parking, marble foyers, and gourmet meals; the Freedom Forum, a nonprofit foundation based in Arlington, Virginia, has a new $15 million building with $1 million worth of artwork; the new AARP (American Association of Retired Persons) building has been dubbed the "Taj Mahal" of Washington, D.C. for its fancy turrets and a fortune spent on furniture.[28]

The second interesting thing that the new Y exemplifies beyond its use of tax money to support the affluent is its stated belief that all recreation, health and wellness, and other related activities are in fact "charitable." One of the cultural and ideological trends that sustain the sanctified sector is equating the needs of the middle class (or even upper middle class) with those who are truly needy. The Los Angeles Y's director responded to criticism of the public subsidizing their affluent clientele by saying, "In my opinion, 100 percent of what we do is charitable. The definition of charity under which we operate is improving the wellness of the community."[29] This director likely believes what he is saying and not just practicing good public relations.

While the trend toward affluent and middle-class narcissism and self-involvement, often at the expense of the poor and disadvantaged in the United States, is usually associated with the 1970s and 1980s, three social scientists studying community chests in 1957 suggested how the linguistic style of American charity had already confused the concept of need:

> The use of "need" also permits the blurring of a distinction that has been of considerable importance in the history of the Western world . . . this is the distinction between rendering aid (especially in cases of acute and obvious distress . . . ) and striving to make people better or happier. The word "need" is associated with such words as "the needy" and "necessitous" which have historic association with the most deprived and disadvantaged elements in any community at a given time and place. When the word is extended in meaning so that the children whose parents are in the top half of the community's income pyramid "need" a camp, the community "needs" a symphony orchestra, and the town's leadership "needs" to be made to understand about poliomyelitis or coronary occlusions, quite obviously there is some hoped-for carryover of meaning from one usage to the other, and some serious attendant confusion . . . the users of the "need" vocabulary frequently seek refuge in a shift from the "needs" of the ultimate beneficiaries to the "needs of the agencies". . . . The concept is . . . vague as to meaning . . .[30]

This linguistic sleight-of-hand is an important tactic of the nonprofit sector. Among other things, it obscures what was ostensibly the mission of these organizations and the justification for tax exemption: that charity was aiding some group which needed help and could not afford to pay for it. Hospitals, clinics, family service agencies, and other charities were given advantages by the public that were not given to private auto companies or grocery stores on this basis.

Of course, I am not saying that all services should be private or taxed; on the contrary, the public sector—as in other nations—could make universal benefits available to all its citizens. Most European countries provide not only social welfare benefits such as health care but also many other services such as recreation and entertainment which are openly government sponsored and available to all. The difference is, this is a social and political decision made to provide such services in a more egalitarian fashion. In the US, however, since government policies which lead to the subsidization of organizations like the Y are hidden from view through public ignorance and an ideology of sanctity, it is unlikely that lower-class joggers will demand the same quality of running tracks the affluent enjoy.

## THE HIGH COST
### OF HAVING A SANCTIFIED SECTOR

Ultimately there would be nothing wrong with having hundreds of thousands of nonprofit organizations, some of which obviously do good work, if such a social organization did not preclude a more equitable system of social welfare. The most salient issues include: the high financial cost of having a glorious nonprofit sector such as the gentrified Y, since it removes funds which in other nations would be available for public spending; the structural bias of the nonprofit sector, like the YMCA, which tends to favor the middle class and contradict the glorifying rhetoric that ideologically supports charity; and the social policy favoring the proliferation of private organizations, which leads to a fragmented service system and causes considerable confusion and lack of quality service to the many needy groups in our society.

### Public Financing, Private Governance

It can be argued that the American system of providing this much health care, education, social services, and other human services through a nonprofit system comes at the expense of what could be achieved for all citizens through a more vibrant and better funded public sector. Of course, antagonism towards using tax money to help the poor is part of the brief that conservatives use to support "a thousand points of light" while denouncing government spending and organization as bureaucratic, inefficient, and corrupt. Yet, the nonprofit sector as a whole does not advertise itself as an alternative to government. Mostly liberal in political view (certainly this is true of most of the leadership of the social service, arts, health care, and educational sectors), many nonprofit leaders urge higher government spending *and* higher nonprofit support. And some surveys indicate that a large number of people simultaneously support governmental aid and charitable aid.[31] Ironically then, the nonprofit sector comfortably strides the liberal/conservative divide by quietly accepting large sums of government monies as well as indirect subsidies. Theoretically one would expect conservatives to voice some disapproval of giving sums like fifty thousand dollars to a social agency for a per capita payment for one foster child, as an example of government waste. Theoretically, one would expect liberals to argue that government could perform this function far cheaper and better than a large nonprofit, and, perhaps, even that the natural mother of the child might do better than either. Yet such critiques are extremely marginal to our political debate.

Government policy as noted earlier has *always* supported and subsidized private charity in America; as Michael Katz among others stresses, historically they have had a symbiotic relation. Hence, as noted in chapters 1 and 2, the federal government turned over Indian education and social welfare to the churches, and local governments sometimes turned over administration of public funds to private agencies such as happened with mothers' pensions. What is surprising to modern observers is that the New Deal period was (at least as presented in most historical texts) supposed to have changed US policy from the old "laissez-faire" consensus to a new more interventionist state. The New Deal was to have placed major social welfare responsibility onto the public sector, primarily through the Social Security Act (with unemployment insurance, AFDC, and state human service support as well as the provision of pensions for the elderly and disabled). Charity was expected to remain, of course, but to be mostly a service for those who sought particular or specialized auspices (religious schools or services, for example) or to provide services such as counseling and advice, which at the time were a relatively small part of the welfare state and of marginal interest to reformers.

The irony is that between 1935 and the rise of the New Right in the 1970s, liberals themselves gave critical support to the charitable sector, allowing it to grow. Often left out of most accounts of the 1930s is FDR's active support for the tax deduction that charitable organizations were able to achieve from the new higher income taxes, a significant milestone. As we have seen, this was one development that aided the rise of the foundation as a social form. FDR also pioneered personally one of the largest and, criticized at the time as one of the most spendthrift charities, the March of Dimes.[32] Also left out of many social welfare histories is the key role of post–World War II legislation—the GI Bill and the Hill-Burton Act—in subsidizing private and nonprofit education and health care in America by providing huge grants for construction to the latter, and by the former's massive support of veterans at private educational institutions. In the 1960s, liberal legislation again aided the nonprofit sector. The War on Poverty eschewed government income transfers or job programs and began the current approach of contracting funds out to nonprofit community agencies.[33] The development of Medicare and Medicaid as a consumer voucher to fund primarily private or nonprofit providers also caused a dramatic surge in private and nonprofit health care institutions and practitioners.

Only beginning in the 1970s did the movement to reduce government spending through the use of private parties come to be associated with budget cutting in the public sector. Words like "privatization" and "contracting out" entered the lexicon of social welfare discussions for the first time.[34] The chief result of these developments—which link, in some ways, the liberal Great Society and the conservative Reagan/Bush years—is that services once assumed by most people to be government responsibilities now have become private. Even prisons and correctional institutions, in-patient mental health care, much physical health care, and now even welfare initiatives ("welfare to work") are fodder for private, for-profit businesses. Although partisan disputes have occurred over privatization, little dispute has occurred over contracting out large segments of public work to nonprofits.

While certainly liberals have sometimes objected to making a city hospital or a prison "private," the same groups seem to have little problem with the government reimbursing major nonprofit providers or with contracting out to private or nonprofit providers. To take an example, since American health care works on a fee-for-service system, it is a bit hard to see why reimbursing Columbia Presbyterian Hospital (a nonprofit) at $450 a night per patient for a bed is so different from providing this same money to Humana Inc. or the Hospital Corporation of America (for-profit services) for similar services. Or to take prisons, more and more services even in ostensibly public prisons are being contracted out to both private for-profit and nonprofit agencies; for example, a profit-making company takes the laundry service, while a nonprofit provides health care or counseling.[35]

Because of state and local efforts at privatization and contracting out, not only do more for-profit companies engage in human service work, but more work previously done by government has been farmed out to the nonprofit sector. Contrary to the mythmakers of the "independent sector," we now have a system in which large parts of the nonprofit world are not independent at all, but governmentally financed. Lester Salamon has estimated that 61 percent of government human service funding is now through the private, nonprofit sector.[36] Of the many agencies Americans associate with charity, a majority are government financed: Volunteers of America is 96 percent, United Cerebral Palsy (UCP) 80 percent, CARE 78 percent, Catholic Charities 65 percent, and Save the Children 60 percent.[37] A late-1980s United Way survey found that expenditures in the following types of nonprofit agencies were from government: 52 percent of day care, 64 percent of drug abuse clinics, 59 percent of legal aid, 65 percent of mental health, 71 percent of social welfare planning, 68 percent of mentally retarded services, 51 percent of settlement housing and neighborhood centers,

56 percent of Urban League affiliates, and 51 percent of women's crisis agencies.[38] Of course not all parts of the nonprofit world receive such dramatic support. Religious organizations (as opposed to agencies founded by religious groups but which now provide services) are not governmentally funded at all, and arts and cultural organizations have seen a steep decline in government money.

The key question raised by all this is, why is the government investing such huge sums of money into services being run by private parties? As of its latest complete estimates (1992), the nonprofit sector had annual revenues of well over $500 billion a year, approximately equal to the gross domestic product of Canada, and more than the nations of China, Brazil, and Spain.[39] Using a combination of the official *Nonprofit Almanac's* estimate of direct government subsidies in 1992 ($160 billion out of $508 billion as of their latest figures from 1992) and adding in a range of indirect subsidies that include tax exemptions for contributions on a federal, state, and local level; exemption from local property taxes, and from federal and state corporate taxes these organizations would pay if they were not considered nonprofit, I arrive at a range of subsidy that is likely in the area of $220 to $250 billion.[40] This itself does not track other indirect subsidies to the nonprofits such as exemption from sales tax, reduced postal rates, freedom from antitrust, copyright, and some employee benefit laws, immunity from some tort liabilities, preference in receiving some government contracts and grants, and free time and space for advertising.

This means in lay terms that you, the taxpayer, are footing a bill for nonprofit providers that would be enough to more than *double* all federal spending on income security (excluding Social Security). In other words, if we simply asked the nonprofit sector to support itself on private donations or fees alone, we could at least double our public provision of income annually to the needy through programs such as unemployment insurance, supplemental security income, food stamps, welfare programs, and so on.[41]

Of course these figures are based on the assumption that taxation would not change private revenues, contributions, and other finances of the nonprofit world, which is clearly unrealistic because these tax exemptions are critical not only to private givers but to the very existence of nonprofit agencies. A second set of issues is whether the services delivered by the nonprofits are already so sacrosanct that they would have to be provided in any event. It is untenable politically to imagine withdrawing public support from elite nonprofit universities, art museums, or symphonies of the nation to spend it on other purposes. The point to be made here, however, is that it is American *government policy* to support nonprofits in combination with their historic tendency to provide therapeutic services rather than income support, even in the human service sector, that helps explain our nation's weak commitment to giving material resources to its citizens. Our nation is committed to a set of institutions that range from elite nonprofits (museums, symphonies) to human service institutions that produce mostly counseling and support services (see below). This policy decision lies undebated as politicians often intone that there is no money for programs to provide material aid to poor or working-class people.

Cities across the country have begun to reevaluate nonprofits' exemption from property and sales taxes; and in this period of government fiscal stringency some municipalities and other political units have managed to negotiate service fees from nonprofits to replace a small percentage of revenues lost. Revenue losses resulting from nonprofit tax exemption are considerable. For example, 39 percent of Pittsburgh's tax base and 40 percent of Syracuse's is exempt. In New York City, a city council proposal sought to remove all tax exemptions given to "elite nonprofit institutions" defined as organizations with executives earning more than $130,000 annually. It did not pass.[42]

It would also be unrealistic and not necessarily desirable, of course, for no nonprofit sector to exist. To this author, there seems to be a stronger justification for nonprofits in the areas of religion and arts and culture than, for example, in any necessity to have a nonprofit health care or social service sector. The key question is, what assumptions we are to make about the so-called independent sector. If we look beyond the ideological haze, what we are doing is taking tax money and simply giving it to, for example, the YMCA or CARE. A great deal of public accountability is sacrificed and given over to a private board of directors and appointed executives. Amazingly, many people seem to believe that the Y, CARE, Catholic Charities, and the Salvation Army spend the public's money more wisely than local, state, or federal officials. This essentially means that the public is trusting businesspeople, highly paid executives, and boards of directors to do what is best for all citizens. Although referring to what was then "federated giving," John R. Seeley et al.'s critical view of charity in 1957 is still worth quoting: "One suspects, [there is] only one major difference between private and public philanthropy—at least nominally [the public sector] is under the control of the voter as donor-taxpayer, while the administration of private philanthropy . . . [is] largely under the control of a small elite group. Thus the difference . . . is essentially very nearly between taxation with representation and without. . . ."[43]

As we will return to in chapter 6, this simple and correct generalization is complicated for many by the fact that, unlike in 1957, now many nonprofits are perceived to be "progressive" in politics or considered by some to be sanctified because of their social movement origins. Hence some who may criticize the Y, CARE, and Catholic Charities would be angered if tax exemptions for health centers for women or AIDS service organizations were abandoned.

## The Middle-Class Beneficiaries of Charity

As my examination of the YMCA showed, many services the nonprofit sector provides are not to the poor but to middle income people. Of course, this fact shouldn't cause us much surprise given some of the nonprofit world's domains. Funding for the arts and culture mostly benefits those in the upper part of the nation's class structure, and educational funding for universities and private primary and secondary schools also serve the more affluent.[44] Nor would one expect that the considerable support provided by the government to "civic, social, and fraternal organizations" from the VFW to the NCAA to Mothers Against Drunk Driving be concentrated among the poor. It may well be argued that considerable public benefit is obtained by supporting the Metropolitan Museum of Art, the Washington Philharmonic, Harvard University, Choate, and other nonprofits, but service to the poor is not among these.

Where income differentials between clients served by the public sector and the nonprofit sector are most striking are in the social service and health sectors of the nonprofit world. Historically, after the passage of Social Security and other public programs in the 1930s, it was understood at least by social welfare experts that more middle-class people would seek help in family service and mental health agencies, while poor people interested in counseling were more likely to be served through government offices. Nor in the years from the 1930s through 1960s would we be surprised to find a private hospital telling a charity patient to go to a public hospital. In the Northeast particularly, where public hospitals like Bellevue and Boston City Hospital existed side-by-side with large nonprofits like Cornell, New York Hospital, Mass General, and Beth Israel, it was not uncommon for ambulance drivers to ask about health insurance and income before taking a patient to the hospital. But what may be somewhat surprising is that such policies have not changed as dramatically since the 1960s and 1970s as reformers hoped. It is true that the Medicaid and Medicare programs (as well as increased government pressure, and court decisions on the provision of charity care) have made overt discrimination against the poor by large institutions such as hospitals less common. Yet as a summary of data on the use of health and mental health services by David Saklevar and Richard Frank show, in each type of health care utilization, the public sector serves a higher percentage of the poor than do nonprofits (who in turn serve more than for-profits). Government also serves a higher percentage of the unemployed than the nonprofits, and, when education is used as an indicator, the lower the education (which usually correlates with social class), the more likely the patient will be served in the public sector instead of either the voluntary or private (for-profit) sectors.[45]

The data on social services are even more dramatic than those concerning health care. To take only two examples, Family Services of America studied its member agencies in the late 1980s and found that only 20 percent of its clients fell in the bottom third of the income curve.[46] In a statistical analysis compiled by Lester

Salamon on all human service nonprofits, only 27 percent of the agencies focused their work on the poor, and 20 percent had some poor clients, but 53 percent had few or no poor clients. Further, consistent with "charity's" history, only one in six agencies provided *any* material assistance (food, shelter, income), while the remainder provided none, solely offering counseling, information and referral, or recreation.[47] Importantly, Salamon found—as other experts have—that it is *government* funding that forces nonprofits to serve the poor, contrary to what the average citizen's conception of charity may be. As Salamon puts it, "the data seem to suggest that one of the major factors accounting for what limited focus the nonprofit human sector gives to the poor is the availability of government financial support."[48] The power of the government to pressure voluntary agencies was one of the strongest achievements of the 1960s reform era. Unable to achieve a national health care program, reformers achieved the Medicaid program, which in turn reimburses voluntary agencies; unable to alter the social structures, community action agencies or Head Start programs were channeled through nonprofit community agencies. A longitudinal study would no doubt show that compared to forty years ago, health care and social service agencies do serve at least somewhat more lower income people than they did then. But such limited change still trails behind what could be achieved in equity if government simply provided all services itself.

It is difficult in this limited space to describe all the reasons why nonprofits generally serve middle income people better than the poor. In part, cultural reasons must be mentioned since, for example, attendance at arts and cultural events and civic meetings is correlated with social class. For many pragmatic and sociological reasons, a nursing aide working a night shift (much less a welfare mother with small children) is unlikely to be found either at the ballet or symphony concert, or at the VFW or MADD monthly meeting. Second, the nonprofit sector historically developed as the prime domain of professionals in America, or as Henry Mintzberg puts it, the nonprofits are typically "professional bureaucracies."[49] Professionals historically have found the more interesting "cases" to be those clients/patients/consumers who are most like them in

social class. Psychiatrists and clinical social workers prefer therapeutic counseling with middle- or upper-class patients to working
with poor patients, who often need time-consuming advocacy
work; physicians prefer not only the higher reimbursement they receive from upper- and middle-class patients but find the affluent
more "compliant" with medical regimens. The professorate as a
profession grew from the early elite universities, and high prestige
accrues from working with the affluent at institutions such as Harvard, MIT, and Yale. The less educated throughout the universe of
schools are likely to provoke the least interest, except for a few idealistic teachers. It is not surprising to find more acclaimed professors at the graduate level than the undergraduate, and at the college
level than the vocational school level. To put professional self-
interest in the most charitable way possible, each profession prizes
those consumers who most value what they do and who most respond to what they are "professing"; they avoid those who are least
willing or able to use their services or who are perhaps the most
skeptical.

Finally, American culture and political economy have combined with professional and middle-class ideology to center the
*purpose* of most nonprofits away from what is most needed by vul-
nerable members of society, again serving the therapeutic rather
than material needs of people. For example, many people contribute to health charities such as the "Big Three," the American Cancer Society, American Heart Association, and the American Lung
Association. Yet what exactly do these huge nonprofits (as of 1991,
ACS held fund balances of $491.7 million; the AHA, 264.6 million;
and the ALA, 136.2 million) provide?[50] Many people—including
poor people and working-class Americans—may believe that these
groups provide aid to the ill or at least do research on cures for diseases. However, generally they do neither. They provide almost no
material support for those suffering from cancer, heart, or lung disease; and while they do support a small amount of research, it is the
public sector which performs almost all research (95 percent of disease research is done through the National Institutes of Health and
other public auspices).[51]

So where is all this money going? What the big health charities primarily provide is public education and information aimed at health care professionals. No one would argue that there isn't value in health education about how to avoid cancer, heart, and lung disease or in the dissemination of information to medical practitioners. But the extent to which these charities take both taxpayer money and lower-income people's contributions in order to support continuing education for physicians or send out updates to hospitals is, as James Bennett and James DiLorenzo remark, a clear example of "Robin Hood in reverse."[52] Like the Y's justification for spending large amounts of taxpayer money to finance middle-class exercise as "charity," there is a peculiarly American middle-class ideology that voluntary organizations tap into. While on the one hand a desperate fear of death and illness (probably much greater than in other cultures) presses Americans to give far more money to health causes than do others, a self-reinforcing ideology obtains. It holds that the ill or potentially ill need neither money nor insurance nor perhaps even a cure, but rather public education about what to do or not do to avoid disease. As a result, Americans pay for countless campaigns of repetitious health advice. This advice—particularly to see your physician frequently, to buy certain vitamins or drugs—obviously benefits professionals and for-profits immensely. For a variety of cultural and educational reasons, these constant health warnings are often least effective with the poor, young, or ill educated. Yet the lack of controversy which accompanies health advice, and probably the usefulness of its ideology as a way to blame the victim—you are ill because you smoked cigarettes or ate fatty foods or practiced unsafe sex—propels the vast investment of funds into charities which focus on educating or haranguing the public.

Both the Y and the health charities exemplify how organizational, professional, and social class interest symbiotically interact in the nonprofit sector to benefit middle-class people far more than the stereotypical notion of "charity" would have us believe. Since the mythology about what these organizations provide is so embedded in the public mind through media and political praise, there is little debate about what *could* be done with the large amount of public money organizations such as the YMCA or American Cancer Society receive.

## The Fragmentation and Duplication of Services

One of the great attractions of American capitalism is its wide range of consumer choices; visitors from other countries often remark on the dozens of brands of toothpaste, coffee, or beer on the shelves in our stores. The nonprofit world, combined with an even more recent proliferation of for-profit services, has made securing social, psychological, or health services every bit as complex as deciding what car to buy. Social welfare and health experts acknowledge that, unlike the choice of cars, many negative results occur from fragmentation and confusion in the human sector area. Obviously the needs of someone evicted from their home, a woman battered by her partner, or a person suffering a severe psychiatric break are quite different from a consumer buying a new car. Their need for help is not only of a higher urgency than for someone choosing a product, but everyone agrees that limited consumer information in these areas prevents a purely capitalist choice, and the loss of time and energy the confusion creates often exacerbates the problem. The stigma of seeking help further discourages clients, so that they are likely to leave the human service system altogether if enough barriers are put in the way. Staffers in almost all social programs complain that people who need services avoid seeking them due to stigma (issues such as mental health, poverty, domestic violence, and AIDS, to name just a few), so agencies put a lot of energy and funding into public service announcements and outreach efforts both to normalize the social issue and inform people about where to find help.

A quick viewing of my local yellow pages (for the relatively small city of Portland, Maine, population 70,000)[53] suggests the level of complexity and multiplicity in the health and human services sector. Spread out across 98 different categories in the yellow pages are more than 300 different organizations and agencies; to take some examples, there are 38 entries for alcoholism information and treatment services; three-and-one-half pages (I gave up counting!) for marriage, family, child, and individual counseling (almost all private practitioners); 21 entries for drug abuse and addiction services; 15 entries for mental health services; 28 for nursing homes; 26 for rehabilitation services; 14 for children's services; and 28 listings under human services. Of course, some issues have few services and hence are not hard to find. For example, there are not many abortion providers nor many agencies in my area listed under AIDS services. Still, if one takes the case of a woman with a child who recently lost her job, where should she turn? Should it be to "Career and Vocational Counseling," "Child Care Centers," "Child Guidance," "Employment Agencies," "Employment Counseling," "Employment Training Service," "Government Offices," "Mental Health Services," "Social and Human Services," including under it such subtitles as "Children's Services," "Community Services," "Crisis Intervention Services," "Family and Individual Services," "Food Assistance," "Homeless Persons Services," "Housing Assistance," "Human Services," "Mental Health Services," "Philanthropic Services," "Vocational Services," "Women's Services," and "Youth Services"; or "Social Workers," "Stress Management Programs," "Training–Human Resources," or "Youth Organizations and Centers?" And—once our prospective client has chosen a category—she still would have to wade through multiple individual agency names under each category!

This well-known and oft discussed labyrinth of "services" has led the American social welfare system to embrace the employment of a large number of "traffic cops" and separate organizations to do nothing more than direct the flow. One-fifth of all the agencies do nothing but "information and referral," that is, tell our overwhelmed client which agency they might want to try out. Added to this huge bureaucracy of referrers is the growing employment since the 1980s of "case managers." Used extensively in agencies serving the poor, the mentally ill, and developmentally disabled, and now more and more domestic-violence victims, and people with AIDS and other health problems, professionally trained people are employed to help individuals keep track of and coordinate their many social agencies and caseworkers. It is not uncommon for mental health consumers to have social workers and case managers from

six or seven different agencies! It seems amazing that both the social service "system" and its academic experts tolerate and support
this; can one imagine, say, the police or fire departments having a
quarter of their personnel tied up in giving out information about
crime and fires rather than actually performing police or firefight-
ing? Yet as Bertram Weisbord notes: "existing policy reflects an
implicit and questionable assumption: that in none of the hundreds
of activities in which nonprofits engage are there economies of
scale that even *might* justify restricting the number of nonprofits
beyond whatever effects occur through natural forces. . . .[54]

A second major problem is created by this fragmented and du-
plicative system: it is not only true that the poor person, battered
woman, or individual in ill health may drop out of the system entirely rather than submit to telling their story to half a dozen people
and being shuffled around from agency to agency; it is also true
that, despite the large list of organizations, the services most ur-
gently needed are still critically absent, particularly for the poor.
Should a person in need call the many agencies in the phone book
for help, they would find that most demand either private payment
or reimbursement by insurance. If our prospective client indeed is
a woman with a child who has lost her job and now has little funds
and no health insurance, much of the entire listing can be tossed
away. If our client is lucky enough to have a good social worker, she
would be sent immediately to the *public sector* where eligibility for
unemployment insurance, Medicaid, food stamps, and what is left
of "welfare" would be determined. If she is either served only by
Medicaid or is ineligible for any insurance, she can forget many of
the 98 categories such as Alcoholism Treatment, Career and Vocational Counseling, Child Guidance, Counseling, Drug Abuse and
Addiction, Eating Disorders, Employee Assistance, Mental Health
Services, Psychologists, Psychotherapists, and Social Workers (at
least in my local area).[55]
   The irony is apparent: despite the appearance of so much, there
is so little. Since the for-profit and not-for-profit system will usually
not provide service at no cost, the fragmented system obscures the
fact that many citizens have to turn to this equally confusing listing

in the phone book: "Government Offices: See White pages section for the following listings: Authorities & Commissions; City under Name; County under Name; Federal under 'United States Government'; State under 'Maine, State of' and Town under name of Town."

It is really only the more affluent who may be able to avail themselves of the three-and-a-half pages of therapists and the many choices in stress management or career counseling in my phone book. But even for the affluent it is not clear that this is at all desirable; as many middle- or upper-class people who have ever sought help can attest, the fragmentation and complexity is not pleasant when a serious issue or problem arises.

## THE PARADOX OF SUCCESS

The status and élan of the voluntary sector has always stood in stark contrast to the two other types of organizational forms: the government and for-profit business. The success of the nonprofit world in the United States has helped discredit government as a form, yet has not discredited the for-profit sector. Instead it has helped pave the way for commercialization of personal services.

For the first several hundred years of the charitable sector in the United States, church, philanthropic, and some political leaders again and again argued the superiority of "charity" over the government sector. The "private sector alternative to socialism" war was fought and appears to have been won. The fact that nonprofits actually serve the middle class better than the poor has, ironically, only reinforced their support. In a self-fulfilling prophecy, many areas of government service are tainted by association with low income, racial minority, and deviant populations. Hence public hospitals are avoided, for they often are associated with poverty and epidemic disease; people who can afford to often seek out nonprofit or for-profit hospitals. A more affluent or better insured person with a psychiatric problem avoids the state mental hospital at all costs and goes instead to a private facility or psychotherapist. Parents in many areas of the country put their children in private schools to avoid the stigmatized public ones. A complex historical process has, on the one hand, starved the public sector of sufficient money to adequately serve the nation's needs, but money is not quite a total answer. Even where government works well in providing service, it is rarely credited.[56]

The most popular feature of government in the United States is often its military or police arm. In a simple analogy, if the government sector and the nonprofit sector were pictured as siblings, the government would be the powerful, warlike brother good at enforcing order, but not the one you'd go to with your problems; while the nonprofit would be the sensitive sister who can provide a crying shoulder for those in need. The irony of the nonprofit world's success is that while it has clearly helped to undermine support for government in America, it may be fading in comparison with another growing sibling, the business sector. It is as if this third sibling, once characterized as bright and efficient but self-serving, has now taken enough sensitivity training and been in therapy long enough, that, hey, they can be trusted with our problems, too.

This historical process is an interesting one. The nonprofit sanctity relies on a concept of "honor" that stems from a combination of its religious origins and the status of the professional caregivers (physicians, teachers, social workers, clergy, etc.) who dominate this sector. For decades, the reason we trusted our bodies to a hospital was that it usually was run by not-for-profit administrators and professionals with a code of ethics. We went to a family service agency or mental health center and shared our innermost thoughts, but implicitly trusted the professionals and administrators of these nonprofit organizations to keep our problems confidential and not exploit us. When we brought our children to school or our elderly relatives to a nursing or old age home, usually again it was to a nonprofit organization that garnered our trust through their auspices and professional leadership. This honor is still very present today in the American mind and can be seen in the value of endorsements by certain nonprofits sought after by profitable businesses: Johnson & Johnson seeks out the Arthritis Foundation's endorsement for its products; producers of bottled water, designer watches, and swimwear seek out the Red Cross's endorsement; products from Nicoderm patches to Florida orange juice have gained the American Cancer Society's stamp of approval; and hotels, motels, restaurants, and auto body shops seek out the American Automobile Association's endorsement.[57]

Yet a strange thing began to happen in the last few decades in America. Nonprofits have implicitly relied on the assumption that the public would not trust profit-making businesses with their personal problems. People presumably would be reluctant to send their elderly relatives to businesses for their personal care; to leave their children all day with a for-profit business; or bring their ill relatives and friends to a for-profit hospital. But this is exactly what has taken place, particularly since the 1960s. Some of this expansion can be attributed to an expansion of need (as women increasingly entered the labor force, more day care was needed; as the population aged, more nursing homes and other geriatric services were in demand). The profit-making sector moved into the breach, finding surprising success in some areas.

But the for-profits' very success probably would not have occurred without government. Medicare and Medicaid were the key factors in providing new funds for the nursing home industry and later the private hospital industry. In other areas of the economy such as child care, only the absence of publicly provided service combined with tax credits has helped launch a private industry. Nonprofit expert Dennis Young argues that nonprofits can be seen as "experimental activity" when "it is unclear whether it can be made profitable." Since nonprofits are relatively easy to start and low in capital needs, they are extremely flexible vehicles which can be turned into profit generators as more and more physicians, health care administrators, psychiatrists and social workers, child care providers, and even correctional experts are proving.[58] Young's point is well taken. There were many nonprofit nursing and old age homes forty years ago, but for-profits followed when ways to make large profits became known. With the exception of a few elite and specialized places, mental hospitals and alcoholism treatment facilities were public or nonprofit once. Now many of these facilities are highly profitable.

Ironically, the nonprofits' reliance on vague process goals based on sentiment ("we help people") and its symbiosis with professionalism as honor may someday be seen as having backfired as more and more services become actual for-profit businesses. No longer does it appear odd for people to use for-profit child care centers, clinics, hospitals, or nursing homes as well as a host of private practitioners for all sorts of personal services and therapeutic counseling. As nonprofits moved to be more profitable and like businesses, businesses have adopted a rhetoric of caring and a symbiotic relation with the professions (medicine, law, psychology, social work, nursing, psychiatry, accounting, pharmacy, even education), which helps them borrow some elements of sanctity and honor. That is, if one wants counseling, what difference does it make whether you seek out a mental health center or private clinician Jane Doe? You have heard that Ms. Doe is excellent, and don't begrudge her fee for seeing you. In fact, the nonprofit mental health center, like the public sector, may come to be seen in a negative light as well: you may be put on a waiting list, and you can't be assured of which practitioner you will see at the center. Similarly, despite the battle currently raging over managed care and HMOs, for-profit medicine is likely here to stay, with the major competition being between insurance industry profits and physicians' groups, the latter seeking to retain some power and financial gain. Certainly, on issues like affluent and middle-class people's choice of physicians, the public supports government regulation—perhaps even some strong laws—but given the huge success of for-profit hospital and nursing home chains in America, there is little reason to believe the majority of the public oppose for-profit medicine per se.

The nonprofit sector may turn out to be an intermediate historical form. Where high capital costs exist such as in hospitals, there are strong advantages for professionals and managers to retain this form for their own financial interest. With the nonprofit entity picking up the high cost of expensive equipment, liability costs, training of a labor force, and other inputs, physicians gain by being freed to concentrate solely on their individual high fees. Nonprofit universities may also be secure; considerable capital would have to be raised by faculty or others to purchase the larger institutions, and considerable risk would have to be absorbed as well as lost opportunity cost. Students as well as patients have also come to expect considerable ancillary services which are out of the realm of faculty to supply, such as good cafeterias, sports arenas, residences, health centers on campus, and so on. Where capital needs are relatively low, however, for example in child care, psychotherapy, or recreational programs, there may be little incentive for professionals or administrators to retain the nonprofit form.[59]

One would be more sympathetic to the nonprofit world if in fact its own agenda weren't so self-interested. As it stands, nonprofit status has become a "trademark," such as a brand name used in endorsements. Clearly some people like to see that the AAA, ACS, or Red Cross has endorsed a consumer product. Some people may always prefer to send their children to a nonprofit school or day care center or send their elders to a religious or public nursing home. Yet in America there are many trusted trademarks now, and for-profit businesses have succeeded on their own to achieve "honor." As was noted in the last chapter with cause related marketing, corporations may be able to directly garner wealth and power with a new style of sensitive-seeming, charitable action. For if there are trusted trademarks in the nonprofit world from Harvard to the YMCA to the American Cancer Society, aren't Microsoft, Saab, Ben and Jerry's, and Kodak also trusted corporate trademarks? There is little reason to believe that if any one of these companies opened a health clinic or school, they would be rejected by consumers. Having helped defeat the notion that certain human services should be *public* services, the nonprofit sector should garner little sympathy for its current plight in competition with private business. It laid the groundwork for it.

# 6—Incorporating the Critics: Clients, Social Movements, and the "Contract State"

> *One of the key mechanisms for transforming social movements from independent adversaries of the state to collaborators is the service contract. . . . Once militant groups . . . find themselves caught in the contradiction of the welfare state . . . [becoming] adjunct[s] of state and local governments seeking to enhance their own legitimacy . . . like anti-poverty groups and other community organizations since the 1960s, [they] have been effectively demobilized by these relationships.*
>
> Stanley Aronowitz[1]

Unquestionably, the nonprofit sector has changed dramatically over time. Today its diversity and scope differs markedly not only from its origins but even from the 1950s and early 1960s. Charity could once have been viewed primarily as a pursuit of the middle class or affluent who gave money and volunteered their time out of sentiments of piety and noblesse oblige. Today not only has the variety of nonprofit, human service, and therapeutic organizations expanded, but they have been dramatically democratized. In many American communities today, one can give to or volunteer for a nonprofit organization that reflects the person's ethnic or racial background, sexual orientation, religious choice, and sometimes specific political belief. While boards of directors and the leaderships of nonprofits have hardly been as democratized as volunteering or giving, there are certainly agencies around that recruit volunteers or staff among a range of classes and races. Americans now seem to be able to choose from such a wide variety of social causes—from disease eradication to religious study, from historical restoration of a one-room schoolhouse to building an alumni center at an Ivy League institution, from promoting world peace to gun control—that the past association between charity and a particular political viewpoint or class status has been virtually erased.

Yet the democratization of charity is also a paradox. Historically, the two groups that most objected to the paternalism of charity—the recipients of social service (the poor, disabled, and other clients) and those on the political Left—might be expected to be most uncomfortable with an ideology that glorifies service and voluntarism. As we have seen in earlier chapters, for much of American history most criticism made of the charitable enterprise came from these sources. Yet in the last three decades the revolt which began in the 1960s—in part a revolt against paternalistic treatment of many client groups—has come to be turned into its opposite, the encapsulation of oppositional groups within the landscape of social service and therapeutic endeavors.

Oddly enough, these days it is the organized representatives of social movements and client groups who often form the most visible vanguard of defense of our fragmented labyrinth of nonprofits, mostly funded by contracts from the state or private grants. Former or current activists within a variety of social movements (racial minorities, women, gay and lesbian, disability groups, for example) have turned into nonprofit contractors. Protesters have become administrators, social workers, and board members who worry about balancing budgets, managing organizational charts, and having adequate professional supervision. How did these changes come about—so relatively swiftly?

## THE PARADOXICAL LEGACY
## OF THE 1960S AND 1970S

There is no question that dramatically important changes occurred in the 1960s and 1970s that changed the relationship between the state and client groups, between professionals and their patients or clients, and between private groups such as nonprofits and their clients. As Ira Glasser noted, the very foundation of the legal rights of "clients" changed in the 1960s and 1970s. Previously,

> violations of individual rights that would have created an instantaneous
> political and legal clamor had they been perpetrated by the police went

unrecognized when they were perpetrated by social service professionals. Because such professionals were presumed to be acting in the
"best interests" of their "clients," no one thought to question the excesses of their power. They were not cops . . . [they acted] in loco
parentis. . . . So a tradition grew up. The Bill of Rights existed, but
did not apply to service institutions.[2]

In 1969, sociologists Marie Haug and Marvin Sussman saw a "revolt of the client" against professionals and their organizations:

> Students, the poor, and the black community no longer accept uncriti-
> cally the service offerings of the establishment. . . . [we call this]
> the revolt of the client . . . In hospitals, schools, colleges, and the
> ghettoes, the clients are rejecting . . . both the practitioner's work
> autonomy and his organizational authority in the role of administra-
> tor. . . . Nowadays individual clients do not drop out; they get to-
> gether, sit in, and confront the functionaries of service organizations.[3]

In the period between the early 1960s to the mid-1970s, important legal victories (some of which have since been eroded) as well
as significant changes occurred in professional and organizational
practice. These included not only civil rights victories for protected minorities and rights for groups like students, children, and
the disabled, but also the imposition of broad limits on the power
of the state, private organizations, and professionals to impose
treatment, act without the informed consent of patients, or deny
due process protections for those receiving social benefits or to
those in prison, drug treatment centers, halfway houses, institutions, and group homes. As the civil rights and antiwar movements
of the 1960s sparked other movements—the women's movement,
the gay and lesbian movement, the disabled and elderly people's
movements, consumer, and environmental movements of the late
1960s and early 1970s—officials of government, nonprofit organizations, corporations, and professionals from physicians to teachers to social workers lost some of the power they had held in earlier
decades. They also began, in varying degrees, to include client, patient, and student input in planning their own service, health, and
education programs.

The two major causes for the dramatic changes in the nonprofit
sector were the movement to incorporate client/patient/consumer

input which was driven by government policy and the agitation of the 1960s and 1970s, and the development of mechanisms (through both government contracting and private funding) to pay some "grassroots" or "indigenous" people and even some radical activists to work for service agencies. These new agencies ranged from community action agencies started by the War on Poverty to self-help organizations to clinics or shelters run by feminist activists. Yet it should give us pause in evaluating American human services to note how quickly these changes have been eroded or even reversed, and by the 1980s and 1990s turned into paper rights for consumers or, as Michael Lipsky presciently observed, into "rights . . . often technical and remote rather than practical."[4] Similarly, how different in any truly substantive way, beyond style and rhetoric, the new social agencies turned out to be in the long run needs some examination. Obviously, many baby boomers came into human service work or community organizing with idealistic views. But looking back, many who remained have been absorbed within the mechanics of the social service system — its complex rules and funding formulas, its disincentives towards actual activism — rather than actually "changing the system from within."[5]

I suggest that this paradox is similar to how previous periods of social unrest led to a series of structural mechanisms to weaken and channel social protest. In the 1930s, for example, one of the most militant periods of worker history in the United States (including general strikes in some cities and sit-down strikes) led to the widespread unionization of industry, which in turn led to the opposite of militancy: a "trade-off" between union security and administered contracts that limited and channeled militance, such as laws outlawing the most radical worker actions. In a parallel, the 1960s' movements eventually led to a contract system in which activist groups became funded — but in return were depoliticized and absorbed within a system of bureaucratic and patronage relationships with the state, and private sector organizations such as foundations, United Ways, and other grantors.

The Economic Opportunity Act of 1964, better known as the War on Poverty, was a pioneering effort to change government funding mechanisms, and in turn, how nonprofit social agencies would function. Intentionally bypassing the normal channels of funding (through states and municipalities), the Office of Economic Opportunity (OEO) provided direct contracts to community agencies at a grassroots level.[6] Particularly controversial but critical to the history of the 1960s was the act's embrace of "maximum feasible participation" of the poor, which meant that poor people and other clients would themselves have to have some representation in social agencies.

The approach of the OEO and much subsequent legislation of the 1960s remains controversial to this day. Some observers such as Daniel Patrick Moynihan charged that elites stimulated social unrest, thus "causing" radicalism and militancy by irresponsibly raising expectations and funding activists and protestors.[7] Years later, President George Bush, visiting in the aftermath of the 1992 riots in Los Angeles, still blamed the policies of Lyndon Johnson for the riots. However, it is important to recall that at the time the legislation was also mocked by many on the Left. Saul Alinsky, the community organizer, called it a "macabre masquerade,"[8] while Stanley Aronowitz, then a community activist, attacked the programs as worthless except for their employment of radicals.[9] Peter Marris and Martin Rein, two well-respected left-leaning social welfare experts, were particularly scathing about community action (the most controversial aspect of the War on Poverty), charging that it "was essentially patronizing and conservative" rather than radical.[10]

But if one moves beyond the specific debates, an interesting and important phenomenon was occurring in this period. While initially radicals and not a few liberals denounced the programs as providing too little concrete aid, such as jobs and income benefits, gradually the notion of "participation" melded rather well with the movements of the 1960s and 1970s. From student movements to racial minority movements to the women's movement, "power to the people" and "let the people decide" was in the air. The "people," or at least some of them, were demanding change and control, and this was often operationalized as "consumer" or "community" control. The well-known battles over school systems in the 1960s, such as the famous Ocean Hill–Brownsville conflict in New York City, and demands for community control over police forces are examples. Universities, confronted with militant students burning ROTC buildings or occupying buildings to protest racism, began to respond to "student power" and provide student seats on committees and senates. Later the women's movement was particularly influential in confronting institutions in which women had little or no power or representation. From medical care to the media to the boardroom to the legislature, "participation" was a key demand.

Although most Americans, except extreme conservatives, would today agree that many of the demands of these activist groups had some merit and led to, depending on one's specific views, long overdue reforms or at least some positive changes, there were always paradoxes, contradictions, and dissent to the idea of "participation" even within the social movements themselves.

The first issue concerns what was then called "co-optation." That is, to what degree were the ideas of those represented on boards, committees, and other structures of what was then called the "establishment" really meaningful change? Was it participation without substance, window dressing, a way to make the leaders feel good? Even if it were more than this, would it actually change the balance of power within society—for the poor, racial minorities, and so on? At universities the more radical students often scoffed at participation. When I was at Columbia University in the late 1960s, participation on university committees by students was mocked by groups like Students for a Democratic Society, quite rightly as it turned out because of how easily it was transformed into a substitute for substantive social change. Haug and Sussman, while praising what they called the "client revolt," noted that "the patients councils' in hospitals, the indigenous community representation on boards, and the placement of students on curriculum committees were meant to socialize the dissidents into the special organizational knowledge of inner professional circles."[11] Jeffrey Galper, another leftist observer, saw "the War on Poverty . . . as an attempt to channel the civil rights struggles and the nascent social upheavals of the early 1960s into the social engineering context of welfare state planning."[12]

A second set of issues that, of course, could not be debated or even anticipated at the time was, what did "participation" or "representation" mean in the absence of viable social movements. It is one thing for a radical student to be on a committee when activist movements are on campus, for neighborhood minority militants to attend meetings while groups such as the Black Panther Party are on the street, or for poor mothers to gain seats on agency councils while the National Welfare Rights Organization (NWRO) recruits members. But, with the notable exceptions of the womens' and gay and lesbian movements, by the mid-1970s much of the organizing of active movements was over. Left in the wake of the movements' decline were many people—ranging from poor people trained in community action programs to more affluent students who went to college or graduate school—who had skills in human services or nonprofit work who wanted roles, but whose constituencies were no longer active on the streets.

Hence the ambiguity of the results of "power to the people" or the more operationalized "consumer rights." The results can be seen as "radical" in a "process" light, but as "conservative" in a structural light. The achievements in process are dramatic: how a poor person entering a social agency or a woman entering a health clinic is treated is noticeably different today compared to thirty years ago in terms of respect and adherence to more formalized sets of policies and rights. But to point out the obvious, if a client enters the agency only to be told that no social benefits are available (increasingly the reality), it is obvious that the process goals have not really helped the poor very much. Or if the woman entering a health clinic is told that her coverage is limited due to managed care or lack of health insurance, again one wonders how far "process" has really taken her. So while agencies and institutions throughout the land provide a rhetoric of inclusion or even "empowerment," paradoxically much has worsened in our society in terms of the material conditions of people. The buzzword "empowerment" in fact can be claimed by the Right, Left, and Center because process goals are so malleable and ambiguous.

## FROM CLIENT "REVOLT"
## TO CLIENT ENCAPSULATION

Each period of social unrest in American history has placed different groups at the forefront of protest; each has achieved important social reforms, which led to relatively rapid efforts at containment. Many of these containment efforts are beyond the scope of this book; they relate primarily to national political and electoral coalitions that absorb more radical dissent. However, at a local level, groups showing the potential for militance or radicalism are also contained by local elites and political leaders who otherwise may lose legitimacy if social unrest continues.

As Frances Fox Piven and Richard Cloward argue in *Poor People's Movements*, power arrangements are most threatened when insurgency is spontaneous, unpredictable, and without clear leadership that can be restrained by law or rewarded by largesse. Whether the unrest is food riots in Medieval Europe, sit-down strikes in factories in the 1930s or ghetto riots of the 1960s, those in power strive not only to repress and control rebellions. They also try to organize and channel disorder into less threatening forums.[13]

Many of those who hold power will always resist these more pragmatic choices, as many corporate leaders resisted trade unionism in the United States. However, more enlightened elites not only see the dangers of continued out-and-out resistance, but see potential gains from a more carefully controlled and contained system of ongoing negotiation. So, in the example of collective bargaining, eventually through the contract system and key labor law legislation (for example, the Wagner Act and the Taft-Hartley Act), the possibility of worker unrest was channeled into a ritualized process of bargaining occurring only in certain years, and, even more important, control over the rank and file was lodged within the union leadership itself, helping to prevent untoward militance from erupting. This includes a legal obligation by union leadership to prevent strikes during the life of the contract.

Such channeling, however, is rarely figured out in advance. It often happens by a combination of trial and error, accident, and serendipity. Between the mid-1960s and mid-1970s, many mechanisms for controlling social change were tried. They included some old-fashioned violence such as the repression of the Black Panther Party and the shooting of student protesters. Eventually, however, two more enlightened and successful strategies emerged that drew on the social service system. The first was an effort to give representation to previously excluded groups that could be contained and controlled, and that would promote leadership with a self-interest in adhering to the law and normal channels of politics. Second, and more subtly, was the move to replace substantive economic and political change with vague service and therapeutic goals that were less costly and ultimately less challenging to the status quo.

At first the organizing of clients—whether through councils, community boards, or community representation on boards of directors—seemed quite radical. Indeed, these efforts were sometimes bitterly opposed by politicians and professionals. Yet many astute political leaders began to see value in such efforts as a way to stifle and encapsulate protest. In his study of New York City in the 1960s, for example, Ira Katznelson credits Mayor Lindsay's administration with understanding that in order to blunt the free-flowing unrest that plagued New York's ghettos in that period, organized and orderly community programs were needed:

> At issue was the attempt to take the radical impulse away from the politics of race by the creation of mechanisms of participation at the community level that had the capability to limit conflicts to a community orientation, to separate issues from each other, and to stress a politics of distribution—in short to reduce race to ethnicity in the traditional community-bounded sense.[14]

Those who work with the poor realize that "consumers" who are interested in long-term political and bureaucratic struggle are a small minority in any period, and such a stance in particular does not tend to characterize those who are most militant and angry. As Marris and Rein so well said of the leaders thrown up by the various poverty programs, they tended to not really be representative of the poor:

Anyone who could hold his own in a committee of public officials, business leaders, the mayor and project directors, was unlikely to still be
poor and uneducated . . . if these representatives can make their influence effective in so formal a setting, they may lose their understanding
with their constituents. By achieving influence itself, such a representative of the poor loses many of the characteristics which identify him as
one with those he represents.[15]

But the problem of participation and the inevitable embour-
geoisement of power holders goes well beyond issues related to the
poor or to ghettos. When both public sector contracts with private
nonprofits and increased patronage of community agencies by private parties emerged, the structure of having to engage in competition for scarce funds, the legal requirements of bookkeeping, and
rules for professional standards and levels of bureaucracy led away
from militancy toward a new reliance on political patronage which
would affect all community agencies. In John Mollenkompf's interesting study of New York City in the 1980s, he points out that the
nonprofits (the "third party government") constitute a not insig-
nificant part of the municipal budget and an important constituent
in the struggle for political power. Far from radical, these nonprofit
groups, particularly those which were once truly community-
based—organizations of poor people, women's organizations, and
minority groups rather than the Ys or Catholic Charities, for
example—had gone through a "progressive decay" in the 1970s
and had been "absorbed into city government" and shifted their
mission "from advocacy to service and their constituents became
clients."[16]

Just as corporations at times were able to pick and choose which
unions or union leaders to negotiate with, actively discouraging the
more radical and militant leaders, government contracting allows
public authorities to monitor the behavior of nonprofits; to pick
and choose among agencies to fund; and to condition aid on patronage. Commenting on the conservatism of New York's agencies,
Mollenkompf notes, "[they] avoid associating with those who
might challenge political incumbents. At most they lobby to increase program funding or change program design. They do not

cross functional or geographic boundaries to support political insurgents."[17]

The depoliticization of political advocacy movements and their fragmentation in New York City mirrors my experience in a much smaller city. The most "liberal" or "progressive" agencies are often the most disappointing in relation to how fragmented and dispersed they have become as divided interest groups. Each agency vies with another for funds, alongside sanitation contractors and solid waste systems. Each social service agency cozies up to a series of political leaders for government contracts each year, whether they be from the city council, county commission, or from state and federal officials. Similarly, social agency executives also wine and dine local bankers, real estate magnates, and CEOs in the area, hoping to attract donations or extract grants.

To begin with, as noted above, few people remain as representatives on boards or councils for long, particularly if they are militant. My experience with organizations for the homeless and poor in my city is that only "morally favored clients" (as Lipsky calls them) tend to remain active in the organization for long. Of course, client populations are fluid. Over time many people leave the system either because they no longer need aid or because they resist punitive and hostile restrictions or they drop out of agency favor. Few clients desire to go to long, boring meetings run by parliamentary procedures that include recitation of budget reports and discussions of where grants may come from. Those few who find themselves socialized to a more middle-class role often enjoy the power and status they gain as anointed "clients." As I noted in my research on "North City," such leaders were viewed with great skepticism by many of the poor and often lost any true claim to indigenous leadership after such "hobnobbing."[18]

But the encapsulation of client activism within mundane bureaucratic tasks, or even more frequently, micro-level conflict, is also apparent at agencies not specifically established for the poor. Over the years I have served on a board of an agency for the developmentally disabled and also have been familiar with a consumer-run mental health club.[19] In neither of these agencies—even at the consumer-run mental health agency, which in many ways represents the optimum of "consumer control" touted since the 1960s—does "politics" in a macro sense really come up. Most often its boards and committee meetings focus on micro-level issues of organization—hiring staff and directors, filling out forms, worrying about next month's budget, meeting fire codes, managing conflict between people within the agency and even deciding which consumers must be banned from receiving services. The only time I have seen actual political discussion come up in any of the agencies mentioned is when they worry about their funding, usually at the end of a fiscal cycle when their contracts are up for renewal.

Since agencies are organized along functional lines, service groups have little identification with one another. Homeless or poverty groups have almost no contact with local developmental disability groups or with AIDS groups or with domestic violence groups or with programs for the elderly. In the past decade, I can remember only once when agencies in different functional areas may have even contacted each other. This occurred when across-the-board budget cuts were threatened in 1991. Usually, even agencies in the same subfield (mental health, developmental disability, aging, child welfare) do not cooperate with each other. In fact, since they are often in competition with one another for funding, it is far more frequent to hear critical attacks on sister agencies. I have heard hallway conversations such as, "Hey, did you hear how they screwed up their grant," or "I hear X agency is going into the Y subfield, we better move there first." When members of these groups are politically active at all—which does happen once in awhile, particularly at the mental health club—it is about *their* funding. It is almost never about broader social and human needs for all poor people or all disabled people or all aged people, much less an even broader vision that transcends clienthood.

But another important point must be made here. In none of these organizations I have used as examples do professionals fight for income or material benefits for the *actual* clients or consumers involved. Organizations for the homeless and poor are concerned about their funding for food for soup kitchens, per diem payments for shelters they sponsor, and reimbursement for staff; organizations for the developmentally disabled and psychiatrically-labeled similarly anxiously await their contracts for their per diem room rates or for hiring new staff. These may be worthy causes, but what is absent from almost all discussion is benefits that might accrue directly to the people they serve: welfare, SSI or Social Security payments, housing vouchers, and so on. The structure of social agency organization produces notions of collective need that are *corporate* (that is, of benefit to the organization), not redistributive to the individuals the agency serves.[20] While occasionally officials of social agencies will sign a petition against budget cuts in welfare or other income programs, almost no agency in the community where I live spends much time fighting for material client benefits. Rather, they fight for more service contract money for their own professional areas.

While contracting out by the public sector is among the most ingenious methods of containment, it is hardly the only one. As touched on in chapter 5, private organizations that play a major role in dispensing resources have also played an important direct and indirect role in absorbing and containing dissent. As with the more astute political actors, the more advanced foundation and other private charitable agencies realized that inclusion rather than repression was the way to absorb some of the 1960s social unrest. The Rockefellers used their foundations, for example, to "take the side of the angels in contemporary issues." Cutting back their involvement in the arts, culture, and conservation, the foundations moved to focus on urban problems such as welfare, low-income housing, and ghetto education. Further, the Rockefellers decided that "an intensified bid should be made to attract more bright young men from diverse backgrounds. Even militants and radicals should be brought in."[21]

Certainly one can give credit to the farsightedness of the foundations, United Ways, corporations, and others who saw the wisdom of integrating their staffs and hiring some of the poor, even radicals and dissenters. But as the phrase "he who pays the piper calls the tune" so well underscores, these funders will not back—

with rare exception—activities that promote a radical political agenda to alleviate social problems. In fact, as Bert Weisbord points out, about the *only* legal stricture enforced on nonprofits since the 1970s is that they maintain their nonpolitical status.[22] Ironically for those who entered the nonprofits with a high level of idealism, while nonprofits *may* make profits and engage in all sorts of complex financial schemes, sponsoring a demonstration or sit-down or sit-in will usually be avoided by nonprofits in order to preserve their tax-exempt status and their relationship with public and private funders. As Craig Jenkins summarizes, private giving serves as a control device over political radicalism:

> Patronage has tended to convert the advocacy organizations into centralized service purveyors, demobilizing masses by emphasizing services and projecting images of elite responsiveness. Elite patrons clearly have a decisive say over the advocates. . . . The nonprofits have had their greatest impact in raising issues, not controlling policy decisions or their implementation. In short, elite patronage is a form of political control.[23]

Participation by various client groups is obviously a positive development in the government of social service. But it also can be profoundly confusing to many clients and has often been a tokenist and cost-free gesture. Significantly, government and private powers can no longer say what they will about different groups at their meetings, must often conduct "needs assessments" and surveys, and are forced to at least go through the motions of client involvement. But the fact that such changes in the social services have come about *at the very same time* that social welfare programs, particularly of a material kind, have been eroding, demonstrates their lack of real import.

Fragmented, disjointed from one another, obsequious to local and state power, social service agencies, even with consumer representation, hardly can counter the dominant conservative ideology. Some experts suggest that the fragmentation of services and the "contract state" actually fit quite well into the conservative times of the 1980s and 1990s.[24] Characteristically blunt, Theresa Funiciello argues that while the poor failed to gain the guaranteed income they struggled for in the late 1960s, social agencies have won a guaranteed income for themselves, even in the era of cut-backs.[25] Ironically, at a time of few major social movements at the bottom of society, clients have come to rely on these organizations for the limited amount of advocacy or protest that does occur when human service budgets are cut. If the poor and other consumers were more directly organized on their own behalf rather than being spoken for by social service, foundation officials, local public offi-cials, and advocacy groups, perhaps such deep cuts in social wel-fare benefits would not have occurred.

## THE LEFT, SOCIAL WELFARE, AND SOCIAL SERVICES

The last several decades have seen a surprising new consensus emerge about social services being a kind of overall solution to so-cial ills. As will be recalled, however, *social welfare* as material aid to poor and working citizens in the form of income, medical, or other resources has been historically quite distinct from *social ser-vices* such as advice, counseling, and other therapeutic endeavors.

Traditionally in the United States and throughout the world, leftist parties supported social welfare measures for several reasons. First is the protection that social wages paid for by the state pro-vided to the working class. Pensions, unemployment insurance, relief, and health and other insurances protected workers from ex-ploitation by employers. Such measures set a floor on wages and working conditions, and promoted class solidarity and the bar-gaining power of workers. Second, redistribution of money from the affluent to those lower in class was thought to be promoted by progressive taxation and by the provision of cash and in-kind ben-efits to the poor and working class. Marxists may have always been more skeptical that true redistribution was possible under capital-ism, but even Marx and Engels included demands for a progressive income tax and workers' rights to education in their *Communist Manifesto*. Third, many leftists believed in the strategic value of winning benefits. As with trade unionism, radicals thought that

worker victories for social benefits helped increase class consciousness and prepared the working class for power.[26]

Only in recent years has there been an attempt to develop a leftist justification for the social services, and here advocates must
stretch the definition of "left" fairly far to find much historical support for their position.[27] On the one hand, there is no reason for
leftists to be against the provision of social services any more than
they would be against other services for people from medical care
to fire protection. On the other hand, we have noted the historic
use of charity workers as agents of social control. Further, American history is replete with conservative efforts to confuse problems
of income, employment, and other material need with individual
concerns such as psychological well-being and personal failing.
These discourses are very much linked to the therapeutic language
and ideology of social services.

Jeffrey Galper points out two cautions about social services in
his 1975 book, *The Politics of Social Services*. First, social services
generally are cheaper and easier "solutions" to society's problems
than social welfare:

> The substitution of inexpensive social services for more vital and critical
> services is another mechanism by which we make do with scarce re-
> sources and simultaneously deflect greater political consciousness.
> Fully meeting people's needs in any area of service would entail not only
> more expense than the society is prepared to allow . . . but . . .
> would require a radically altered society. . . . Hence, the counseling
> components of social service programs tend to receive more support
> than those which involve the distribution of harder resources like
> money, jobs, and houses.[28]

Second, the fight for pensions, unemployment benefits, or the
minimum wage has often united working-class, poor, and even
middle-income groups, but social service approaches often indi-
vidualize problems or divide classes and communities, removing
collective struggle from the table:

> . . . the social services function to encourage people to redefine their
> needs and their views of what a solution to their problems entails, so that
> inexpensive and politically accommodating services can replace expen-

sive and politically disruptive services. . . . It places the solution of social problems in the context of the private bargaining situation in which the client tries to personally secure those resources that can make life easier through some kind of purchasing arrangement, or, at least, through a private negotiation. As such, it focuses away from the nature of the society at large or from necessary changes in the client's environment that go beyond what any one person can provide for another.[29]

The struggle for large-scale collective income and job security gains for the poorer classes was believed to be conducive to class consciousness, but what about the establishment of a counseling center or a drug treatment program as service advocates often propose? It is hard to say. It could be that a new counseling center is a positive thing, or perhaps not. Much depends on how the issue is framed—whether its creation stemmed from true popular demand or from state and professional initiative. If, in fact, the issues are framed in such a way as to imply that a counseling center or drug treatment program can replace struggles for social equality, such services may serve to manipulate public opinion by centering the problem on bad, weak, or harmful individuals.

Some caution is in order. The word *services* and the concepts of social or human services are malleable and arguably mean different things in 1999 than they did in 1959 or 1979. No doubt some people do refer to noncash resources such as medical care and day care as "services." Certainly these are issues for which collective struggle and social gains can be made. Other service issues may or may not be "political" in a clear organizing sense, but will always remain necessary such as care for abandoned and neglected children or for profoundly developmentally disabled people. Complicating the discussion further is the vast expansion in the definition of "human need" that has developed in recent decades.[30]

Despite such complexity, I believe that more than a semantic misunderstanding is occurring. I believe a fundamental reconfiguration in thought has occurred in which some liberal and leftist activists, and many people in the human service and helping professions, have allowed and encouraged a confusion between material benefits and intangible "services." The latter, conveniently for professionals, are funded primarily through nonprofit agencies or directly to professionals themselves as private practitioners, not directly to clients or consumers.

## THE LEFT'S EMBRACE OF
## SOCIAL SERVICES AS "POLITICAL"

Beginning in the 1960s, several parts of the Left began to develop a very different outlook on social services. Most notable among these were the new social movements emerging out of the New Left, in particular the women's movement, the gay and lesbian movement, and the self-help movement in both its oppositional form (one thinks of the Mental Patients Liberation Front and other consumer groups) and less radical representations (encounter and recovery groups). Further, a large number of baby boomers, once participants in the New Left or minority movements, entered the human service professions from the 1960s on.

The social movements that arose in the 1960s and early 1970s came about during a period of general economic prosperity. Issues central to the unrest of the past — unemployment, poverty, destitution — were not as urgent. The New Left emerged, in fact, as a reaction to the Old Left of social democrats and Marxists, with their concerns about social welfare issues and their view of the working class as the vanguard. New Leftists and other post-1960s movements have often grafted the "poor" onto a list of "vanguards"; but if not an afterthought, the connection between the middle-class Left and the poorer classes was (and remains) tenuous at best.[31]

Many positive outcomes resulted from the various social movements that emerged in the post-1960s period. These include the revelation that people are oppressed not just by class systems and macro-level social policies but within their noneconomic roles as well. The idea that "the personal is political" was popularized by the women's movement. The movements for women's, minority group, gay and lesbian, and disabled people's rights, for example, all saw the social services and health systems as important arenas for struggle. Both the need for new services and rights such as abortion and birth control, day care, battered women's shelters, rape crisis centers, and the need for new forms of organizations, "alternative services" such as drop-in centers or woman-run clinics, became central issues to the politics of the 1970s and after.

Yet if the Old Left had vastly overstated the working class as an engine for change, the newer movements vastly overstated the role of the new vanguards. Politics came not only to *include* the social services, but sometimes seemed to be *only* the social services. In one particularly odd strain of this tendency, a combination of self-help, lifestyle-ism, and counterculture seemed to associate all positive values with the new service demands:

> A new service consciousness appears to have erupted with large numbers of the population concerned on an everyday basis with institutions related to mental health, health, day care, drugs, ranging even so far as the development of services to assist people facing death. . . . The groups that are reflecting the new, more advanced values of the society (the minorities, the women, the youth, and to some extent the educated affluents) have expressed considerable interest in service issues. . . . In essence, service is a major agenda for all of them, although in different ways for each. . . . The human services, because of their basic intent (benefits for the people) and mechanism for achieving this objective (relations among people) have important positive intrinsic potential.[32]

Although the optimism of self-help gurus Alan Gartner and Frank Riessman quoted above did not characterize all of the New Left or new social movements, its vast overstatement of the role of human service issues and workers would become quite common.

Oddly unexamined is the self-interest that the new social movements and human service workers had in promoting a vanguard role for themselves and, less consistently, their clients. In her 1984 book on social services as a radical left issue, Ann Withorn criticizes the Old Left for its lack of involvement in services. Withorn posits a unique role for service workers:

> It may be that sensitive, politically aware service workers have a critical and unique social role to play. It may be we, and not comrades with complex economic analyses and more narrowly materialistic conceptions of change, who can best articulate a political ideology and appeal to the masses of people who are feeling personally isolated and without permission to acknowledge their basic social needs.[33]

Steve Burghardt, another leftist in social work, waxes even more stirring on the capabilities of the radical human service worker: "Our pivotal 'insurrectionary' role can be to produce relationships between clients and workers that run counter to dominant social relationships produced elsewhere."[34]

I myself was among those guilty of such hyperbole.[35] To some extent many of us were protesting earlier notions of the social services as being only an instrument of social control and our perceived exclusion as professional workers from the old Marxist vanguard. Some youthful exaggeration should be expected. But it is surprising how little insight we had into our own self-interest. It has, as the years have gone by, been amply demonstrated by the upward mobility of many former activists in the social services as well as in academia, journalism, and government.

Why should human service workers or educators or doctors be seen as having some special role in social change?[36] No doubt people who counsel, who care for the homeless or battered women, who work at nursing homes and retirement centers, or who work with abused or neglected children are generally very good people performing useful roles. But many groups in society do "good" work. Why weren't firefighters, emergency medical technicians, air traffic controllers, structural engineers, mechanics, farmers, cooks, artists, masons, or carpenters embraced as vanguards? The "pivotal role" proposed for the human service worker, educator, or physician cast aside all sociological analysis of power and replaced it with the residue of Christian sentiment.

Although the halcyon days of the 1960s and 1970s are over, interestingly the literature by proponents of radical service work or defenders of social movement organizations[37] still generally fail to define what radical actions or social change actually flows from their work. Most often they simply assert forcefully their "goodness." Sympathetic observers of these groups often ignore the absence of a clear political ideology and the substitution of paid employment or voluntarism for the political demands and protests which characterized earlier movements. For example, in a breathless account of the Gay Men's Health Crisis (GMHC) in New

York, Philip Kayal admits that "gays taking the initiative to serve others in need reflects a value emphasized by all American religions and complements the country's Protestant and capitalistic character."[38] But still he insists that AIDS activism is different:

> AIDS volunteers are, by definition, in an authenticating experience as growing, connected persons. As such, gays become political actors. This empowerment through connectedness makes it possible to say *no* to misanthropic oppression and rejection and *yes* to survival as gay people. GMHC's development discredits the claim that voluntary action is an apolitical, secular activity.[39]

Kayal insists that "bearing witness" to the AIDS crisis is *political*, but his definition of "political" is essentially religious and mystical. In fact, his own study of the many GMHC volunteers found that they do not share his view. Acknowledging that his data shows that "the vast majority of volunteers do not generally root their activity in the political and social reality of AIDS and being gay," Kayal simply asserts, "This does not mean that gay/AIDS volunteerism is not political work, because it certainly is, if not in intent then at least in consequences." He adds later that "apparently the relationship of volunteerism to the politicization process remains unconscious."[40] Essentially, Kayal argues that gay voluntarism is "political" because he says it is so!

Accounts of feminist service organizations are similar. In an interesting analysis of three Massachusetts health centers between the 1970s and early 1990s, Cheryl Hyde notes the waning of explicit socialist-feminist ideology and suggests that it has become true that "agency orientations shaped movement orientations, a reversal of the relationship between these tendencies during the formative years."[41] Since these health centers had to secure funding, retain good relations with state or private organizations in their operating environment, and function as businesses, many original goals were cast aside in the conservative 1980s. But like Kayal, she defends the agencies against the arguments of co-optation or "goal displacement" mostly by assertion. Providing no clear definition of what would be "radical" politically or how we might judge the potential of social service as a strategic arena of political action, she concludes that since the clinics are still around and doing good work and receiving the support of local "progressives," co-optation or goal displacement has not occurred.[42]

## THE PRIMACY OF
## SENTIMENT TRIUMPHS AGAIN

Clearly, there are many reasons why the social services and non-profit sector took on such an élan in recent decades. These include the entry of a large number of activists into nonprofit agencies in the last few decades, sometimes after they experienced negative work experiences in the public sector.[43] Second, both the relative ease of creating new agencies and the opposition of conservative governments—for example, the AIDS crisis and the response of the Reagan period—led social movements to create their own or-ganizations rather than rely on government. Like jobs in the trade unions or with the New Deal government in the 1930s and 1940s, many liberals and leftists began to view these work sites as almost sacred realms, sometimes ignoring very real problems and contra-dictions which occur there as with all work in our society.[44]

But I would argue that it is primarily the quasi-religious "laying on" of hands and relational closeness (true to the religious tradition of Christianity) that seems to best explain the élan of the nonprofits and service work. Those who believe social service or volunteering or education are "liberating" are harking back to the Christian tra-dition discussed in chapter 3, whether they are personally religious or not. Once again, *being with* the poor or disabled or ill is seen as an end in itself. How else can we interpret statements such as this one by a volunteer quoted in the *Washington Post*, who says, "Go-ing out and serving homeless people is the most radical, hands-on thing you can do."[45] "Radical" in what sense? It seems to be the evocation of a personal closeness—again ends substituted for means—that is occurring. Sentiment replaces more profound his-torical or structural thought about how social change might come about.

Today's younger generation of activists, human service workers, and volunteers has seen no major radical movements in two decades and consequently has come to mistake the missionary zeal of service work with politics. For neophytes, the constant assertion that nonprofit social service agencies are somehow "political" reinforces the mistaking of bureaucratic organizations for social movements. The new generations do yearn for some meaningful activity. But the absence of large-scale social and political movement as well as the influence of elder siblings and the media has made the idea that volunteering with the homeless, with Habitat for Humanity, with people who have AIDS, or with battered women is about the most "radical" thing a person can do. And, what other models do young people in their teens and twenties now have? At best they may remember Live Aid or Hands across America, or they engage in local walks in their communities for good causes. "Doing good" has become, in the absence of active oppositional movements, the "only game in town" for those who want to embrace some cause broader than themselves.

## REPRISE:
## MORALIZING AN IMMORAL SYSTEM

In the preceding four chapters I have explored some of the changes as well as consistencies in the vastly expanded charitable enterprise. Obviously some positive changes have occurred in what today is called the nonprofit sector. We can applaud the gradual lessening of the stern Christian stewardship that so characterized early America. Today even the older moralistic organizations like the Salvation Army must share a place at the table with AIDS activists at a United Way dinner.

But there is a big "catch" to this new democracy in the nonprofits. The stern Christian stewardship is very much alive and well and increasingly represented by the twin forces of a repressive state and a harsh marketplace. As many activists found jobs with nonprofit contractors, what have been the major political changes of the last decades for many poor people and racial minorities? One can point to the return of capital punishment, the massive growth in prisons and other correctional facilities exemplified by the war on drugs, the consistent cutback of social welfare benefits in scope and size, and the decline of the labor movement as deindustrialization and the power of capital has waxed successfully. These are not really moral times no matter what gloss we put on them.

The paradox of so much claimed morality at a time of immorality could certainly not be planned. But the growth of the nonprofit sector at the same time that material conditions for the lower third of Americans have deteriorated supports a conclusion that the charitable sector legitimizes the other two sectors (capital and government) and also drains off energy, intellectual as well as physical, from any opposition to the developments mentioned above.

Just as the Medieval church for over a millennium served as a safety valve for idealistic young men who rejected the service of noblemen or the practice of warfare and hence entered monasteries or other church service, today the moralization of one sector (the nonprofit) balances and moralizes its opposites: the warlike correctional state and the competitive, unfeeling marketplace. For most middle-class Americans who have any sympathy for those in need, "giving" is a stance that is seen as the only alternative to doing nothing. Challenging the massive incarceration of the poor and African-Americans or the lack of power for workers at their jobs are no longer even subjects of much political debate. Nor do these issues seem to stir volunteers or donors. As the public sector is more and more stripped of any role that is seen as positive, thousands of potential public servants and perhaps millions of potential political activists abandon the state to its correctional mission—to arrest, punish, or divert into treatment—while they focus on the moral mission of giving a check to their favorite cause, volunteering once a week at a shelter, or preparing for a career in a human service or educational setting.

The morality of our new (secular) missions and monasteries rests, however, on the abandonment of considering the immorality of other systems. Since it is relatively easy to set up a soup kitchen, many middle-class idealists—and not a few poor people—agree that this is the solution to the problems of poverty, homelessness, or hunger. Hidden from view, even from discussion, is how the organization of private business could be changed or how the policies of the state and federal government could be altered. These issues seem too overwhelming, too far from home, and, for many, not even relevant. As the Church balanced feudal power and the monarch's military might, the institutions of charity and the élan of one-on-one service today serve a similar role.

# 7—Moving beyond Clichés

*Conceptions and words that have long ago lost their original meaning con-tinue through centuries to dominate mankind. Especially is this true if these conceptions have become commonplace, if they have been instilled in our beings from our infancy as great and irrefutable verities. The average mind is easily content with inherited and acquired things, or with the dicta of parents and teachers, because it is much easier to imitate than create.*

American anarchist Emma Goldman[1]

## BACK TO TINA TURNER´S QUESTION

In naming this book *What's Love Got to do with It?*, I admit to drawing shamelessly from popular culture. Nevertheless, the question as it relates to charity is a serious one. If "love" is un-derstood as a strong emotional sentiment which draws some people to others, there is no doubt that in most cases volunteers and paid workers at soup kitchens, homeless and battered wom-en's shelters, AIDS hospices, child welfare agencies, and social ser-vice programs for the elderly are motivated by love. In a sense, then, the answer to Tina Turner's question may well be "some-thing" or even, "Quite a bit."

Yet as a society we have become more skeptical about profes-sions of love. We realize that whether in romantic love, political campaigns, advertising slogans, or religious appeals, words of love and sentiment come cheap. There may be no quick way to identify what "real love" is, but we do realize that an entire context is nec-essary to evaluate "love." We know that the abusive partner may not only claim to love but sincerely believe he loves. So even in ro-mantic love, only over a long period of time, perhaps retrospec-tively, might we eventually say "it seems they were in love."

Yet, in an era when relationships between people are troubled enough that Turner can doubt whether "love" is nothing more than a "secondhand emotion," shouldn't we be skeptical when so many protestations of love emanate from high-level officials and af-fluent philanthropists? In retrospect, we now judge many historical practices of "helping people," such as those discussed in chapters 1 and 2, as primarily shaped by needs for control and power. The "love" of the missionary for the Indian and the early visitor for the poor seems to hold only ironic meanings for us, the way a lover who has experienced trauma from an ex-partner can hear "their" song only with bitterness. It is not the point whether individuals in these eras were well-meaning, but rather the overall social context in which their actions took place.

It is in this regard that the voluntary nonprofit sector as a social institution is at fault. As we saw in chapters 1 and 2, institutions which spoke in the name of love and moral improvement actually served as vehicles of repressive benevolence against those who were different from the Christian "civilized" norm. As discussed in chapters 4, 5, and 6, nonprofit institutions often serve the interests of the well-off (such as wealthy donors, influential boards of trustees or directors, and middle-class constituents) more than they do the presumed beneficiaries, such as poor people. While today's nonprofit world may seem to be a great advance over charity's repression of Indians or poor people centuries ago, the developments of recent years are in some ways even sadder than the prior history. First, they suggest how little progress in social organization we have made as a society. Second, today's volunteers and workers generally disavow the ethnocentric and strongly repressive views of the older American missionaries. That the fight for social justice has met with so little success despite the involvement of good people demonstrates more plainly than ever the fundamental weakness of the nonprofit sector as a vehicle for change.

Charity viewed as an institution takes raw recruits, often idealistic, and places them in a highly traditional regulated relationship to clients, patients, consumers, or other recipients. While it urges some incontestably good advice on its workers and volunteers, it also limits their action and controls their interaction in important ways. While we might all agree that professional and bureaucratic organization helps weed out some who might abuse clients, it also screens out those who might want to talk politics with clients, who might suggest that they "bite the hand that feeds them," or raise criticisms of institutional structures. In fact, as trained people know, sometimes the organizations weed out the most idealistic because they simply seek to chat with and learn from people called "clients," or because they are likely to ally themselves with clients in disputes with the agency. In the social work profession, for example, students are often told they are too idealistic or "overidentified" with their clients; less often, if at all, are they told they are *too* identified with their organization or *too* professional.[2] The range of emotion structured by charity may appear unlimited to the neophyte or analogous to familial or romantic love. But any trained human service worker or volunteer knows that this is not what human service work is about: the worker or volunteer who stays with the organization more than a short time follows rules, carries out agency policy, and performs limited and routinized tasks that the organization mandates. High idealism usually fades to conforming with rules, development of small-scale political and organizational skills, and professional credentialism. In other cases, "burnout," anger, or disillusionment occur. It can be argued that charitable organizations, rather than fostering love, serve to limit and tame it.

## ALTERNATIVES TO CHARITY

One of the conventions of Western society is that we always tend to compare actions to inaction rather than one set of acts against another. One reason why voluntarism or serving as a human service worker is so glorified in our culture is that these individuals are seen as *acting* (that is, not just doing nothing while people suffer). So the guiding assumption is that without vehicles to enlist people into volunteering or working in charity, the disabled, the ill, the poor, and others would suffer. But it is also possible to compare this manner of expressing compassion ("love") with other methods of expressing or implementing feelings and beliefs.

We can compare charity and social service with two other sets of social action: social movements and campaigns for a public social welfare system that would ensure a decent life for all citizens.

## Social Movements

What if all the energy that went into volunteering and working at millions of positions in the nonprofit economy were channeled elsewhere? What if these people were recruited as organizers of social action that demanded more for the needy? What if the challenge was seen as attempting to change society for the better rather than merely ladling out soup at a kitchen or making sandwiches at a shelter?

I was struck by a comment made by activist attorney Lloyd Rees on an ABC television special after the William Aramony scandal broke at the United Way of America in 1992. He compared labor and civil rights activist Cesar Chavez with the leaders of charities, such as William Aramony. Declaring that Chavez had taken a salary of only $6,707 a year as opposed to the hundreds of thousands of dollars a year that high-level charity officials receive, Rees suggested that Chavez had "done more for poor people than all the others [charity officials] combined."[3] Perhaps the comparison seems unfair at first; we can't all be a charismatic Cesar Chavez, but it does raise an important question. What if not only Chavez but other figures in American history such as Martin Luther King, Thomas Paine, Eugene V. Debs, Margaret Sanger, or Mother Jones had been content to serve at soup kitchens or join a religious mission somewhere? What if they had become therapists or professional administrators?

Why is it in Western society that the Mother Teresa figure is seen as a symbol of love, but those who organize people toward action, or those who write about injustice, or those who protest injustice are usually treated as dangers to society or, at best, misguided cranks? Social movements started by ordinary people have made positive changes in the conditions of working people, the poor, racial minorities, women, the disabled and elderly, and many others. Without the committed and persistent unrest among labor and the unemployed during the 1930s, there most likely would be no Social Security pensions, unemployment insurance, or rights to organize a union; without the ghetto riots and welfare rights movements of the 1960s, it is unlikely that many of the social programs of the 1960s and 1970s would have been created.[4] It is significant to note that most of America's social welfare legislation was passed into law only during two brief periods—from 1934 to 1938 and 1964 to 1973—both periods of marked social unrest and political instability.

But throughout most of the West, Christian sentiment is heroized while those involved in conflictual movements are villainized. Occasionally, such as in the case of Martin Luther King, a retrospective halo is placed on a few of these movement leaders who displayed sufficient loyalty to Christianity during their lives. But this occurs only after death and primarily for reasons of political expediency. In most cases, agitators and organizers are not held as having anything to do with "love" at all. Even if one excludes figures who are obviously controversial—such as Debs, Goldman, or Malcolm X—it is still rare for sanctity to fall on social movements or their leaders. Tom Paine may have been a revolutionary leader admired in retrospect, but he is not glorified in the way Mother Teresa is. John L. Lewis, the great labor organizer, is probably unknown to most schoolchildren, and if he is mentioned at all in school, chances are he would not be portrayed in a positive light. Why can't "love" be associated with labor organizing (Chavez, Lewis), with political leadership (Paine, Goldman, Debs), with social movement leadership (King, Malcolm X) or with brave innovation (like Sanger and birth control) rather than only with those who adhere to conventionality?

In fact "love" turns out to be political. Just as until recently same-sex love was rejected as immoral and unnatural, social actions taken to demonstrate love and compassion are socially constructed as such only through political compliance with dominant norms. Love is limited to its association with Christian symbolism and considered unrelated to other actions which arguably may be more important, effective, and courageous than charity. Absent a commitment to Christianity and its symbols of conciliation and sentiment, there is no ideological space for movements and their leaders to be enshrined in the American pantheon.

## Public Social Welfare

Just as sentiment grounded in traditional Christianity and the gestures of charity seem more heroic than social movements, so too charity seems to surpass any vision of a society that shares its store of resources, a vision at the heart of many political theories from social democracy to communism. Why is a society that punishes its poorest people—ushering them into prisons and homeless shelters rather than providing them with income or material resources—considered a society motivated by "love"? Why are societies that make efforts to distribute their wealth not accorded such praise?

To take one example, Norway uses its oil wealth to provide a rich public social welfare system including a family allowance of $1,620 per child (to all families); forty-two weeks of paid maternity leave; retirement pay at a generous level to homemakers who did not work outside the home; a year off with pay every decade for workers to retrain; and a health care system which limits personal costs to $187-a-year per individual.[5] Or to take another example, I quote an observer's comments about France:

> The benefits of living in a country where the government was expected to furnish all essential social services were obvious. . . . French mothers—whether married or single, rich or poor—received the equivalent of $150 a month from the government for each of their children under age eighteen. Apartment owners could not evict tenants who were behind in their rent during the winter months. Office workers had a right to a desk by the window where they could see the sunrise or sunset. Employers in Paris were required to pay for half the commuting costs of their employees. Everyone was entitled to a vacation, usually lasting five weeks. In the case of poorer families, the government subsidized the holiday, including the costs of transportation to the mountains or the Mediterranean.[6]

It is well-known to social scientists that those nations which provide generous social welfare systems know little of homelessness, hunger, poverty, or high rates of violent crime. The only response Americans (of conservative, moderate, or liberal stripe) tend to muster to this information are comments such as, "Aren't the taxes too high there?" or "Aren't the governments too strong?" Suddenly, when asked to potentially express "love" through concrete financial action, a new reticence takes over. "Let's not get carried away."

Policy experts have long debated America's lack of a strong social welfare system, usually the rubric of "American exceptionalism." To the many causes for the historic weakness of the American welfare state, I note that in addition to the usual explanations—heterogeneity of our country by nationality, ethnicity, and religion; individualism and a cowboy settler mentality; and the weakness of trade unionism, socialism, and labor parties—the meagerness of the American public social welfare system is also explained by our love affair with charity, voluntarism, and nonprofit organization. America's private system of organization of social services, universities, hospitals, and other health care facilities is a brake upon any effort to construct a fairer, better society. As was evident in the health care debate several years ago, private parties are so strong in America that even mild reforms are often scotched. In addition to the raw political power of both the nonprofit sector and the private for-profit sector examined in earlier chapters, there is the power of the charitable ideology. A combination of charity, therapy, and correction is held to be necessary in the United States to solve a host of social problems. Some descriptors (the aged, a homeless woman and child) conjure up the romance of charity, while others (the drug user, the male vagrant) conjure up correctional strategies, and some (such as mental illness or children who are insufficiently passive and submissive in school) suggest some modicum of therapy and correction. But very few people favor delivering cash to people in need.

Except in some small circles, it is considered silly to suggest that money or resources would help the above groups (the catchall "throwing money at problems"). The relation between lack of money and homelessness and child abuse, between poverty and crime, long term drug use, and serious mental disability is rarely acknowledged by Americans today. To acknowledge some of these facts would challenge too much of Americans' symbolic understanding and ideology. It would imply that social class and economic structure dictate many of our social problems, not primarily our morals, character, or Christian sentiment.

## BEYOND SYMBOLISM

America's proud faith in its independence and lack of a welfare state comes at a considerable price. To cite just several examples, we trip over millions of people a year living on our streets rather than build more affordable housing or provide other genuinely useful aid to poor people; we must worry about the millions of people who avoid health care facilities because they are without insurance, and could communicate their diseases to others; and we spend a fortune to house a large segment of our population in correctional institutions since we allow so many people to grow up in poverty.

As much as our political leaders, religious figures, social service administrators, and united way chieftains pat themselves on the back and exhort us to volunteer our time or give to charity, there are some relatively simple answers to many social problems that most Americans will not entertain. To take just two examples, organizing more of the workforce into strong unions to push up wages and fringe benefits, and forcing a higher rate of corporate taxation to provide income, housing, and health care for all Americans, would do far more good than a thousand charitable campaigns.

We know that cross-national studies show a correlation between the strength of worker organization—in trade unions and labor parties—and the level of the welfare state.[7] A weak, cowered labor force that is primarily unorganized, as currently exists today in America, cannot force business to improve workers' wages and benefits. Much less is it able to press to raise the minimum wage or increase unemployment benefits, pensions, health care insurance, and other aid to the rest of the working class. With all the economic problems in Europe and elsewhere in the world, nations with strongly organized unions and working-class parties have done best in developing and preserving benefits for all citizens, not just union members. The problem for Americans is that to organize for themselves means conflict with their employers (at least in the short term) rather than expressions of "love."

Similarly, instead of waxing rhapsodic about corporations giving

1 percent of their pre-tax billions to charity,[8] a serious campaign to force big business to finance the benefits that many European workers and their families *already* receive would be a most valuable way for the rich to display their "love." Americans *could* demand family allowances, paid maternity leaves, national health insurance, unemployment pay that actually replaces most wages lost when out of work, and so on. Key to a movement at some point around these issues will have to be the *universality* of benefits (that is, all citizens need to gain some benefits) and *equity* in finance (that the tax burden is not borne primarily by those not affluent).

It's true at the moment that these ideas seem radical. Political debate more often focuses on how much to cut the public benefits that remain. Until the billions in resources tied up in corporate accounts (and in areas of government finance) are held to have something to do with expressing "love," all the sentimental dialogue about "helping people" will be just that; a symbolic and clichéd manner to show that one is doing good without accomplishing very much.

# —Notes

## INTRODUCTION

1. Arendt, H., *On Revolution.* New York: Viking, 1963, pp. 74–75.

2. Thoreau, H. D., *Walden and Essays on Civil Disobedience.* New York: Airmont Publishing Co., 1965, pp. 59–60.

3. Reagan quoted in frontispiece in Brilliant, E., *The United Way: Dilemmas of Organized Charity.* New York: Columbia University Press, 1990.

4. Clinton quoted in Purdum, T., (*New York Times*) "Volunteering Gets Powerful Push," in *Portland Press Herald,* January 25, 1997, 2A.

5. The quotes from de Tocqueville (from *Democracy in America*) and Bremner are in Bremner, R., *American Philanthropy.* Chicago: University of Chicago Press, 1960, p. 42 and p. 1 respectively.

6. McCarthy, K., (ed.), *Lady Bountiful Revisited: Women, Philanthropy, and Power.* New Brunswick, NJ: Rutgers University Press, 1990, p. ix.

7. Wencour, S., Cook, R., & Steketee, N., "Fund-Raising at the Workplace," *Social Policy,* 14:4, (spring 1984): p. 57.

8. Debs cited in Lagemann, E. C., *The Politics of Knowledge: The Carnegie Corporation, Philanthropy, and Public Policy.* Middletown, CT: Wesleyan University Press, 1989, pp. 23–24.

9. Lundberg, F., *The Rich and Super-Rich.* New York: Bantam, 1968, pp. 465–66.

10. Polsky, A., *The Rise of the Therapeutic State.* Princeton: Princeton University Press, 1991.

11. For a brief review of the "seamier" side of American social welfare history, see my "Welfare 'Reform' or Putting the Letter 'P' Back on the Poor," in *Flying Horse* (1997) 1:2, pp. 54–56, also in the *Bangor Daily News,* September 9, 1996, p. 12. The "charity trains" refer to the origin of American foster care in the placing out of poor immigrant children (often against the parent's will) from the Eastern cities to the West started by Charles Loring Brace and the Children's Aid Society in the 1870s, and recently the subject of a PBS documentary.

12. Tonry, M., *Malign Neglect: Race, Crime, and Punishment in America.* Oxford University Press, 1995, presents one of the best critiques of how corrections has replaced social welfare as the dominant force, at least in many African-American communities. Tonry's early chapters provide good data on the percentage of African-American men in the correctional system, particularly since the "war on drugs."

13. DeLoria, V., *Custer Died for Your Sins: An Indian Manifesto.* London: Macmillan, 1969, see especially pp. 101–2.

14. Cited in Wood, *The Arrogance of Faith: Christianity and Race in America from the Colonial Era to the Twentieth Century.* New York: Knopf, 1990, p. 19.

15. McKnight, J., *The Careless Society: Community and its Counterfeits.* New York: Basic Books, 1995, p. 176.

16. Piven, F. & Cloward, R., *Regulating the Poor: The Functions of Public Welfare.* New York: Vintage, 1993 [Orig. 1971], p. xvii.

17. Piven and Cloward are also among the most seminal critics of the sentimental historiography of social welfare. On social welfare historians in particular, see their "Humanitarianism in History: A Response to Critics," in Trattner, W., ed., *Social Welfare or Social Control?* Knoxville, TN: University of Tennessee Press, 1983.
18. The best social welfare history that critiques the tendency to see public social welfare and private aid as totally separate is Michael Katz's *In The Shadow of the Poorhouse* (New York: Basic Books, 1986). I had initially intended in this book to cover both the well-understood use of the word "charity" as private efforts to aid the poor, the American government's symbiotic relation with it, and, departing most from prevailing wisdom, "charity" as representing the new government style of giving a therapeutic response to all social problems. That is, while classically scholars have stressed the change from "charity" to "welfare state," in fact, the sentiment and character reform objectives of charity have so permeated government policy that this word may best describe the therapeutic and service objectives of the neoliberal state. However, I did decide to limit my main focus to the private voluntary sector.
19. An important sociological dictum of W. I. Thomas.
20. This phrase was the actual motto of the Boston Associated Charities but was widely cited by all the Charity Organization Societies (COS) of the late nineteenth and early twentieth centuries. The friendly visitor—the usually unpaid predecessor to today's social worker—was meant to influence the poor or immigrant family by teaching or giving advice, not by distributing alms or money. See Lubove, R., *The Professional Altruist: The Emergence of Social Work as a Career, 1880–1930*. New York: Athenum, 1975, chapters 1 and 2.

CHAPTER 1

1. Quoted in Kvasnicka, R. & Viola, H., *The Commissioners of Indian Affairs, 1824–1977*. Lincoln: University of Nebraska Press, 1979, p. 54.
2. Jaimes cited in preface to Ward Churchill's *Fantasies of the Master Race*. Monroe, ME: Common Courage Press, 1992, p. 3.
3. DeLoria, V., *Custer Died for Your Sins*, 1969, p. 101.
4. From Thomas Morton's "New Canaan" reproduced in Washburn, W., *The Indian and the White Man*. Garden City, NY: Doubleday, 1964, pp. 38–39.
5. From John Heckewelder, originally from "Account of the History, Manners, and Customs of the Indian Nations, Who Once Inhabited Pennsylvania and the Neighbouring States," reproduced as document 20 in Ibid., pp. 63–65.
6. See discussion of the religious debates in Europe in Mander, J., *In the Absence of the Sacred*. San Francisco: Sierra Books, 1991, p. 199.
7. Under the "Doctrine of Discovery," the papal bulls asserted that ordinarily the indigenous peoples of a "discovered" land should keep their land, unless, of course, they refused to trade with the settlers, refused to accept religious missionaries, or began a fight with the various authorities. This Catholic ruling then did not always play out very differently from Protestant practice. The interpretation that the "savages" had to agree to accept the dominion of the monarchs and Christianity allowed for any resistance to justify violence. In some cases, Spanish explorers read (in Spanish) the manifesto of the doctrine of discovery from their ships. Indigenous peoples, neither understanding the language or meaning of such speech, were usu-

ally friendly but had no intention of giving up their own ways. After a period — days in some cases, longer in other areas — this became clear to European explorers and often violence erupted.

8. Churchill, W., *Struggle for the Land*. Monroe, ME: Common Courage Press, 1993, pp. 37–38.

9. Quote of Powell and preceding discussion of Morgan in Hoxie, F., *A Final Promise: The Campaign to Assimilate the Indians, 1880–1920*. Cambridge: Cambridge University Press, 1989, pp. 17–23.

10. Slotkin, R., *Regeneration Through Violence*. New York: Harper Perennial, 1996.

11. See Ward Churchill's "And They Did it Like Dogs in the Dirt" (review of the movie *Black Robe*) in *Indians Are Us? Culture and Genocide in Native North America*. Monroe, ME: Common Courage Press, 1994, pp. 115–37.

12. One example of a Catholic missionary who opposed the government's policies during the terrible "trail of tears" in the 1830s (when Indians were forcibly moved from their homelands to the West) was Father Andrew Petit, who stayed with the Potawatomi nation as they were pushed thousands of miles west and died with them. See "Apostle to the People of Fire," in Jahoda, G., *The Trail of Tears*. New York: Random House, 1975, pp. 190–208.

13. Cited in Wood, *Arrogance of Faith*, pp. 18–20.

14. Slotkin, *Regeneration Through Violence*, p. 51.

15. Quoted in Zinn, H., *A People's History of the United States*. New York: Harper and Row, 1980, p. 14.

16. As is evident in the essays in Calloway, C., ed., *After King Philip's War: Presence and Persistence in Indian New England* (Hanover, NH: University Press of New England, 1997), resistance in New England never ceased, but King Philip's War did mark the end of the possibility of indigenous military success against the settlers.

17. Wood, *The Arrogance of Faith*, pp. 262–63.

18. From the records of the Governor and Company of the Massachusetts Bay in New England, reproduced as Document 45 in Washburn, *The Indian and the White Man*, p. 184.

19. DeLoria, *Custer Died for Your Sins*, p. 109.

20. Ibid, p. 10.

21. Ibid, p. 102.

22. Josephy, A., *The Nez Perce Indians and the Opening of the Northwest*. Boston: Houghton-Miflin, 1997, pp. 83–84.

23. Ibid, pp. 126–28.

24. Ibid, p. 131.

25. Ibid, p. 160.

26. Ibid, pp. 161, 164.

27. Ibid, p. 230.

28. Ibid.

29. Ibid, p. 218.

30. Ibid, p. 223.

31. Ibid, p. 234.

32. Ibid, p. 245.

33. Ibid, p. 281.

34. Hoxie, F., *A Final Promise: The Campaign to Assimilate the Indians, 1880–1920.* See particularly pp. 10–14.

35. Ibid, pp. xi–xii.

36. Ibid, p. 11.

37. Quoted in Mander, J., *In the Absence of the Sacred,* pp. 275–76.

38. Quoted in Ibid, p. 276.

39. Hoxie, F., *A Final Promise,* p. 180.

40. Kvasnicka & Viola, *The Commissioners of Indian Affairs, 1824–1977,* p. 198.

41. Hoxie, F. *A Final Promise,* p. 195.

42. Churchill, W., "In the Matter of Julius Streicher," in *Indians Are Us? Culture and Genocide in Native North America,* pp. 76–77.

43. For the missions approach to African-Americans, quite similar in repressive impact to Indians, see Van Horne, J., ed., *Religious Philanthropy and Colonial Slavery* (Urbana, IL: University of Illinois Press, 1985). In using "whites" as a label, I do not mean to exclude other groups or the complex amalgam of heritages that is actually the reality of "race," hence I place the quotes here on whites. The key point is that many people not stigmatized by their evident racial category were objects of character reform as noted in the text.

44. DeLoria, *Custer Died for Your Sins,* pp. 239–40.

45. Cited in Slotkin, *Regeneration Through Violence,* p 65.

46. Ibid, p. 254.

47. For a very readable account of how the Indians influenced the Constitution, see Weatherford, J., *Indian Givers: How the Indians of America Transformed the World* (New York: Crown, 1988). In 1988 both houses of Congress passed resolutions "Acknowledging the contribution of the Iroquois Confederation to the development of the United States Constitution." Senate Con. Resolution 76.

48. Mather cited in Bremner, *American Philanthropy,* pp. 12–14.

49. C. E. Wright, *The Transformation of Charity in Postrevolutionary New England.* Boston: Northeastern University Press, 1992, pp. 177–79.

50. Calloway, C., *After King Philip's War: Presence and Persistence in Indian New England,* p. 9.

51. O'Brien, J., "'Divorced' from the Land: Resistance and Survival of Indian Women in Eighteenth-Century New England," in Ibid, p. 153.

CHAPTER 2

1. Richmond, M., *Friendly Visiting Among the Poor.* Montclair, NJ: Patterson Smith, 1969 [orig 1899], p. 151.

2. Lowell quoted in Katz, M., *In The Shadow of the Poorhouse,* p. 80.

3. Perhaps among the more comprehensive descriptions of some of the harsh treatments of the poor are Schneider, D., *The History of Public Welfare in New York State* (New York State: New York, 1939), and Deustch, A., *The Mentally Ill in America* (New York: Columbia University Press, 1949). Deustch gives a particularly detailed treatment of the "dumping" of mentally ill paupers and the auctioning off of the poor. For discussion of the treadmill, see Schneider, pp. 151–55.

4. This is essentially the framework developed in the works of Frances Fox Piven and Richard Cloward, particularly in *Regulating the Poor: The Functions of Public Wel-*

*fare and Poor People's Movements: Why They Succeed, How They Fail* (New York: Pantheon, 1977). We are quite obviously (and have been since the late 1970s) in a down cycle of history in which lack of militant protest by the poor, weakness in labor and other supporters of reform, and the strength of corporate power have eroded gains made by the lower classes in the 1960s and early 1970s.

5. See, for example, the frequent use of public works in New York in the 1850s and 1860s to contain social unrest described in Bernstein, *New York City Draft Riots* (New York: Oxford University Press, 1990), pp. 99, 138–42; Schneider (*The History of Public Welfare in New York State*) describes the use of public works in New York City to aid the poor as early as 1807 (p. 170).

6. Reverend Chapin was New York City's leading Universalist minister. This quote is cited in Horlick, A., *Country Boys and Merchant Princes: The Social Control of Young Men in New York*. Lewisburg, PA: Bucknell University Press, 1975, p. 54.

7. Winthrop and Penn quoted in Bremner, *American Philanthropy*, pp. 8–10.

8. Although the distinction between the "deserving" and "undeserving" poor (or in some statutes the "worthy" and "unworthy") has a long history emanating from the English Poor Laws, widows, orphans, the elderly, and others presumably deserving often ended up being treated quite harshly, for example, by being placed in poorhouses, auctioned off, and so on. Perhaps the best explanation for this contradiction is given by Michael Katz: "In essence, social policy advocated shutting up the old and sick away from their friends and relatives to deter the working class from seeking poor relief." (Katz, 1986, p. 25). Put in an even harsher light, the commissioners of the New York almshouse stated in 1875, "Care has been taken not to diminish the terrors of this last resort of poverty, because it has been deemed better that a few should test the minimum rate at which existence can be preserved, than that the many should find the poorhouse so comfortable a home that they would brave the shame . . ." Cited in Schneider and Deustch, volume 2 of *The History of Public Welfare in New York State*, p. 38.

9. Franklin quoted in Olasky, M., *The Tragedy of American Compassion*. Washington, D.C.: Regnery Publishing, Inc., 1992, p. 43.

10. Rush quoted in Alexander, J., *Render them Submissive: Responses to Poverty in Philadelphia*. Amherst: University of Massachusetts, 1980, p. 6.

11. Wright, C., *The Transformation of Charity in Postrevolutionary New England*, see particularly p. 5 and p. 60.

12. Rothman, D., *The Discovery of the Asylum*. Boston: Little, Brown and Company, 1971, pp. xviii–xix.

13. Beecher quoted in Boyer, P., *Urban Masses and the Moral Order in America, 1820–1920*. Cambridge, MA: Harvard University Press, 1978, pp. 12–13.

14. Bethune quoted in Ibid, p. 119.

15. Gurteen quoted in Ibid, p. 145.

16. Quoted in Bernstein, I., *The New York City Draft Riots*, p. 235.

17. Reverend Prime cited in Horlick, *Country Boys*, pp. 62–63.

18. Brace, C. L., *The Dangerous Classes of New York and Twenty Years of Work Among Them*. New York: Wynkoop & Hallenback, 1880, pp. 22–23.

19. For seminal accounts of the Jacksonian period attack on outdoor relief, see Rothman, *Discovery of the Asylum*, and Katz, M., *In the Shadow of the Poorhouse*.

Although historians often focus on the Yates Report in New York and Quincy Report in Massachusetts, the history indicates success in eliminating outdoor relief in many states including the ones mentioned.

20. Two of the best accounts of charity leaders' attacks on outdoor relief occur in "Brooklyn and the War Against Outdoor Relief," in Katz, *In the Shadow*, pp. 47–54, and in Schneider & Deutsch (volume 2), *The History of Public Welfare in New York State*, see chapters 3, 4, 6, and 11 through 13 for the virulence of New York's charity leaders in fighting both outdoor relief and the mothers' pension movement in New York. The data reporting that ten cities had cut outdoor relief (along with significant reductions in aid in three other cities) comes from Fredric Almy, a leader of Buffalo's Charity Organization Society who did an 1899 survey, cited in Katz, p. 43.

21. Bernstein, *The New York City Draft Riots*, pp. 68–71.

22. There certainly was endemic corruption in the operation of many political machines in the days before civil service and other reforms. In this sense the reformers' and philanthropists' charge that outdoor relief was "political," that is, that it rewarded campaign supporters or fellow ethnic group members or sought to buy votes, was true in many cases. But looked at from a more humane perspective, outdoor relief along with other features of political machines such as patronage jobs allowed urban immigrants to survive. The repressive aspects of "good government" campaigns lie in their lack of any sympathy for the poor or working classes, who are urged to simply "pull themselves up by their own bootstraps."

For a wonderful example of a twentieth-century politician whose career as mayor, governor, and congressman was marked by a dedication to "outdoor relief" for his supporters and by the the bitter opposition of reformers, see Beatty, J., *The Rascal King: The Life and Times of James Michael Curley, 1874–1958* (Reading, MA: Addison-Wesley, 1992). A story, perhaps apocryphal, of Curley's weekly meetings outside city hall with a poor Boston Irish man who drank too much to give him a few dollars surreptitiously as a "loan" (in order not to embarrass him) reflects some of the social class, ethnic, and religious differences in almsgiving and views of aid.

23. Katz, *In the Shadow*, pp. 47–54.

24. See chapter 11 of Schneider & Deutsch (volume 2), *The History of Public Welfare in New York State*, quote on p. 182.

25. The first chapter of Piven, F. & Cloward, R., *Regulating the Poor: The Functions of Public Welfare*, provide some historical sense of how both the religious/secular and public/private sectors experimented with dividing up the poor and developing a system of visitation and surveillance.

26. Quote is from Schneider, pp. 187–88; see also McCarthy, K., ed., *Lady Bountiful Revisited*, chapter 1.

27. Alexander, *Render Them Submissive*, p. 139.

28. Gurteen quoted in Katz, *In the Shadow*, p. 76.

29. Carson, M., *Settlement Folk*. Chicago: University of Chicago Press, 1990, p. 1, p. 5.

30. Gurteen quoted in Boyer, *Urban Masses*, p. 151.

31. Hill quoted in Bremner, *American Philanthropy*, p. 100.

32. Jacques Donzelot's best-known work is *The Policing of Families* (New York:

Pantheon, 1979). The quote is from Polsky, *The Rise of the Therapeutic State*, pp. 58–59.

33. Stadum, *Poor Women and Their Families: Hard Working Charity Cases, 1900–1930*, Albany, NY: SUNY Press, 1992, pp. 8–12. Neither Stadum nor I are suggesting that this case was *typical* of *all* contacts with the Associated Charities, but the Pernet case illustrates how much control the charities came to have over the lives of poor women.

34. The case records come from an unidentified agency in Connecticut. See O' Keefe, D., "Annals of Social Work," *American Heritage* 36 (1985): pp. 100–101. They are fragments of case records, so admittedly do not represent all actions taken with each client by the agency.

35. Recent feminist scholarship has tended to reinterpret nineteenth and early-twentieth-century charity from a gender lens. An analysis almost uncritical of women visitors is McCarthy, K., ed., *Lady Bountiful Revisited*. More nuanced and interesting are Gordon, L., *Heroes of Their Own Lives*, New York: Viking Press, 1988; Ginzberg, L., *Women and the Work of Benevolence*, New Haven: Yale University Press, 1990, and Pleck, E., *Domestic Tyranny: The Making of American Social Policy against Family Violence*, New York: Oxford, 1987. The latter three books, for example, suggest that charitable intervention could strongly aid abused and neglected women, but all acknowledge that such efforts were always framed along class lines and poor women often paid a major price for their involvement with charity officials and visitors.

36. Stadum, *Poor Women and Their Families*, p. 149.

37. Dubofsky, M., *When Workers Organize: New York City in the Progressive Era*. Amherst: University of Massachusetts Press, 1968, p. 26.

38. Gompers cited in Withorn, A., *Serving the People: Social Services and Social Change*. New York: Columbia University Press, 1984, p.13.

39. Reed quoted in Katz, *In the Shadow of the Poorhouse*, p. 84.

40. See particularly the work of Mimi Abramovitz (*Regulating the Lives of Women*, Boston: South End Press, 1996) on gender discrimination in Social Security and other pieces of social welfare legislation, and the work of Jill Quadagno (*The Color of Welfare*, New York: Oxford University Press, 1994) on the racial biases of social welfare legislation.

41. The strongest proponent of returning to the nineteenth-century model is Marvin Olasky. See particularly his *The Tragedy of American Compassion* (1992) which carries an endorsement from Newt Gingrich and an introduction by Charles Murray. But liberals and feminists also have taken umbrage at critical presentations of the past. For example, the attacks by liberal social welfare historians on the work of Frances Fox Piven and Richard Cloward assembled in Trattner, W., ed., *Social Welfare or Social Control?* (1983), particularly by Trattner, Muriel & Ralph Pumphrey, and James Leiby, and the reinterpretations of the friendly visitor by McCarthy, ed., 1990 (above), indicate that at least some social welfare historians, social work academics, and feminist writers are uncomfortable with the harsh realities of the nineteenth century and Progressive Period and prefer a more sentimental account.

PART II:

THE SURPRISING SUCCESS OF CHARITY AS SYMBOLISM

1. Pinchot quoted in Smith, S. & Lipsky, M., *Nonprofits for Hire*. Cambridge, MA: Harvard University Press, 1994, p. 15.
2. Zinn, H., *A People's History of the United States*, p. 62.
3. Ibid, p. 238.
4. James Paterson uses surveys from the 1930s, 1960s, and 1970s to indicate that the American view of poverty and social welfare have not changed very radically. For example, even in the 1930s (p. 45), polls show that the public supported work requirements over the dole and local control over federal entitlements. Similarly in the 1960s and 1970s, beliefs about welfare and the poor remained fairly stereotypic and characterological among a majority of Americans. See pp. 109, 157–58, and 202 in Paterson, J., *America's Struggle Against Poverty, 1900–1985*. Cambridge, MA: Harvard University Press, 1986.

CHAPTER 3

1. Day, D., *The Long Loneliness*. New York: Harper, 1952, p. 150.
2. Camilio Torres in Gerrasi, J., ed., *Revolutionary Priest: The Complete Writings and Messages of Camilo Torres*. New York: Vintage, 1971, p. 313.
3. As Karl Marx put it in "The Communism of the Paper Rheinischer Beobachter" in 1847, "The social principles of Christianity justified slavery of Antiquity, glorified the serfdom of the Middle Ages and equally know, when necessary, how to defend the oppression of the proletariat, although they make a pitiful face over it." (See *Marx and Engels on Religion*. New York: Schoken, 1964, p. 83). Most major sociologists of religion tend to agree. Both Max Weber and Ernest Troeltsch distinguished sects and oppositional salvation religions, which are often "radical" in a broad sense, from established churches, which are generally cooperative with secular power. The record of the major church bodies in America on a host of issues from slavery to Indian repression to the incarceration of Japanese-Americans to the rights of business to repress strikes has not been a good one. The church does better in retrospect, condemning past oppressions. Significant change has taken place within certain Protestant denominations since the 1960s. Their relative liberalism in the last two decades has been partly provoked by the overall move to the Right in the nation's political debate as well as the polarization with Protestant fundamentalism. However, even the most liberal Protestant churches' or Jewish synagogues' or Catholic Bishops' statements have not exactly been of a revolutionary or anticapitalist nature.
4. Mother Teresa quotes from Christopher Hitchens' irreverent *The Missionary Position: Mother Teresa in Theory and Practice*. London: Verso, 1995, pp. 10–11, 95.
5. Troeltsch, E., *The Social Teaching of the Christian Churches*. London: George Allen and Unwin, Ltd., 1956, p. 134.
6. Biblical quotes from Meeks, W., *The Origins of Christian Morality: The First Two Centuries*. New Haven: Yale University Press, 1993, p. 50.
7. Martin Luther quoted in Tawney, *Religion and The Rise of Capitalism*. New York: Penguin, 1926, p. 84.

8. Vincent de Paul quoted in Washburn, H., *The Religious Motive in Philanthropy*. Freeport, NY: Books for Libraries Press, 1970, p. 21.

9. It is again important to distinguish organized churches from millennial movements, as do Weber, Troeltsch, Marx and Engels, and most sociologists of religion.

10. See, for example, the description of the Catholic worker movement in Murray, H., *Do Not Neglect Hospitality: The Catholic Worker and the Homeless*, Philadelphia: Temple University Press, 1990. Murray, a self-professed radical, offers no concrete political program, objectives, demands, or proposals other than "being with" those in need.

11. Aries, P. & Duby, G., *The History of Private Life*. Cambridge: Belknap Press, 1988, volume 1, p. 262.

12. Cited in Carter, R., *The Gentle Legions*. Garden City, NY: Doubleday, 1961, pp. 29–30.

13. Cited in Geremek, B., *Poverty: A History*. Oxford: Basil Blackwell, 1994, p. 20.

14. Ibid, p. 35.

15. Tawney, *Religion and The Rise of Capitalism*, p. 33.

16. One of the best descriptions of the relative glorification and tolerance for the poor in precapitalist times is in chapter 1 of Miller, H., *On the Fringe: The Dispossessed in America*. Lexington, MA: D.C. Heath, 1991, pp. 1–23. In fact, almost all social welfare textbooks support the notion that there was both a decline in conditions for the poor and a severe loss of status as the feudal era ended and capitalism arose.

17. Aries & Duby, *The History of Private Life*, volume 2, p. 66.

18. Ramsey, B., "Almsgiving in the Latin Church: The Late Fourth and Early Fifth Centuries," *Theological Studies* 43 (1982): p. 252.

19. Aries & Duby, *The History of Private Life*, volume 1, pp. 278–79.

20. Both quotes (Byrne and Roche) from Mann, A., *Yankee Reformers in the Urban Age: Social Reform in Boston, 1880–1900*. New York: Harper and Row, 1954, p. 26 and p. 49.

21. Ibid, p. 75. See also the descriptions of late-nineteenth-century and twentieth-century religious radicals and their hostility to the organized church in Craig, R., *Religion and Radical Politics: An Alternative Tradition in the United States*, Philadelphia: Temple University Press, 1992. The radical change in both Protestantism and Catholicism in the late nineteenth century, from representing a rather conservative political position to a mild-to-moderate liberalism (in modern terms), was greatly provoked by the loss of legitimacy occurring in both the American and European churches at that time as socialist movements gained adherents, sometimes at the expense of the church.

22. Troeltsch, E., *The Social Teaching of the Christian Churches*, p. 201. Of course, separation of realms of life are relative. Although the most idealistic and ascetic aspects of Christianity dwelled apart from the public realm of church/kingdom, as the text suggests, Catholicism had a tremendous political and economic influence during feudalism, which weakened considerably with the advent of capitalism.

23. Tawney, *Religion and The Rise of Capitalism*, pp. 199, 229. Theorists differ on the degree to which Protestantism was a necessary condition for the rise of capitalism. Weber's classical treatment in *The Protestant Ethic and the Spirit of Capitalism* argued this, but writers from Tawney to Geremek (above) have modified or dissented

from aspects of the Weberian thesis. Unquestionably though, whether an inevitability is to be imputed or not or an incompatibility between Medieval Catholicism and capitalism is complete or not, in Western history the glorification of trade, banking, and profit occurred in the Protestant dominated regions of Europe first.

24. Tawney, *Religion and the Rise of Capitalism*, p. 163.

25. Weber, M., *Economy and Society*. Berkeley: University of California Press, 1978, volume 1, p. 585.

CHAPTER 4

1. Steinbeck quoted in Nielsen, W., *The Big Foundations*. New York: Columbia University Press, 1972, p. 311.

2. See, for example, statistics from 1990 in Clotfelter, C., *Who Benefits from the Nonprofit Sector?*, Chicago: University of Chicago Press, 1992. Those earning under $10,000 a year actually contribute a higher percentage of their income than those earning more, though at over the $100,000-a-year point the curve again approaches the lowest income group. Of course, the patterns of giving are quite different between the poor and rich, with more contributions of the poor being church-related while most of the rich's money goes to cultural and educational institutions.

3. Hall, P. D., *Inventing the Nonprofit Sector*. Baltimore: Johns Hopkins Press, 1992. See particularly pp. 17–30; see also Marcus, C. (with Hall), *Lives in Trust: The Fortunes of Dynastic Families in the Late Twentieth-Century America*, Boulder, CO: Westview, 1992, pp. 60–81.

4. Hall, *Inventing the Nonprofit*, pp. 28–30.

5. Marcus, *Lives in Trust*, pp. 64–69.

6. Both Wright in *The Transformation of Charity in Postrevolutionary New England*, and Marcus in Ibid use the term "fiduciary model" as a near synonym for "trusteeship." Possibly the fiduciary concept is broader since it extends the notion of "trust" to those who eventually came to sit on boards who were not named as "trustees." Historically, the control of nonprofits expanded to include many professionals and hence includes the term "board of directors" as well as boards of trustees. Both trustees and directors have over time been held to only a very broad set of vague guidelines ("prudent man rule") over their organizations.

7. Hall, *Inventing the Nonprofit Sector*, pp. 176–77.

8. See Kang, C. & Cnaan, R., "New Findings on Large Human Service Organization Boards of Trustees," *Administration in Social Work* 19:3 (1995): pp. 17–44.

9. This estimate is from Smith & Lipsky, *Nonprofits for Hire*, p. 8. Of course there are many types of boards, and these include many mutual benefit organizations (unions, fraternal organizations, social clubs) and political and trade groups as well as classical nonprofit charities.

10. As I will return to, the clients of charitable agencies certainly don't elect their boards of directors. In recent years it has become less unusual to have "client" or "consumer" representation, although some agencies do this in a tokenistic way.

11. Gladden quoted in Bremner, *American Philanthropy*, pp. 112–13.

12. Cited in Lichtenstein, N., *The Most Dangerous Man in Detroit*. New York: Basic Books, 1995, pp. 1–3.

13. Patman cited in Hall, *Inventing the Nonprofit Sector*, pp. 70–71.

14. See particularly Karl, B. & Katz, S., "The American Private Philanthropic Foundation and the Public Sphere, 1890–1930," *Minerva* 19 (1981): p. 245.

15. Karl & Katz quoted in Colwell, M. A., *Private Foundations and Public Policy*. New York: Garland Publishing, 1993, p. 32.

16. Rockefeller, J. D., *Random Reminiscences of Men and Events*. New York: Doubleday, Page and Co., 1909, pp. 185, 187.

17. Marcus, *Lives in Trust*, p. 280.

18. Nielsen, *The Big Foundations*, chapter 11, see particularly pp. 192–193.

19. Lundberg, F., *The Rich and Super-Rich*, pp. 524–25.

20. Quoted in Marcus, *Lives in Trust*, p. 323.

21. Rockefeller, *Random Reminiscences*, p. 184.

22. Lubove, *The Professional Altruist*, p. 190.

23. With the one notable exception thus far of the Vietnam War.

24. Procter quoted in Lubove, *The Professional Altruist*, p. 194; the phrase "militant civic patriotism" is also from Ibid.

25. Ibid, p. 182, see his chapter 7 generally.

26. Hoover and the Red Cross incident recounted in Bremner, *American Philanthropy*, pp. 145–46.

27. Seeley, J., Junker, B., & Jones, R. W., *Community Chest: A Case Study in Philanthropy*. Toronto: University of Toronto Press, 1957, p. 33.

28. On the "mythmaking" within the United Way and its lack of "grassroots" nature, see Brilliant, *The United Way*, pp. 28–29, 32. See also Carter, *Gentle Legions*, pp. 264–66 for the same point.

29. Brilliant's data, Ibid, (see Appendix H-2, p. 310–11, for example) suggests corporate CEOs and corporate vice presidents or managers make up 41 percent of the top volunteer groups in 131 local United Ways, with professionals and "middle management/supervisory" employees being another 22 percent. Hence we are talking about very small numbers from other groups, for example 4.3 percent union officials, 5.3 percent homemakers, etc. A more recent study by Kang & Cnaan, "New Findings," (1995) finds that United Ways had the highest corporate concentration of the agencies studied (they were compared with family service agencies, the YMCA and YWCAs). Using a categorization of "upper-upper level" management and "middle-upper level," the United Ways stood at 48 percent and 27 percent (a total of 75 percent) as compared with 43 and 23 for the Ys (66 percent) and 27 and 17 percent for family service agencies (44 percent). See table 2, pp. 28–29. Of course, all these data have imperfections since occupational status alone may not tell us much. For example, boards often have people described as "homemakers" who are spouses of corporate executives or political figures, or list as "community members" retired executives or financiers.

30. Carter, *Gentle Legions*, p. 249.

31. This point about the early edict for chain stores to become active in community chests, Red Crosses, and other organizations is made in Boorstein, D., *The Americans: The Democratic Experience*. New York: Vintage, 1974, p. 112.

32. Brilliant, *The United Way*, p. 35.

33. Ibid, p. 167.

34. Quoted in Carter, *Gentle Legions*, p. 277.

35. Brilliant, *The United Way*, p. 166.

36. Smith, H., "Corporate Contributions to the Year 2000: Growth or Decline?" in Hodgkinson, V. & Lyman, R., eds., *The Future of the Nonprofit Sector*. San Francisco: Jossey-Bass, 1989, p. 335.

37. Here I am not exploring the presumably positive ramifications the idea of "corporate responsibility" has had in terms of some corporate practices relative to the environment, civil rights, consumer safety, and so on, but only on giving.

38. Gifts by corporations have been remarkably consistent for the last three or four decades. Peter Dobkin Hall (*Inventing the Nonprofit*, p. 80) points out that despite Reagan's specific call for greater voluntarism, corporate contributions to charity remained below the 2 percent of gross income mark that it was expected to meet. Looked at as a percentage of all private giving, corporate donations have ranged between 4.5 and 5.5 percent of all contributions, not much when compared to, say, Australia, where companies make up one-third of all giving, or Japan where corporations finance most social welfare (see Oster, S., *Strategic Management for Nonprofit Organizations: Theory and Cases*. New York: Oxford University Press, 1995, Table 8.1 on Total Giving, pp. 108–9, comparison with Japan and Australia, p. 107).

39. Mescon, T., Tilson, D., & Desman, R., "Corporate Philanthropy: A Strategic Approach to the Bottom Line" in America, R., ed., *Philanthropy and Economic Development*. Westport, CT: Greenwood Press, 1995, pp. 59–63 in particular.

40. See Funiciello, T., *Tyranny of Kindness*, New York: Atlantic Monthly, 1993, pp. 130–42 for a scathing critique of Second Harvest; see also Weisbord, B., *The Nonprofit Economy* (Cambridge: Harvard University Press, 1988), p. 12, on Second Harvest.

41. Quoted in Bertsch, K., "Community-Based Development—Avoiding Resource Misuse and Abuse in America," in America, *Philanthropy and Economic Development*, p. 41.

42. Krentler, K., "Cause-Related Marketing: Advantages and Pitfalls for Nonprofits," in Hodgkinson & Lyman, *The Future of the Non-Profit Sector*, pp. 368–71 particularly.

43. This fear is expressed in Ibid, and some of the contributors in America (above). However, it should be noted that with current tax laws, companies probably will be limited in how much they can use cause related marketing in place of the full charitable deduction they receive in giving to a foundation or nonprofit charity. Future giving will no doubt depend both on federal tax policies and different corporate profit profiles.

44. This is not at all to suggest that there have not been dramatic changes in giving over the years, both by many wealthy families and corporations, and more significantly perhaps in the nature of philanthropic efforts over the years. For example, in the late 1960s the Rockefeller charities moved a great deal of money into ghetto programs, racial issues, welfare, and housing, and correspondingly reduced their arts and cultural offerings. Nevertheless, given the fairly steady aggregate rate of corporate donations and philanthropic effort, legitimation arguments are weakened to some extent, as it would seem that legitimation would be more essential in periods of social unrest than in periods of quiescence, such as currently.

45. Nielsen, *The Big Foundations*, pp. 312–16 generally, quote from p. 312.

46. Marcus, *Lives in Trust*, p. 9. While Marcus is particularly interested in private family dynastic wealth, his point holds, I believe, for the nonprofit sector generally as being a central cultural legitimation of wealth and power. New wealth seeks to emulate the esteem of old wealth and, hence, tends to mimic the traditional patterns of older families.

47. Carnegie quote in Lagemann, *The Politics of Knowledge*, p. 16.

48. Rockefeller, *Random Reminiscences*, p. 141.

49. The first quote is from Odendahl, T., *Charity Begins at Home: Generosity and Self-Interest among the Philanthropic Elite*, New York: Basic Books, 1990, p. 26; DiMaggio & Useem quoted on p. 41.

50. Ostrower, *Why the Wealthy Give: The Culture of Elite Philanthropy*. Princeton: Princeton University Press, 1995, p. 36.

51. Odendahl, T., "Charitable Giving Patterns by Elites in the United States," in Hodgkinson & Lyman, *The Future of the Non-Profit Sector*, p. 421.

52. It should be noted that giving to the poor actually represents only a tiny percentage of elite philanthropy, since giving to culture and education are the primary areas the very rich give to. So in the example I give of homelessness, this is an even smaller percentage of charitable endeavor.

But even with the most active and progressive groups, in my own experience, which includes doing quite a few speaking engagements about homelessness and poverty in New England, the point I am making is particularly poignant. I find that people frequently nod or cheer in response to even radical explanations of homelessness. Yet over and over again they find issues of economics and social structure too overwhelming in practice, and see the continued embrace of the soup kitchen or shelter work or counseling as the major thing they can do. See chapter 6 for a closer examination of the social service sphere as a substitute for social movement or political work.

53. Almost all serious analyses of homelessness and poverty suggest that issues of income, power, and employment are at stake. Building houses and not shelters, providing income, not soup kitchens, is not merely some radical "pie in the sky" program but is arguably the *only* way to eradicate homelessness in America. For critiques of "shelterization" and soup kitchen solutions see Hoch, C. & Slayton, R., *New Homeless and Old*, Philadelphia: Temple University Press, 1989, Marcuse, P., "Neutralizing Homelessness," *Socialist Review* 18:1 (1988): pp. 69–95, and Hopper, K. & Baumohl, J., "Held in Abeyance: Rethinking Homelessness and Advocacy," *American Behavioral Scientist* 37:4 (1994): pp. 522–52.

54. As one example, in my many years of teaching social work, I have taught students in a class in which they are required to do a project in organizational change and/or community organization. Almost invariably their field work supervisors (social workers including administrators and clinicians) advise students to expand agency services in some small way. Students rarely, with the exception of the occasional radical, question that the growth of the agency or service relates to the actual needs of clients. Proposals for change are often minimal, such as adding apples to soup kitchens or new rules of conduct at shelters.

55. Odendahl, *Charity Begins at Home,* p. 9.

56. I believe that the many clichés of our culture about accepting gifts — "Beggars can't be choosers," "Don't look a gift horse in the mouth," "Don't bite the hand that feeds,"—while perhaps reflecting some general discomfort with gifts, also suggest the dangers of the weaker party not accepting the charitable gift. In the Western social script, rejection constitutes hubris (as implied in the first two clichés) or even danger (in the last one). While it is true that these clichés are used in situations other than charity today (certainly we may use them in family, friendship, and work situations), they do imply that rejection of philanthropy takes a strong degree of courage on the part of recipients.

CHAPTER 5

1. Odendahl, *Charity Begins at Home*, p. 44.
2. Funiciello, *Tyranny of Kindness*, p. 255.
3. Pierce quoted in Karl & Katz, "The American Private Philanthropic Foundation," p. 240.
4. Polls from the early 1980s showing more public confidence in charity than government are cited in Katz, *In the Shadow*, p. 280; polls from the late 1980s cited in Ostrower, *Why the Wealthy Give*, p. 128.
5. Quote from Carter, *Gentle Legions*, p. 243. There is a certain outrageousness about events for charity that appeals to the fun-loving, even postmodernist, humor of Americans. In a parallel to the reveling of the old popular holidays of Europe, sports and charity seem to be among the few institutions in which people can let loose and (within limits) do as they please.
6. Examples of nonprofits are from Hawks, J., *For a Good Cause? How Charitable Institutions become Powerful Economic Bullies*. Secaucus, NJ: Hawks Communications, 1997, p. 27, 28, 29, 32, 58.
7. Ibid, p. 15; Employment figures from Independent Sector, *Nonprofit Almanac: Dimensions of the Independent Sector*. San Francisco: Jossey-Bass, 1996, p. 44.
8. *Newsweek* magazine quoted in Bennett, J. & DiLorenzo, T., *Unfair Competition: The Profits of Nonprofits*. Lanham, MD: Hamilton Press, 1989, pp. 17–18.
9. *Philadelphia Inquirer* study quoted in Hawks, *For a Good Cause?*, p. 35.
10. Tuckman and Chang, "Accumulating Financial Surpluses in Nonprofit Organizations," in Young, D., Hollister, R., Hodgkinson, V., *Governing, Leading, and Managing Nonprofit Organizations*. San Francisco: Jossey-Bass, 1993, p. 258.
11. Weisbord, *The Nonprofit Economy*, p. 164.
12. Hawks, *For a Good Cause?*, p. 28. The general point is that it is to the benefit of organizational executives and boards of directors to show lower revenues in their for-profit subsidiary (since they are taxed), moving them to the nonprofit arm. On the other hand, the more costs that can be loaded onto the profit-making subsidiary, the more fund surpluses (generally unregulated) can be placed on the ledgers of the nonprofit.
13. Brilliant, *The United Way*, p. 77; see also Dinerman, B., "The Ignorant Philanthropists," *The Nation* (March 30, 1970): pp. 369–72.
14. Funiciello, *Tyranny of Kindness*, p. 251.
15. IRS figures from Hawks, *For a Good Cause?*, p. 15.
16. Figures are from Independent Sector, *Nonprofit Almanac*, 1992 edition, p. 198.

17. The best overall source on the politics of the new "contract state" is Smith & Lipsky, *Nonprofits for Hire.*

18. Hawks, *For a Good Cause?*, p. 25, quotes a US Small Business Administration (SBA) study which indicates that 76 percent of nonprofit revenue are from fees for service. The *Nonprofit Almanac* does not provide exactly comparable data, but if one combines their figures (p. 159 of the 1996 edition) of 39 percent private payments and 31 percent government payments by grants or contracts, one can arrive at a 70 percent figure, assuming that much of the governmental funding is fee for service or per capita payment as well.

19. I don't want to fall into the considerable nostalgia in the social science literature about the old "nonprofits." As chapters 1, 2, and 4 suggest, much of this nostalgia is misplaced. The old trustee-dominated hospital and other charities always favored the more respectable over the poor, and there are harrowing stories of discrimination by disease (such as TB and venereal diseases) as well as by race and class. The prime change as social scientist Charles Perrow found in his study of a Western nonprofit hospital over time has been the movement of power from trustees to doctors to the newly emergent administrators (cited in Oster, *Strategic Management for Nonprofit Organizations*, p. 152). Some of the nostalgia for the old style nonprofit generally may be that of professionals from physicians to social workers to nurses who have seen their autonomy erode in the nonprofit as increased financial viability has become key.

20. Salamon, L., "The Changing Partnership Between the Voluntary Sector and the Welfare State," in Hodgkinson & Lyman, *The Future of the Non-Profit Sector*, p. 55.

21. Quote from Kevin O'Connell, an owner of a private health fitness club who is suing the YMCA for unfair competition, in Hawks, *For a Good Cause?*, p. 109.

22. Zald, M. & Denton, P. "From Evangelism to General Services: The Transformation of the YMCA," in Zald & McCarthy, *Social Movements in an Organizational Society: Collected Essays*. New Brunswick: Transaction Books, 1987 pp. 143–60.

23. See, for example, Cloward, R. and Epstein, I., "Private Social Welfare's Disengagement from the Poor: The Case of Family Adjustment Agencies," in Zald, M., ed., *Social Welfare Institutions*, New York: John Wiley and Sons, 1965. Other older agencies I have discussed — the Charity Organization Societies which became the United Ways and Family Service Organizations, the Boy and Girl Scouts, the Boys Clubs, and the Red Cross — were also extensively criticized.

24. Quoted in Bennett & DiLorenzo, *Unfair Competition*, p. 109.

25. Ibid.

26. Ibid, p. 103, 105.

27. Ibid, on the D.C. Y, see pp. 104–5; Los Angeles, p. 107; Baltimore, p. 108; quote on p. 110.

28. Hawks, *For a Good Cause?*, pp. xii–xiii.

29. Quoted in Bennett & DiLorenzo, *Unfair Competition*, p. 106.

30. Seeley, Junker, & Jones, *Community Chest*, p. 125.

31. See, for example, the survey in Table 2.26 of Independent Sector, *Nonprofit Almanac*, 1992, p. 86, which shows 81 percent of Americans agreeing with a question about the obligation of government to care for the needy, while at the same time 75 percent support an obligation to give to charity.

32. Roosevelt's close friend and appointee as head of the massive anti-polio drive, Basil O'Conner, was apparently the William Aramony of his time. See Carter, *Gentle Legions*, pp. 95–104.

33. Historians Bruce Jansson and James Patterson both recount Sargent Shriver's (then director of OEO) appeals to LBJ for public works jobs or income programs, which were flatly rejected by the President. See Jansson, B., *The Reluctant Welfare State*, Belmont, CA: Wadsworth, 1988, p. 221, and Patterson, J., *America's Struggle Against Poverty*, p. 141.

34. These words are sometimes used interchangeably, but generally "privatization" is a term used to describe a rather permanent end to government responsibility for a service with its consequent takeover by private parties. "Contracting out" is a time-limited contract offered by government to provide service, and often includes non-profit organizations as those receiving contracts as well as for-profit providers. Although historically the social welfare sector was not thought to avail itself of profits, the widespread privatization of prisons and mental hospitals, for example, indicate otherwise. Less profitable ventures such as group homes for those with AIDS or dependent children or shelters for the homeless tend to be contracted out to nonprofit organizations.

35. There is certainly a difference of scale between wholesale surrender of a government function — hospitals or prisons — and piecemeal surrender of responsibility that contracting out represents. But, they are part of the same trend to reduce government spending by, among other things, reducing the use of public employees, particularly unionized labor.

36. Salamon quote on p. 161 of Hawks, *For a Good Cause?*

37. Ibid, p. 128.

38. Cited in Moskowitz, J., "Increasing Government Support for Nonprofits: Is it Worth the Cost?" in Hodgkinson & Lyman, *The Future of the Non-Profit Sector*, p. 276.

39. The latest figures on the size of the nonprofit sector annual revenues are $508.5 billion (*Nonprofit Almanac 1996–1997*, Table 4.2, p. 190). The Conference Board figures on gross domestic product from December 1991 are $500.3 billion for Canada, $393 billion for China, $375.1 billion for Brazil, and $358.3 billion for Spain. Put another way, the nonprofit sector would itself be larger in revenue than the GDP of all nations except the US, Japan, Germany, France, Italy, and the UK.

40. Independent Sector, *Nonprofit Almanac 1996–1997*, Table 4.2, p. 190, provides a figure of $159.4 billion in public sector contributions to nonprofits in 1992, the latest year available. A putative list of revenues forgone by the government would include at least $29 to $37 billion that go to the charitable deduction on federal taxes; between $20 and $56 billion in untaxed revenue on what nonprofits themselves make, depending on what assumptions are used (should the nearly $200 billion in 1992 beyond government and private donations be taxed, or only the fund balances over operating income?), and (using an old estimate) between $10 and $15 billion in lost local property taxes. See James Ferris & Elizabeth Graddy, "Fading Distinctions among the Nonprofit, Government, and For-Profit Sectors," in Hodgkinson & Lyman, *The Future of the Non-Profit Sector*, p. 133, for the latter figure. All other figures are based on Independent Sector's data cited above. None of this includes

forgone state and local taxes, sales taxes, and other items listed in the text. The range of public sector support for the nonprofit sector (in the 40 to 50 percent area) is consistent with other estimates.

There are admittedly many complexities and problems with these calculations. Clearly the $104 billion contributed by private donors in 1994 (Independent Sector, Table 4.1, p. 189) would probably decline rapidly if taxed at my putative 28 or 36 percent rates. Nor is it clear how those revenues in fees above and beyond government and private donations (nearly $200 billion in 1992, not to mention $56 billion in interest and investment income) would be treated if the tax exemptions were lifted.

41. The federal budget for income security (excluding Social Security) was $220.5 billion in 1995; the subsidized amount of the nonprofit sector is in fact nearly at the $335.8 billion spent for Social Security that year. See US Government Budget.

42. Hawks, *For a Good Cause?*, p. 39, 165.

43. Seeley et al., *Community Chest*, p. 379.

44. See Netzer, D., "Arts and Culture," and Schwartz, S. & Baum, S., "Education," in Clotfelter, *Who Benefits from the Nonprofit Sector?* It is the case in terms of education that heavy federal and state subsidies reduce the class differentials within colleges and universities considerably. But as Schwartz and Baum point out, since college attendance is skewed by social class to begin with, the net difference between those who attend nonprofit universities and the general public is quite high.

45. Saklevar, D. & Frank, R., "Health Services," in Ibid, pp. 41, 44. There are again considerable differences of degree between different services. Public and nonprofit mental health services (both inpatient and out) appear to be in particularly stark contrast by social class compared to some of the (physical) health services.

46. Salamon, L., "Social Services," in Ibid, p. 144.

47. Ibid, see Table 5.7, p. 147. Similar figures from the Urban Institute are cited in Bennett & DiLorenzo, *Unfair Competition*, p. 12.

48. Ibid, p. 157. Government funding not only requires formal nondiscrimination compliance on the part of nonprofits, but eliminates some of the surrogates used as barriers to services (agencies that serve only the mildly neurotic, or only people from affluent neighborhoods, etc.) by dint of their contract demands and monitoring.

49. Cited in Oster, *Strategic Management for Nonprofit*, p. 69.

50. Figures from Bennett & DiLorenzo, *Unhealthy Charities: Hazardous to Your Health and Wealth*. New York: Basic Books, 1994, p. 83.

51. Ibid, p. 13.

52. Ibid, p. 139.

53. Obviously the directory covers a broader region, but the entire metropolitan area's population is no more than 250,000.

54. Weisbord, *The Nonprofit Economy*, p. 81.

55. This is admittedly a broad generalization which is subject to differences between geographic areas of the nation and different fluctuations in services and programs. In the area where I live, many service providers accept *no* Medicaid patients, and many of the rest have a formal or informal "cap" on Medicaid or charity cases. Since it is now politically and culturally frowned upon to advertise these prejudices, many alcoholism treatment centers, child guidance clinics, counselors and psychothera-

pists, drug treatment and eating disorder centers, mental health clinics, and other programs tend to place many poorer clients on a long waiting list or refer them elsewhere. In many cases those at the bottom of society with a severe problem do not hang around for four or six months to approach the agency again about where they are on the waiting list, nor are they necessarily available at home waiting for their "number to come up" for treatment or assistance.

56. Even clear success stories, such as the ability of state universities to produce superior or equally well-trained students compared to elite schools, are treated as exceptions to the rule by the press. "Government" is often *not* invoked at all when treating popular services such as schools, universities, Head Start, or police or military issues.

57. Examples are from Hawks, *For a Good Cause?*, pp. xiv, 101–2.

58. Young, D., "Beyond Tax Exemption: A Focus on Organizational Performance Versus Legal Status," in Hodgkinson & Lyman, *The Future of the Non-Profit Sector*, pp. 188–89. One assumes that Young's point is relevant to a modern capitalist economy, not to our earlier history, since we have seen the nonprofit form preceded by many for-profit forms in the earlier centuries of American history.

59. Capital investment is hardly the only issue. Some areas of the nonprofit world are clearly much more profitable than others; for example, small businesses are clamoring about the Y's physical fitness programs because this is such a lucrative area; but it is hard to imagine that shelters for battered women will soon, if ever, be for-profits. Another barrier to conversion to for-profit status beyond profit and capital expenditure are the opportunity costs and organizational difficulties. For example, cancer doctors have a strong interest in there being an American Cancer Society, but considerable time and energy would have to be sacrificed from probably more lucrative endeavors (certainly for oncologists) for such an organization to be run as a for-profit venture. It would also entail considerable risk.

CHAPTER 6

1. Aronowitz, S. *The Death and Rebirth of American Radicalism*. New York: Routeledge, 1996, pp. 133–34.

2. Glasser, I., "The Prisoners of Benevolence," in Gaylin, W. et al., *Doing Good: The Limits of Benevolence*. New York: Pantheon, 1981, pp. 112–13.

3. Haug, M. & Sussman, M., "Professional Autonomy and the Revolt of the Client," *Social Problems* 17 (Fall 1969): pp. 153, 155. One can debate how much the 1960s really represented a "revolt of the client" as separate from the social movements of civil rights, black power, the student and antiwar, and womens' movements, for example. Still, whether as part of these movements or an indirect offshoot, tremendous changes did occur in relation to the treatment of clients, patients, students, and other consumers of service.

4. Lipsky, M., *Street Level Bureaucracy*. New York: Russell Sage, 1980, p. 43.

5. "Change from within" can be identified as a reformist response to both those in the late 1960s who sought to "smash" or abolish the "system," and those who sought to create alternative systems such as the back-to-the-land or commune movement. Within the human service professions such as social work, "change from within" was made into a formal goal by the early 1970s and became a subject of classroom

study (see for example, R. Patti & H. Resnick, "Changing the Agency from Within," *Social Work* 17:7 (1973): pp. 48–57). Summarizing a debate which filled pages at the time, most of the baby boom radicals — if only to survive — obviously entered the "system," but the argument that the system had more impact on vitiating radicalism than the radicals had in changing the system still remains a legitimate critique, and one which has been borne out by time.

6. Both critics and supporters of the War on Poverty agree that the Democratic administration chose to bypass local and state officials to incorporate low-income voters, particularly African-Americans, into the national party. The administration was particularly fearful that government funds would not find their way to low-income blacks in the South or in Northern cities ruled by strong ethnic political patronage machines. See Piven and Cloward, *Regulating the Poor*, particularly chapter 9, and Moynihan, D. P., *Maximum Feasible Misunderstanding*. New York: The Free Press, 1970.

7. Moynihan, Ibid. A critical but more leftist account of the failure of the War on Poverty is contained in Marris, P. & Rein, M., *Dilemmas of Social Reform: Poverty and Community Action in the United States*. Chicago: University of Chicago: 1982.

8. Alinsky quoted in Trattner, W., *From Poor Law to Welfare State*. New York: The Free Press, 1989, p. 302.

9. Aronowitz quoted in Moynihan, *Maximum Feasible*, p. 149.

10. Marris & Rein, *Dilemmas of Social Reform*, p. 269.

11. Haug & Sussman, "Professional Autonomy," p. 158.

12. Galper, J., *The Politics of Social Services*. Englewood Cliffs, NJ: Prentice-Hall, 1975, p. 117.

13. Piven & Cloward, *Poor People's Movements*.

14. Katznelson, I., *City Trenches: Urban Politics and the Patterning of Class in the United States*. New York: Pantheon, 1981, p. 177.

15. Marris & Rein, *Dilemmas of Social Reform*, p. 167.

16. Mollenkompf, J., *A Phoenix in the Ashes: The Rise and Fall of the Koch Coalition in New York City Politics*. Princeton: Princeton University Press, 1992, p. 91.

17. Ibid, p. 160.

18. Wagner, D., *Checkerboard Square: Culture and Resistance in a Homeless Community*. Boulder, CO: Westview Press, 1993, see pp. 136–45.

19. I became familiar with the consumer-run mental health club while performing ethnographic interviews there as part of the work cited above, and have continued to visit and keep in touch with some consumers. However, I am particularly indebted to Marcia B. Cohen's active involvement and writing about the mental health club for much of my insight. The club is the optimal result of the 1960s/1970s goal of consumer participation in that it is ostensibly the consumers (those diagnosed with psychiatric disorders) who run the agency, which provides a drop-in center, meals, vocational training, socialization, and other services.

20. The major exception to this rule (and it is an important one) is with benefits whose rates determine per diem or per capita reimbursement to social agencies and institutions *and* clients as well. The two most frequent examples of related funding mechanisms are the Medicaid and SSI programs. Here a general increase or decrease in these programs would affect financing both within institutions and organi-

zations and for individual recipients. This is not the case with welfare, food stamps, Social Security pensions, and other benefits.

Also I should note, in response to comments by some expert readers, that there are agencies in some cities, mostly advocacy groups rather than direct service groups, that do play an active role in opposing cuts in material benefits. But these noted exceptions do not disprove the general rule.

21. Marcus, *Lives in Trust*, pp. 299–300.

22. Not only must nonprofits *not* engage in partisan politics, they also are barred from "committing, encouraging or inducing acts that are illegal or contrary to public policy" according to IRS rulings. See Weisbord, *The Nonprofit Economy*, p. 120. It is true, of course, that there are many ways around the law in terms of advocacy of issues affecting client groups and legislation. However, when adherence to legal strictures is considered along with the fact that almost all nonprofit human service groups depend on largesse from political and business leaders, few organizations are going to risk getting "cut off" by engaging in militant, unlawful, or radical action.

23. Jenkins cited in Colwell, *Private Foundations and Public Policy*, p. 42.

24. Smith & Lipsky, *Nonprofits for Hire*, p. 208.

25. Funiciello, *Tyranny of Kindness*, p. xviii.

26. An excellent discussion of socialist theory regarding social welfare is in the first chapter of Esping-Andersen, G., *Politics Against Markets: The Social Democratic Road to Power*. Princeton: Princeton University Press, 1985.

27. For example, Ann Withorn (in *Serving the People*) seeks desperately to find such traditions. Despite a valiant effort, Withorn admits that before the 1960s the Women's Christian Temperance Union and the Workmen's Circle are the best examples of what she sees as "radicals" who drew on service models. These two organizations are rarely — to put it mildly — counted among radical organizations in most left-wing analysis. Even the cases she cites from the 1960s, prior to the women's movement, are weak as she correctly notes that Economic Research and Action Project (ERAP), Student Nonviolent Coordinating Committee (SNCC), and other '60s radicals criticized their members and occasional service efforts as "mere social work." It is surprising, given how this work is such a fine effort to defend social service radicalism, to see how little in the way of specifics she provides either as evidence of a leftist tradition for social services or for any concrete test of which programs or efforts should be supported by radicals.

28. Galper, *The Politics of Social Services*, p. 67.

29. Ibid, p. 67, p. 97. It is true that within social work and even a small segment of psychiatry and education, community organization was in vogue for awhile as a way to develop more collective approaches. But again, organizing by service workers is most successful when issues of resources — housing, the environment, health care, taxes — are at stake compared to issues usually thought of as social services.

30. I have in mind here everything from genetic counseling to grief counseling, certainly an expansion that has been a mixed blessing. Some good critiques of the expansion of the human service/human need paradigm as a new consumerism include McKnight, J., *The Careless Society*; Polsky, *The Rise of the Therapeutic State*; S. Peele, *The Diseasing of America*, New York: Lexington, 1989; and Specht, H. & Court-

ney, M., *Unfaithful Angels*, New York: The Free Press, 1994. All these books raise provocative questions for the Left as to whether the usual demand for "more" as being better (more social workers, educators, health care) is always in the interest of consumers.

31. For a good discussion of this issue, one of the few, see David Croteau, *Politics and the Class Divide*, Philadelphia: Temple University Press, 1995. Barbara Ehrenreich in her *Fear of Falling* (New York: Pantheon, 1989) has also commented on how poor and working-class people are viewed through a middle-class perspective.

32. Gartner, A. & Riessman, F., *The Service Society and the Consumer Vanguard*. New York: Harper & Row, 1974, pp. 44, 54–55.

33. Withorn, *Serving the People*, p. xx.

34. Burghardt, S., *The Other Side of Organizing*. Cambridge, MA: Schenkman, 1982, p. 215.

35. See, for example, Wagner, D. & Cohen, M., "Social Workers, Class, and Professionalism," *Catalyst* 1:1 (1978): pp. 25–53. Our article, like a few others in *Catalyst*, argued that it was not necessarily through a special service role, but through human service workers' role as *workers* that social service workers could have an impact. Although it was a slightly different argument, in retrospect, it personally makes for painful reading on a number of levels, including our excessive optimism about the role of social service workers in our society.

36. Probably no theorist was more critical to the development of the glorification of the professional (unintentionally) than educator Paulo Freire (most famous for his *Pedagogy of the Oppressed*). Freire's emphasis on literacy and conscientization seemed to be applied almost uncritically from a less industrial to an advanced capitalist nation, and, more important, seems to have led some followers to stress the noble role of teacher, educator, and other helper over the indigenous peoples themselves. Within psychiatry a small school of radicals clustered in the community mental health movement also claimed a huge purview for themselves. See Dumont, M., "The Changing Face of Professionalism," *Social Policy* 1:1 (May-June 1970): pp. 26–31, and his book *The Absurd Healer*. New York: Viking Press, 1971.

37. Social movement organizations (SMOs) are nonprofit organizations that had their origins in activist movements such as battered women's shelters, womens' health care, many AIDS/HIV programs, disability rights services, and so on.

38. Kayal, P., *Bearing Witness: Gay Men's Health and the Politics of AIDS*. Boulder, CO: Westview Press, 1993, p. 72.

39. Ibid, p. 30.

40. Ibid, p. 126, p. 134.

41. Hyde, C., "The Ideational System of Social Movement Agencies: An Examination of Feminist Health Centers," in Hasenfeld, Y., ed., *Human Services as Complex Organizations*. Newbury Park, CA: Sage Publishers, 1992, p. 139.

42. I do agree with Hyde that "co-optation" or "goal displacement" are charges sometimes glibly made by scholars of organizations and some radicals. However, it is an important step to not only provide a more nuanced characterization of organizations as they change over time with the political environment (which Hyde and others do), but to evaluate more theoretically and historically whether the goals of forming service organizations actually could ever have led to radical politics, and, if so, un-

der what conditions. Most sociological, social work, or organizational literature fails to discuss the latter issue at all, either because it is not of concern to the authors or the observers are so unable to wrestle with their own theoretical or organizational backgrounds.

43. One reason for this is simply that by the late 1970s and after, fewer public sector positions were available for newer workers. But, as Michael Lipsky comments, it is also true that many idealistic young workers entered the public bureaucracies such as welfare centers, ghetto schools, or public hospitals believing they would resemble their desired mission, only to find frustration. He notes that the "grinding down" that young neophyte workers felt in the government sector considerably weakened their idealism. Speaking of their burnout, he says

> . . . generations of thoughtful and potentially self-sacrificing people are disarmed in their social purpose. They come to believe that it is impossible to find conditions conducive to good practice, and that public agencies cannot be otherwise structured. Their choices appear to be to leave public employment for other work or to resign themselves to routine processing of clients while instructing the next generation of idealists that there is little sense in hoping for change or in rendering human services. . . . *Street Level Bureaucracy*, p. 186.

In my study of a small number of radical social workers, (Wagner, *Quest for a Radical Profession*, Lanham, MD: University Press of America, 1990), I also found a high level of frustration with work in the public sector. Indeed, most social workers had left these jobs, yet they believed they were still doing activist political work in the voluntary nonprofit sector. See especially chapters 4 and 5. See also my "Radical Movements in the Social Services: A Theoretical Framework," *Social Service Review* 63:2 (1989): pp. 264–84.

44. I have argued in the above that the social services serve as an important vehicle for absorption of radicals particularly because of their ability to attract idealistic workers, and then demand their loyalty to limited organizational objectives (rather than radical objectives). See Zald, M. & McCarthy, J., "Organizational Intellectuals and the Criticism of Society," *Social Service Review* 46 (1975): pp. 344–62, for a similar argument.

45. *Washington Post* cited in Olasky, *The Tragedy of American Compassion*, p. 207.

### CHAPTER 7

1. Goldman, E., "The Failure of Christianity," from Shulman, A., ed., *Red Emma Speaks*. New York: Schocken Books, 1983, p. 232.

2. I still remember how validating it was to see this thought in print (which, of course, many of us in schools of social work had as well) in Cloward & Piven's introduction to Bailey, R. & Brake, M., *Radical Social Work*, New York: Pantheon, 1975. The introduction was later published in shortened form as "The Acquiescence of Social Work," *Society*, Jan.-Feb. 1977: pp. 55–65.

3. Civil rights attorney Lloyd Rees on Ted Koppel show (ABC News), "The United Way Under Fire," Feb. 27, 1992.

4. The works of Piven and Cloward are most clear on this. Although the process of

how unrest and social movements brought about change in these periods has been contested by some analysts, there seems little fundamental disagreement that to a large extent the passage of social welfare legislation in these periods was strongly structured by social movements and protests.

Between 1934 and 1938, the New Deal initiated a host of public works programs (CCC, PWA, CWA, WPA), the Social Security Act (including old age pensions, unemployment insurance, and federal welfare), the National Labor Relations Act, the Public Housing Act, and the Fair Labor Practices Act (the minimum wage, outlawing child labor, mandating the eight-hour workday and so on), all in response to unrest of labor, the unemployed, and the elderly. Between 1964 and 1973, the following acts and social welfare changes occurred: the Civil Rights Act and the Economic Opportunity Act (including Head Start, community action, legal services for the poor, the Job Corps, neighborhood youth corps, neighborhood health clinics) were passed, Food Stamps, Medicare and Medicaid became available, a guaranteed annual income was proposed (Family Assistance Plan), OSHA (Occupational Safety and Health Act) was established, the Social Security program was indexed to inflation, the Supplemental Security Income program (SSI) was passed, and the Comprehensive Employment and Training Act (CETA) passed. Again generally, the civil rights movement, ghetto riots, labor, and elderly activism can be cited as the chief causes of reform.

5. Ibrahim, Y., "Welfare's Snug Coat Cuts Norwegian Cold," *New York Times*, December 13, 1996, pp. A1, 12.

6. Pells, R., *Not Like Us: How Europeans have Loved, Hated, and Transformed American Culture Since World War II*. New York: Basic Books, 1997, p. 294.

7. The works of Gosta Esping-Andersen and Walter Korpi on comparative welfare states are the most comprehensive in showing correlations between labor organization and the strength of public welfare systems in the Western world. See, for example, Esping-Andersen, *The Three Worlds of Welfare Capitalism*, Princeton: Princeton University Press, 1990; Esping-Andersen, "Power and Distributional Regimes," *Politics and Society* 14:2 (1985); and Korpi, "Power, Politics, and State Autonomy in the Development of Social Citizenship," *American Sociological Review* 54:3 (June 1989), pp. 309–28.

It is true that since the rapid movement of globalization and the allure of privatization, Western European welfare states have reduced their social welfare expenditures. Even with some cuts, as the text indicates, their societies provide far more public benefits than America.

8. In 1993 (the last year data is available for), total corporate contributions to charity were at 1.14 percent of their pre-tax income. Independent Sector, *Nonprofit Almanac*, p. 82.

# Index